MUSTANG

CRESTLINE

RANDY LEFFINGWELL • DAVID NEWHARDT

Originally published as *Mustang: Forty Years*

This edition published in 2010 by
CRESTLINE
A division of BOOK SALES, INC.
276 Fifth Avenue Suite 206
New York, New York 10001
USA

This edition published by arrangement with Motorbooks International, an imprint of MBI Publishing Company.

First published in 2003 by Motorbooks International, an imprint of MBI Publishing Company, 400 First Avenue North, Suite 300, Minneapolis, MN 55401 USA

ISBN-13: 978-0-7858-2696-5
ISBN-10: 0-7858-2696-3

Edited by: Darwin Holmstrom
Designed by: Stephanie Michaud
Associate editor: Peter Schletty
Editorial assistant: Mariam Pourshoushtari

On the front cover: The Boss 302 might have been designed for the track, but it also made a well-balanced street car.

On the back cover:
Top left: With its five hood scoops, the 1970 Shelby was everything but subtle.
Top right: The success of the Mustang meant the baby boomers had arrived as an economic force to be reckoned with.
Bottom left: The next generation of Mustang will feature state-of-the-art mechanical parts, but it will still be recognized as a descendant of the original Mustang.
Bottom right: Engineers put more emphasis on cornering than straight line performance with the SVO Mustang.

Printed in China

ACKNOWLEDGMENTS

We wish to thank our good friends at Ford Public Affairs: Sandra Badgett, Product Manager; Jason Camp, Media Fleet Manager; and John Clinard, Manager, Western Region Public Affairs, Ford Motor Company, Mission Viejo, California, for their ongoing and generous help on this and many projects through the years.

In addition, particularly on this book, we wish to thank Edsel B. Ford II, Board Member, Ford Motor Company, for his thoughts and reflections on forty years of history. Furthermore, we are grateful to Greg Hutting, Project Manager, and Dick Hutting, Chief Designer, Ford Design CA, Valencia, California, for their recollections on the creation of the 2005 concept GT cars.

We also wish to thank John Handy, Senior Vice President, Boys Design; Carson Lev, Director Hot Wheels Adult Licensing, New Business Development; and Mark Jones, Senior Designer Hot Wheels, Mattel, Inc., for the story of "Pony Up."

We further wish to express our deep gratitude to Leslie Mark Kendall, Curator, and Dick Messer, Director, the Petersen Automotive Museum, Los Angeles, California, for their help and encouragement with this project.

In addition, we are most grateful to Dennis Bickmeier, Director of Public Relations, California Speedway, and to Doug Stokes, Director of Communications, Irwindale Speedway, for their cooperation in allowing access to their facilities for our photography.

Without a doubt, it is car owners, collectors, and restorers who make projects like this possible by opening their garages for our requests to photograph their cars. We are deeply grateful to:

Roy Adcox, Arcadia, California; Armando and Erik Benitez, West Covina, California; David Bennett, Westminster, California; Doug and Marianne Bohrer, Visalia, California; Ben Borja, Pasadena, California; George Boskovich, Camarillo, California; Alan Bolte; Mark Brown, Fallbrook, California; Bob Casey, Curator, Henry Ford Museum & Greenfield Village, Dearborn, Michigan; Don and Aileen Chambers, Mustang Country, Paramount, California; Otis and Bettina Chandler, Ojai, California; Tom Chronistop, Garden Grove, California; Steve Davis, Visalia, California; Steven and Debbie Earle, Monterey Historic Automobile Races, Buellton, California; Bob Fria, La Crescenta, California; Henry Fuchs, Vintage Museum of Transportation & Wildlife, Oxnard, California; Kenn Funk, Glendale, California; Brian Gates; Sanford Goff, San Diego, California; Steve Grant, San Pedro, California; Siegfried Grunze, Sylmar, California; Sam Haymart, Roseville, California; George Jacobs, Palm Springs, California; Michael T. Jackson, Los Angeles, California; Reid Jensen; Bob King, Huntington Beach, California; Barry Konier, Orange, California; Dan Krehbiel, Garden Grove, California; Bryan Kreuger, Anaheim, California; David Kunz, Los Angeles, California; Debra Legris, Manhattan Beach, California; Tracey and Janet Lehfeld, Garden Grove, California; Jay Lincoln, La Habra, California; John Lock, Laguna Niguel, California; Kenny Maisano, Laguna Niguel, California; Martin Mazman, Fresno, California; Michael McCafferty, Del Mar, California; Scott H. Merle and Lance Kruljac, Long Beach, California; Richard Miller, Yorba Linda, California; Frank and Linda Morales, Anaheim, California; Mark Mosteller; Gary Patterson, Shelby North American, Las Vegas, Nevada; Robert E. Petersen, Publisher and Founder, Petersen Publishing, Beverly Hills, California; Bryan and Doug Reid, Brea, California; Louis Robinson, San Gabriel, California; Brian Sbardelli, Los Angeles, California; Eric Scott, Escondido, California; David Severin, Woodland Hills, California; Lorraine Kay Smyth,

Laguna Beach, California; Tony Sousa, Los Angeles, California; Michael P. Stewart, Burbank, California; Daniel Swana, Upland, California; Debbie Taylor, Garden Grove, California; Kris Trexler, Los Angeles, California; Jim Wahl, Upland, California; George Watts; Jeffery Weiss, Costa Mesa, California; Don Winans and Linda Yorba.

We both wish to express our gratitude to our colleague Robert Genat, Encinitas, California, for his exceptional photos of the police and drag racing versions of these cars.

In addition, we'd like to express our thanks to Chrome & "R" Color Lab, Los Angeles, California, for their care in processing David's hundreds of rolls of Fuji Velvia film.

Nearly last but at the top of our heroes list, we express our gratitude to Mike Smyth, Pasadena, California, for his enthusiasm, help, and support throughout this entire project.

Finally, we are both grateful to our much better halves, Carolyn Chandler and Susan Foxx-Newhardt, for their patience and encouragement through this process and project.

We both hope you enjoy the results of this great collaboration!

—*Randy Leffingwell*, Santa Barbara, California
—*David Newhardt*, Pasadena, California

Despite the attention-grabbing paint, the 1993 Mustangs used by the California Highway Patrol had identical drivelines and suspensions as the 5.0 Mustang GT available to the public. However, the floor pan around the driver's seat was reinforced, and the underhood sound deadener was deleted. Robert Genat/Zone Five Photo

DEDICATION

For John Clinard

For more than twenty years, John has supported, encouraged, and greatly facilitated media attention to Ford Motor Company and its products, and, on a broader scale, to the entire auto industry and its roles and responsibilities in the world. His own intimate involvement with the SVO Mustang project is just one example of his enthusiasm for performance automobiles, especially the Mustang. He is unique in his industry, and we will always value his intelligence, his wit, his imagination, and his great friendship.

(previous) Following World War II, the Ford division owned the youth market with vehicles like this stylish 1947 Deluxe station wagon. Young Henry Ford II had returned from the U.S. Navy and saved his grandfather's company by powering cars like this into production.

The Thunderbird was one of the most significant and influential automobiles of its day. Its arrival and the competition it represented saved the Chevrolet Corvette from extinction. For Ford Motor Company, it set the company on a path that eventually led to the Mustang.

(August 1946–November 1960)

WAR RECOVERY AND THE BIRTH OF THE BOOM

Ford, General Motors, and Chrysler spent most of World War II producing matériel for U.S. soldiers and for America's allies. They effectively stopped manufacturing private automobiles during 1942. The U.S. war production board kept Detroit's designers occupied drawing tanks, airplanes, and guns. There was little time left to plan for their next automobiles for peacetime.

After the war, soldiers with unspent wartime pay came home to their wives who had stepped into the industrial workforce and built savings accounts from wages earned assembling bombers and jeeps. The half-decade of hardship and hard work had created a strong hunger for new products, especially automobiles. The smaller independent carmakers, Studebaker and Hudson, both of whom had been less occupied with defense production during the war, quickly introduced new models, while the Big Three were forced to dust off 1942 tooling and reintroduce familiar products.

As early as 1946, carmakers noticed a growing desire for something nicer than the re-labeled prewar models. Ford, Chrysler, and Nash introduced limited-production models that evoked the elegance of the custom-body car era during the early 1930s. The carmakers fitted mahogany veneers framed with white ash, yellow birch, or maple. These were probably the first mass-produced personal-luxury cars. Chrysler's Town & Country convertibles and sedans sold

12,000 copies by 1951. Nash sold barely 1,000 Suburbans, but its style, uncharacteristic for stodgy Nash, caught viewers and brought them into dealerships to look at other models. Ford produced 3,500 of its wood-paneled Sportsman convertibles. Mercury Divisions had its own Sportsman but manufactured just 205 of them. Ford division reintroduced its popular, stylish wood-bodied station wagons as well. Showroom traffic suggested to Ford management that the marketplace was interested in distinctive, personal automobiles.

In 1949, chrome and two-tone paint replaced wood in many of the numerous new models introduced that year. Still, the idea of exclusive, factory-special cars, not only from the premium divisions such as Lincoln and Cadillac but also from Chevrolet and Ford, was becoming a staple of the postwar car business.

In November 1952, the population elected General Dwight David Eisenhower, "Ike," as their next president. In July 1954, Eisenhower proposed a $33 billion National Defense Highway system similar to the auto routes and autobahns of Europe. Meant for the efficient movement

of U.S. armed forces, these long, smooth interstate roads fed a hunger for automobiles. Throughout this period, the United States witnessed the birth of a middle class that earned enough money to pay its bills and have some left over. Leisure time became a reality, and the purchase of an automobile became a goal.

U.S. soldiers had encountered sports cars in England and enjoyed their road-holding and liveliness, and also had appreciated their economy. Returning soldiers introduced sports cars to the United States, bringing the diminutive cars home in their personal luggage. Unlike even the smallest U.S.-built cars at the time, these vehicles had individual bucket-type seats and manual transmissions with shift levers on the floor.

For Ford, Chrysler, and General Motors, the floor shift was too reminiscent of the Model T. America had shifted manually before; now prosperous Americans could afford a machine to do the shifting for them. What's more, sports car sales in the United States were nearly inconsequential, amounting to less than one percent of total new car registrations. Italian designer Batista "Pinin" Farina and Englishman Donald Healey introduced a Nash-engine two-seater in 1951. They targeted Nash-Healey production at 200 per year, but it performed poorly and sold slowly. Few Americans noticed when designer Howard "Dutch" Darrin collaborated with Henry J. Kaiser to build a fiberglass-bodied two-seater on the chassis of the Henry J., Kaiser's economy model. Calling it the Kaiser-Darrin, Kaiser presented it in 1953, but it disappeared after the company had completed just 437 of them. Sports cars delivered a mixed message to the American public: carmakers wanted to attract the youth market, but often the cars cost too much and failed to deliver the performances youthful buyers wanted.

Chevrolet took a big gamble when it put its Blue Flame Six in front of its two-speed automatic transmission and surrounded it in a plastic-bodied product it had named after the U.S. and English Navy's convoy escorts, the corvettes. GM capitalized on the Corvette's incredibly limited first year production, emphasizing its exclusivity and inviting only 300 wealthy or highly visible public figures to buy Corvettes in 1953. For some car buyers, the two-seater quickened their pulse; others noted that the Chevrolet's primitive sports car cost nearly as much as Cadillac's brand-new six-passenger El Dorado convertible and hastened their retreat from Chevrolet showrooms. No matter. Chevrolet sold 3,540 Corvettes in 1954, which was enough for GM to give the model another chance. Ford, dismissing the sports

Long-board surfing has been a California preoccupation since before World War II. Ford first manufactured wood-bodied station wagons in 1937. When Ford re-introduced its wood-bodied station wagons after the war, they were available with an inline six or the 100–horsepower flathead V-8.

13

The top trim level available was this Super Deluxe model that offered two sun visors, armrests on each door, and chrome moldings around the windows and inner horn ring. Spotlights were extra dealer options on a car that sold for $1,893 with the 90 horsepower six or $1,972 with the V-8.

car market until it heard GM was entering it, soon provided the competition that ensured the Corvette's future.

Ford Motor Company's board of directors called 28-year-old Henry Ford II home from the navy in late 1943, during the war. The board needed him to run the company his grandfather had founded but now was too ill to manage. The founder died on April 7, 1947, but by that time Henry Ford II's youthful leadership had already moved Ford division ahead of Chevrolet in sales of convertibles and station wagons, a critical indication of Ford's appeal to the younger buyers with and without families. Henry Ford II reacted quickly to the company's problems, but Chevrolet sales totals reached a million cars in 1949, passing Ford for the first time since 1927. By the early 1950s, Ford Motor Company had settled firmly into second spot behind General Motors.

Ford's Design Chief Franklin Q. Hershey had worked as Cadillac's chief of design before Harley Earl, GM's design vice president, terminated him in 1948 (for running a side business making ashtrays). Unlike Earl, Hershey cared little for sports cars or for European exotics. His first job was making custom bodies for Duesenbergs, Packards, and other cars at Walter Murphy Body Company in Pasadena, California. There Hershey developed a passion for the American classics. When a group of Ford designers and engineers formed the Ford Motorsports Club in late 1951, Hershey declined the invitation to join them. A few months later in early 1952, his attitude changed, as Jim and Cheryl Farrell reported in *Ford Design Department – Concept & Show Cars, 1932 – 1961*. Shortly after Hershey took over Ford design, motorsports club member J.R. "Dick" Samsen, who was one of his designers, asked him why Ford didn't build a sports car. Hershey told him the company knew it could not make money on these vehicles. Then one late-winter evening, a close friend who was also a designer still working for GM, dined at Hershey's home and showed Hershey a photograph. It was Chevrolet's new sports car; Hershey knew immediately what he and Ford division had to do. Overnight he became a sports car enthusiast, buying himself a Jaguar XK-120 and studying every other model available.

In March 1952, he hired GM designer Bill Boyer from under Harley Earl's nose to design Ford's response to Chevrolet's new threat. Boyer worked feverishly in a small secure studio with Dick Samsen, Allan Kornmiller, and a few engineers and fabricators. They based their car on Jaguar's XK-120, just as Chevrolet's Bob McLean had done with the Corvette. Boyer, Samsen, and Kornmiller had a full-size clay model ready for Ford management to see in the Dearborn design studio on the morning of January 17, 1953. A few hours before, GM had debuted the Corvette at its Motorama Show in New York City's Waldorf Astoria Hotel.

If Chevrolet had a sports car, Ford decided it would make a better one. The Corvette had plastic side curtains like the English MGs and Triumphs. This was less an aesthetic choice or product-planning decision than an unfortunate side-effect of the car's original door shape and the short lead time between the public unveiling and start of production. Ford's two-seater would have roll-up windows. Chevrolet had worried about an unstable steel supply after labor strikes, and government intercession had wracked the industry in the previous two years. It had selected a novel new material—fiberglass—for its sports car body. Ford, which owned its own ore mines in Canada and operated steel mills at its vast River Rouge plant, knew its supply of steel was secure. Chevrolet, GM's economy division, had only a six-cylinder engine in its lineup; Ford's V-8, already in production, would go into their car. Henry Ford II wanted it that way and Ford division's vice-president and general manager, Lewis D. Crusoe, would see that it got done.

When Ford introduced its Thunderbird on October 22, 1954, the car was an immediate hit. Even though Chevrolet had gotten its new V-8 into the Corvette for 1955, it was clear to everyone, from magazine writers to paying customers, that Ford had guessed much more "right" than had Chevrolet. Ford production designers Robert Maguire and Damon Woods had finished the Thunderbird with clean, simple lines that they adorned with subtle fins looking more like body edges than the illuminated bullets off the back of the Corvette. Chevrolet suffered badly, selling only 675 of its 1955 Corvettes while Ford sold 16,155 of its Thunderbirds. Although T-bird sales slipped about 5 percent for 1956, the 1957 restyling that brought new tail fins, a new interior, and redesigned front bumpers and grille boosted sales to 21,380.

Ford division's General Manager Lewis Crusoe was an astute observer of his customers. A story that author Gary Witzenburg recorded in his book, *Mustang*, illustrates Crusoe's knack for sensing trends.

Ford only offered its Sportsman convertible in the Super Deluxe model, which featured a chrome rub strip along both front and rear fenders. In 1946, this car sold new for $1,982, and Ford manufactured just 723 of them.

Ford framed the mahogany panels in white ash. The body division used cabinet dovetail joints to fit the pieces together. Weatherseals inside the trunk kept contents completely dry, but the wood itself required annual maintenance.

"A few weeks before the 1955 Thunderbird was presented to the public—as product planner Tom Case remembers— Crusoe drove one home to see how it checked out on the road. Following a weekend with the new car, Crusoe called Case into his office on Monday morning.

"'There is one thing wrong with the Thunderbird,' he told Case. 'It's a beautiful car, but we need a rear seat in it. Let's go to work and make a four-passenger 'Bird.'"

Many factors affected Crusoe's conclusions. He worried that Ford's market might follow Corvette down into triple-digit production numbers. What if both companies had overestimated America's interest in sports cars? Even the morality of the day played a role in his decision. In the mid-1950s, nice girls did not date young men without an escort. No matter how wealthy, influential, or eligible a bachelor might be, a two-seat T-bird owner may find his date broken off once the young woman's father saw there was no room in the car for a chaperone.

Case understood that their almost-luxurious sports car could not "grow" into the next generation Sportsman convertible. Ford needed to provide leg room, head room, and comfortable seating for rear passengers, and also to give them a trunk large enough for their baggage. Yet performance that had been exciting with two seats in 1957 should not have to diminish with

The classic Ford V-8 at the time displaced 239 cubic inches. With its standard Holley two-barrel carburetor, the engine produced 100 horsepower at 3,300 rpm.

four-seat versions in 1958. Ford had not fully developed its thin-wall V-8 engine technology. Case knew that for 1958, big power still meant big engines with big weight. By the time Ford division introduced its four-passenger Thunderbird, the car had gained close to 430 pounds. Case made the 1957 300 horsepower-optional V-8 into standard equipment for 1958.

Sales figures proved Crusoe and Case to be right. Even with a mid-year introduction, Ford dealers sold nearly 40,000 cars. Sales more than doubled by the end of 1960. In their 1963 book, *Ford: Decline and Rebirth: 1933 – 1962*, Allan Nevins and Frank Hill quote Crusoe's description of the new Thunderbird: "[It's] more truly a personal or boulevard car for the customer who insists on comfort and yet would like to own a prestige vehicle that incorporates the flair and performance characteristics of a sports car."

Automakers reward shrewd decisions, especially those that bring new customers to their dealers, with a promotion. For Crusoe, recognition arrived just as he conceived of the bigger, better Bird. On January 25, 1955, Ford's board of directors named him executive vice president of Ford's Car and Truck Division, making him responsible for assembly and distribution of all Ford vehicles. Soon after, he also was named chairman of the Product Planning Committee.

Yes, those are electric window lifts. The fully equipped Sportsman jumped up in price to $2,282 for 1947 and, in a measure of the growing wealth of the nation, Ford produced 2,274 cars, nearly three times what it had in 1946.

Robert S. McNamara, a Californian who had joined Ford Motor Company in 1946, had been a Harvard business school professor before the war. During the war, he had been one of 10 officers who ran the U.S. Air Force Office of Statistical Control. McNamara and a group of former officers, headed by former Army Colonel Charles "Tex" Thornton, joined Ford. Thornton and his men made names for themselves during the war, as historians Nevins and Hill described it, when they "built up an office which made every useful fact about [Air Force] planes and their use available practically on demand." At Ford, they sought to put the company's finances in order. Within months of their arrival, the group had questioned everyone, a work procedure that earned them the name "Quiz Kids." Their steady inquiries lead to answers, strategies, policies, and products that saved Ford money and made it profitable. Their name evolved to "Whiz Kids."

While they knew everything about the company, the Whiz Kids knew nothing about the car business. Lewis Crusoe adopted them and, after Thorton left in 1948, McNamara gained increasing financial responsibility in Ford Division. The board named him division vice president and general manager in January 1955, when the board promoted Crusoe to executive vice president.

McNamara's philosophy was that Ford should not produce any automobile that didn't make a profit. He also recognized that Ford could find profit in sales of accessories such as radios, white wall tires, automatic transmissions, and optional hardtops. He concluded that many more buyers wanted these accessories than Ford Motor Company had anticipated. Potential buyers could be enticed to add these items to their future car, he believed.

Ford's answer to the instability of the sports car market was its personal luxury car. Meanwhile a new market—the small-car market—struggled for recognition in the United States. McNamara noticed the inroads that Volkswagen and Renault had made on Ford's sales and on America's highways. Ford division reacted as it had done with the Corvette: quickly and decisively. McNamara introduced his personal project, the Falcon, in 1959, and the compact model sold an astonishing 417,174 cars in its first 12 months. This set a record for first year's sales throughout the auto industry. In the same season, Chrysler introduced its Valiant and Chevrolet brought out its air-cooled rear-engine Corvair. None of these cars had the looks of a show stopper, but in the case of the Falcon, it was not from lack of effort. Ford design had done a number of drawings that conceived the Falcon differently. Roof lines and fenders had a variety of other shapes before McNamara, Crusoe, and Henry Ford II approved a final design. McNamara, however, had no interest in second-guessing design decisions. This was especially

The Mercury division didn't want to be left out of the postwar exuberance and had its own Sportsman. However, while the Ford division produced slightly more than 3,000 of its models through 1948, the Mercury division manufactured just 205 examples.

(**opposite**) *The Thunderbird body, designed by former GM stylist Bill Boyer, made no mistakes. Boyer duplicated the shapes of the taillights in the exhaust pipe frames. The T-bird was introduced with a V-8 engine, something Chevrolet's Corvette had to wait three years to get.*

true when the car's first year sales had been so high. But there were others who asked themselves if even more cars might have sold if it looked better.

One individual who considered those questions was Lido Iacocca. Lee, as everyone knew him, already had made his mark selling cars in Pennsylvania. He had earned an undergraduate degree from Lehigh University and a master's from Princeton, both of these in mechanical engineering. He knew from the time he was 14 that he wanted to work at Ford (he owned a l938 flathead while at Lehigh), and in 1946, he joined the company as a student engineer. But after nine months of his 18-month introduction program at River Rouge, he was disillusioned. Years later he wrote about it in his 1984 book, *Lee Iacocca: An Autobiography*. After spending an entire day making a detailed drawing of a clutch spring, he wondered, "Is this how I want to be spending the rest of my life?

"I wanted to stay at Ford," he continued, "but not in engineering. I was eager to be where the real action was—marketing or sales. I liked working with people more than machines." But Ford would not transfer him to sales, so he quit. A short time later, he rejoined Ford Motor Company, working for Eastern division Sales Manager Charles Beacham.

By 1956, when he was 32, Iacocca had caught McNamara's attention. He had invented a sales promotion—"twenty percent down and $56 a month for a '56 Ford." McNamara, then 39 and Ford division's chief executive since January 1955, instituted the promotion nationwide and later he assessed that Iacocca's "$56 for '56" idea contributed to an additional 72,000 car sales that year. It earned the innovative engineer-turned-salesman an invitation back to Dearborn.

Not long after Iacocca arrived in Detroit, the tenor of the industry and the pride at Ford Motor Company underwent two big changes. Following a horrific auto-racing crash involving a factory-entered Mercedes-Benz in June 1955 at Le Mans, France, every automaker in the United States. became wary of direct involvement in motorsports. While Mercedes-Benz continued in competition through the rest of 1955, it withdrew completely from all racing at the end of the year, and other carmakers saw bad publicity lurking in every corner.

During its February 1957 board meeting, board member and GM Chairman Harlow Curtice suggested to the Automobile Manufacturers Association (AMA) that member companies "take no part in automobile racing or other competitive events involving tests of speed and that they refrain from suggesting speed in passenger car advertising or publicity." He feared the U.S. government would take an unwelcome interest in the auto industry and possibly impose regulations that would hamper the ability to sell cars or improve them. Every member of the AMA ratified Curtice's proposal. It was the auto industry's equivalent of Prohibition, however. None of the members

stopped their activities—they just learned to hide them well.

In this newly conservative atmosphere, Ford Motor Company introduced what it thought was the car that fit this new morality perfectly: the Edsel. In late 1954 and early 1955, Ford commissioned market surveys and sent its designers to street corners to observe what people drove. America's population was increasing and so was consumer income. More families and individuals owned cars now than ever before. The growing middle class had embraced Ford's Thunderbird. Henry Ford II wanted to take back first place. He believed he could do it by slipping a new product line between Mercury and Lincoln.

In late 1954, Ford's board challenged chief designer Roy Brown to "design a car that we can tell is different from everything else on the road." He stood on street corners, watched every other vehicle whiz past, and saw nothing but horizontal grilles. He and his colleagues returned to their studios and began to create. While its radical looks hurt the Edsel, a nationwide economic downturn also killed the car soon after its introduction on September 4, 1957.

Challenged to "design a car that we can tell is different from everything else on the road," chief designer Roy Brown did exactly that, creating the Edsel's iconic and controversial vertical grille. However, the car itself was ill-conceived from the start. Positioning the Edsel both above and below the Mercury lineup confused buyers and even the new Edsel dealers. The car was plagued with small defects that somehow had slipped through engineering and quality control. Worse, a $2 million ad campaign had tantalized people into believing this was the greatest invention in the history of the automobile; yet when the Edsel appeared in the showrooms in August 1957, people just saw an oddly styled, heavily chromed showboat. On top of all that, the nation entered a recession in early 1958 that severely shrunk the demand for any up-market model. Ford President Ernie Breech didn't want the car, and the Ford family didn't want it named after the founder's son, the father of Henry Ford II. When Ford's board pulled the plug on the car on November 22, 1959, it estimated losses at greater than $350 million. It was a hard loss for the company, and Henry Ford II found himself forced back into second place. According to designer Roy Brown in an interview in *Classic and Sports Car* in September 1989, "Mr. Ford wouldn't let anybody in the company talk about it for years."

McNamara's unexciting Falcon continued to roll out of the factory doors. By 1960 though, Chevrolet had upped the ante, improving the image of its staid economy Corvair with the introduction of the Monza, a performance-oriented option package. Turning a blind eye to the AMA ban its own chairman had authored, Chevrolet replaced the featureless bench seat with

Shortly before the T-bird's introduction, Ford division General Manager Lewis Crusoe drove one home. The next day he told product planner Tom Case "There's only one thing wrong with the Thunderbird. It's a beautiful car, but we need a rear seat in it."

two buckets and the two-speed automatic that shifted on the dash with a four-speed on the floor. Design and engineering departments gave the Monza's dashboard more instruments and carpeted the floors. In 1959, McNamara's frugal, utilitarian Falcon had generated almost a third of Ford Motor Company total sales. Yet within two years, it was the pale cousin at the beach on a sunny day, its sales falling precipitously. By 1963, the Falcon represented barely 1/25th of the corporation's sales.

Still, Ford Motor Company again rewarded volume with a promotion. On Wednesday, November 9, 1960, Robert S. McNamara was elected president of Ford Motor Company by the board of directors. By the time the corporation publicly announced McNamara's presidency, the United States had selected a new leader as well. Within a month, President-elect John F. Kennedy asked Ford Motor Company's president-elect McNamara to manage the military he had once served. McNamara accepted the cabinet post of Secretary of Defense on December 13.

On November 2, a week before Kennedy's election, Ford's board also promoted Lee Iacocca to vice president and general manager of Ford Division. For a man who had set goals for himself throughout his life, Iacocca had achieved one of his life ambitions at age 36, and he commented to friends that he was only a year behind his target date.

McNamara left quickly, and Iacocca suddenly felt an unanticipated burden. While his performance had been excellent, he knew he lacked something that all his predecessors had accomplished. "I had no real credentials as a product man," he wrote in his autobiography. "At this point in my career there was no car that people could point to and say: 'Iacocca did that one.'"

Ford began production of its new Thunderbird on September 7, 1954. By the time it stopped on September 16, 1955, Ford had manufactured 16,155 of them.

(previous) Ford Motor Company engineering Vice-President Herb Misch knew the corporation had some great vehicles coming. In the summer of 1962, he decided a concept car, "something that would stop auto show visitors and journalists in their tracks," would help promote the new line. What he got was the Mustang, shown here alongside Dearborn's proving ground fence.

Before Joe Oros, Ford design studio chief, had final approval of the design for the production Mustang, he asked clay modeler Charlie Phaneuf to start on a fastback design. Oros believed "if we really want to make this a sporty car, it had to have a fastback model." Lee Iacocca saw it just as production started on the coupe and convertible, and he approved it on the spot.

(November 1960–October 1962)

GREAT IDEA, WRONG DIRECTION

Lee Iacocca had learned much from Robert McNamara. As Iacocca recalled, no matter what question or situation, McNamara always knew all the facts. But he was also a realist who understood that his subordinates weren't as knowledgeable as he was. "Go home tonight," he once told Iacocca, "and put your great idea on paper. If you can't do that, then you haven't really thought it out." Iacocca did, and he continued to keep notes in a small black book he carried with him. One note referred to a roof-line sketch for McNamara's Falcon that he'd seen but someone had rejected as impractical. It resembled the early T-bird roof with visual appeal. Despite record first-year sales of the Falcon, Iacocca wondered if even more would have sold had the practical car looked more appealing.

Another note questioned the identity of Ford Motor Company. GM promoted their cars' appearances under design bosses Harley Earl and Bill Mitchell. It also heralded something it called its "general excellence." Chrysler boasts were more specific, focusing on the company's engineering. It already had introduced the compact Valiant with its in-line "slant-6" engine, and its hemispherical-head high-performance V-8 engines for the Chrysler 300-series already were legendary.

But what was Ford's defining character? The Fifties had brought luxury to Ford's image and now 1960 saw basic transportation back in the family. McNamara had pushed his Falcon's functionalism so hard that some within Ford wondered if he secretly wanted the car available only in black.

This was the first project out of Ford's Special Projects studio, which was launched in 1954. Conceived as a possible Mercury sports car to parallel the Thunderbird, it was referred to as D-523. After Ford shuttered the Special Projects Studio in 1958, the design staff stored the car until 1961 when someone renamed it the Cougar and sent it off to the show circuit, starting with the 1962 New York auto show.

(opposite) *For designer/modeler Charlie Phaneuf, this was an opportunity to try every design feature and option he knew, including European bulb-type oversize headlights. A number of design cues he initiated here saw production in later years, including the sculpted hood with hold-down pins.*

McNamara was gone, and now Iacocca ran Ford division. He got a strong shove from Henry Ford II to follow the instincts that earned him this job. So Iacocca gathered eight creative department heads to look into the future of Ford division. They met after regular working hours at Dearborn's new Fairlane Inn on Michigan Avenue less than a mile from World Headquarters.

Iacocca invited Don Frey, product planning manager, and his special projects assistant Hal Sperlich. He included market research manager Bob Eggert, along with public relations manager Walter Murphy, marketing manager Chase Morsey, advertising manager John Bowers, and Sid Olson from J. Walter Thompson, Ford's outside advertising agency. Iacocca's eighth weekly dinner guest at the Fairlane Committee, as it soon became known, was special projects manager Jacque Passino. He was Ford's racing director even during the AMA prohibition.

The agendas for these dinners began with the past. Three years earlier, the entire auto industry had embraced Harlow Curtice's ban on racing and speed promotion, yet GM's own Chevrolet and Pontiac divisions were among the worst offenders. Also, Ford's Falcon concerned Iacocca. Chevrolet had seized a performance advantage when it offered the Monza version of its economy Corvair.

"We started watching registrations of the Corvair, which was a dog," Don Frey told Mike Mueller in *Mustang 1964 ½ – 1973*. "I guess in desperation, they put bucket seats in the thing, called it the Monza, and it started to sell. We got the idea that there must be something to it. And that's how it all started, watching Monzas."

Iacocca knew there were no Monza options for Falcon. The car's styling was simply too staid to appeal to a market demanding excitement. Ford division received bags of mail each week that begged for a new two-passenger Thunderbird. Iacocca saw the growing interest among consumers in their cars' appearance and performance. Chase Morsey and Bob Eggert, with help from Frank Zimmerman from marketing, produced countless studies indicating that America's population was changing. The postwar baby boom presented a population approaching the career-starting/car-buying age. Children soon would outnumber their parents; there would be more 15 to 29 year olds than 30 to 39 year olds. Annual incomes would exceed $10,000 in three times as many households from 1960 to 1970. Specific surveys revealed preferences for bucket seats, floor-mounted four-speed manual transmissions, and an end to fins.

Two other concerns nagged at Iacocca. Surveys said the Falcon was stodgy. Iacocca knew that a small car project McNamara had husbanded through development, a new vehicle code-named the Cardinal, was worse. Iacocca knew he had to convince Henry Ford II, who had authorized $36 million

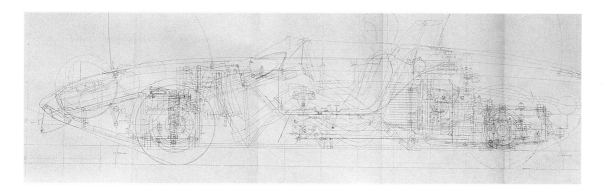

This scale drawing establishes the "hard points": engine air cleaner height, front and rear suspension pivot points, cowl height, seating positions, and other important dimensions of Herb Misch's concept car.

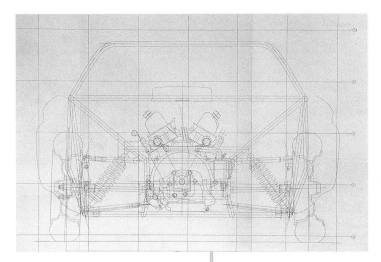

This drawing, looking from the rear of the car forward, shows the English Ford Cardinal/Taunus V-4 engine in place. It also shows how the independent rear suspension mounted to the rear transaxle housing.

to develop the car, to cancel it now. McNamara's Cardinal would use either an in-line four-cylinder engine from Ford of England or a new V-4 designed and manufactured in Germany. Either way, the boxy little coupes and sedans made the Falcon look striking. Ford engineering had designed the Cardinal with front-wheel drive, which provided better use of space within the package. It was innovative and far from being another chrome-plated Edsel, but this was far from 1958. The Cardinal package held no appeal to a nation that turned on to rock-and-roll music, tuned up its 300 horsepower V-8s, and had been transformed by a hatless young president with a chic wife who wore designer fashions.

Henry Ford II swallowed the loss, relegating the Cardinal to European-only distribution. As the Taunus, it sold millions of cars over the next decade in Europe. Iacocca understood that Henry Ford II's decision represented marching orders: Make this new vision of the future a success.

Out of the 14 Fairline Committee dinners came "The Lively Ones," a term and frame of mind that rapidly reinvented the Falcon for 1962. Ford introduced a convertible and offered a vinyl-roof, four-on-the-floor Falcon Futura. The division created similar options for the Fairlane and the new, larger Galaxy models as well. The best news for the Falcon was that engineering had completed the new 221-ci thin-wall V-8, providing much higher horsepower per pound than the previous high-performance V-8s. Falcons with the 221s were called Sprints.

The "Lively Ones" rapidly evolved into a "Total Performance" theme, a three-pronged thrust aimed directly at General Motors and Chrysler, the other vigorous rule bender of the AMA ban. The performance orientation these two had pursued had left Ford behind. Part of this was due to McNamara's cautiousness, but the responsibility rested equally with young image-conscious Henry Ford II. Ford division's marketing efforts through the early 1950s became quality and safety. The Edsel introduced safety wheel rims and self-adjusting brakes. Henry Ford II accepted the ban and McNamara embraced it.

Performance enthusiasts within Ford smelled a rat and they knew that Chevrolet, Pontiac, and Chrysler blatantly continued to support National Association for Stock Car Auto Racing (NASCAR) and United States Auto Club (USAC) efforts through their back doors. Jacque Passino struggled to assist long-time Ford racers Holman-Moody and the Wood brothers, but he had to be cautious to avoid embarrassing the chairman.

Chevrolet and Pontiac laid waste to NASCAR super ovals and Chrysler took home trophies from the drag strips. In Europe, Jaguar, Aston-Martin, and Ferrari took endurance race, hill climb, and rally wins and headlines. Ford was nowhere to be found.

Iacocca approached the chairman again. Henry Ford II waited and then approached General Motors whose top management expressed its regret and dismay that it could not control its division managers who chose to race anyway. Henry Ford II hadn't wanted to be the first carmaker to openly breach the AMA edict, but GM's answer to him didn't wash. He wrote a letter to the AMA in mid-June 1962, notifying the board of directors that Ford would establish its own standards of conduct regarding how the performance of its vehicles would be promoted and advertised.

The Fairlane Committee planned to officially return Ford to racing in NASCAR and drag racing at National Hot Rod Association (NHRA) venues. Next Ford would go after USAC's prestigious

Except for the long side scoops, little of the Mustang I's striking looks carried over into the production Mustang. They appeared here first and became a defining element of Mustang design.

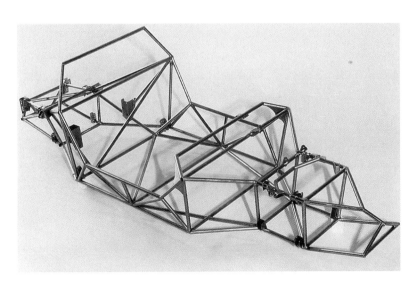

Because the car was born in the minds of engineering and not design, the car became a development model for many techniques not often found in American production automobiles. Among those ideas was this "birdcage" frame, made up of welded-together steel tubes, and when assembled, resembled a birdcage.

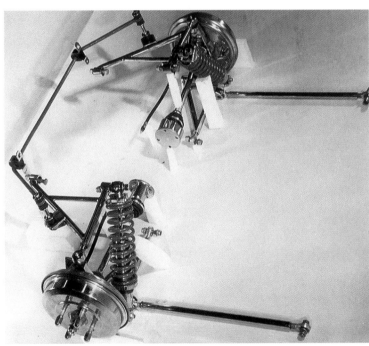

Engineering chief Herb Misch decided to introduce the car at the United States Grand Prix at Watkins Glen, New York. To the engineers working on the project, this encouraged them to build their "show car" like a racer. Roy Lunn and Bob Negstad gave it an independent rear suspension using an upper A-arm with an inverted lower A-arm and coil-over shock absorbers. Engineering settled on a 49-inch rear track.

(opposite) *From the date of approval until the show car's debut was just 22 weeks; 100 working days. While the first the show car's 16 weeks were hurried, the final 6 weeks were frantic in order to complete the Mustang for its introduction at Watkins Glen, New York.*

Indianapolis 500. In addition, it would support sports car racing and, at the J. Walter Thompson ad agency's suggestion, would take the Falcon to Europe to compete in the 1963 Monte Carlo Rally. Ford had a strong presence in Europe with its Taunus; now it was time to show customers over there what Fords could do at speed on snowy mountain passes. Ford's engines would become the stars; "powered by Ford" would come to mean something.

The second thrust of the "Total Performance" philosophy would make something out of the consumer interest in two-seat Thunderbirds. Iacocca went to Ford's styling chief, Eugene Bordinat, to discuss possibilities. Bordinat surprised his visitor. Bob Maguire, co-designer of the 1955 Thunderbird, was now head of advanced styling. He had come up with a concept for a smart, stylish four-passenger coupe. The full-size clay model, code-named the Allegro, had taken some inspiration from the Thunderbird's long nose and the long-nose/short-tail configuration of Lincoln's elegant 1956 Continental Mark II. Maguire put its bucket seats on both sides of the transmission tunnel, allowing him to draw a roof line lower than the Continental's.

Iacocca liked it—the idea more than the car itself. He encouraged Bordinat to explore the possibilities: four seats, two seats, and 2+2 seating where rear leg room might be less than a sedan or standard coupe. Iacocca later went to see Tom Case who had become Falcon planning manager. He asked Case to investigate the factors involved in producing a new four-place car. Case knew that Budd Company had produced bodies for the original Thunderbird. As a variation on the research for Iacocca, and in an attempt to keep costs down by modifying existing body stampings, he wondered if Budd could update the car for new production. Budd produced a prototype. They mounted it onto a modified Falcon chassis and removed the fins and headlight eyebrows from the 1957 Thunderbird body. Called the XT-Bird, its proportions never looked right, and Budd's costs to produce it were too high for its probable sales. Furthermore, Iacocca was not enthusiastic about the two-seater idea, and so Case and Bordinat abandoned the proposal.

Now it was early 1962 and Tom Case had been promoted to manager of special vehicles for Ford and Lincoln-Mercury. Case's study went to product planning manager Don Frey and Hal Sperlich, his special assistant. Frey understood sports cars, having driven an Allard while in the army in 1950. He and Sperlich got the assignment to create a car that would be code-named the "Special Falcon," a sporty car built to sell at $2,500 and weigh 2,500 pounds. Bordinat's group began working on several design ideas.

Executive designer John Najjar and studio manager Gale Halderman worked with design legend Alex Tremulis and a young first-year designer, Syd Mead, in the Corporate Advanced Studio in 1959 and 1960 to create the Gyron. Its most significant feature, beyond the roster of designers who shaped it, was that it operated on two wheels. It was balanced and stabilized by a large horizontal gyroscope.

Retractable headlights made aerodynamic and design sense. The car had a clean nose during daylight hours, which added to its visual appeal.

Even in the abstract, with nothing around it to compare size, the Mustang looks—and is—small. Built on a 90-inch wheelbase, it was just 154.3 inches long overall.

The Mustang I sits outside its permanent home, the Henry Ford Museum. For the first year of its life, it was almost always on the go to promote Ford engineering.

The tubular steel space frame made it easy for John Najjar and Jim Sipple to mount the engine where it made best sense for performance, handling, and fuel economy. This concept hasn't reappeared in any production Ford car, but it went on to influence Ford's most famous racer the GT40.

Department heads began to get excited. "Total Performance" was coming to mean total involvement. During the Model T days of banked board-track racing, "powered by Ford" meant something significant. The expression had weight in the late 1930s and early 1940s with the legendary flat-head V-8s. It was about to mean something again. But how did Iacocca let the consumer know? Outside Ford Motor Company, coincidence and serendipity were poised in wait.

Carroll Shelby, a tall, lanky Texan, wanted to put an American V-8 into a lightweight European sports car to make a reliable race car. Shelby had won countless races, including the 24 Hours of Le Mans in 1959, which he won while driving an Aston-Martin. Though he retired because of a heart condition, he pursued his dream of building high performance racing and road cars. General Motors turned down his proposal to buy Corvette engines and chassis without their fiberglass bodies; it wasn't willing to compromise its Corvette or to risk it being a racing failure. Shelby, who distributed Goodyear racing tires throughout the western United States, had met Ford racing engine manager Dave Evans at the July 4 Pikes Peak Hill Climb. Before this, Shelby had learned that English manufacturer, A.C. Cars, had lost its engine producer. He contacted the company and generated interest in the project. In August 1961, Shelby called on Ford's Evans, Frey, and racing manager Jacque Passino, hoping to acquire some of the new thin-wall 221-ci V-8s. Passino liked Shelby's idea and saw in it a testing and development arrangement that, if successful, would further the concept of "powered by Ford." He approved the sale and shipment of some engines, and Shelby went to work. His first prototype, named the Cobra, ran on January 30, 1962, in England at Silverstone racing circuit.

Still, this was outside the company. How did Iacocca tell consumers what was going on *inside* Ford, that things at the Blue Oval were changing? In late spring, even while Shelby's project had earned favorable magazine attention after its tests at the end of January, it was still called the Shelby A.C. Cobra.

Then in July 1962, a month after Henry Ford II's letter to the AMA and while Shelby was beginning production of his Cobra for racing and street sales, Dan Gurney, a former Porsche Formula One driver from California, arrived in Dearborn with English car builder Colin Chapman. They had an idea of their own. Fourteen months earlier, Jack Brabham had raced a four-cylinder rear-engined Cooper-Climax at Indy that failed to finish. In May 1962, Gurney had driven a rear-engine Buick V-8-powered car for Mickey Thompson that also failed to finish. Engine durability always was the culprit. Gurney and Chapman told Passino they needed a reliable 350 horsepower from a lightweight engine. Their timing was as sharp as Shelby's had been. Don Frey and Dave Evans had watched Gurney in Thompson's car during the race and had reached similar conclusions. Driving home to Dearborn from Indianapolis, they had begun to plan what it would take to build an Indy-winning engine. They did the deal: Chapman's Lotus would be "powered by Ford."

By the time Gurney and Chapman visited Passino, the third element of the "Total Performance" program already had begun during a small meeting held on May 8, just weeks before the 500-mile Indianapolis race. It had been just another coincidence waiting to happen. Ford Motor Company engineering Vice President Herb Misch knew the cars the corporation was bringing out in the fall for the 1963 model year were the first of a series of more appealing automobiles.

Jim Sipple and John Najjar looked at engine possibilities and concluded the compact German Ford V-4 fit best into their midships concept. This configuration emulated the successful prototype sport racings cars of the time.

Misch and Cog Briggs, the public relations liaison for engineering, concluded that a concept vehicle, something that would stop auto show visitors and journalists in their tracks, might help promote the new lineup. Misch, the engineer, even compromised the mechanicals: as a show car, whatever this might be, it didn't even need to run; it only needed to look sensational.

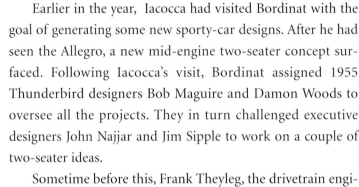

Earlier in the year, Iacocca had visited Bordinat with the goal of generating some new sporty-car designs. After he had seen the Allegro, a new mid-engine two-seater concept surfaced. Following Iacocca's visit, Bordinat assigned 1955 Thunderbird designers Bob Maguire and Damon Woods to oversee all the projects. They in turn challenged executive designers John Najjar and Jim Sipple to work on a couple of two-seater ideas.

Sometime before this, Frank Theyleg, the drivetrain engineer who had supervised development of McNamara's front-drive V-4 Cardinal, had become friends with another front-wheel drive supporter, Royston C. Lunn, an English chassis engineer whom Ford had transferred to Dearborn. Theyleg and Lunn both were sports car enthusiasts and they wondered if the Cardinal V-4, with its transaxle, might be useful in a mid-engine, lightweight sports car, yet they were realists. They understood that when the Cardinal was killed, "Total Performance" took over Ford division attention. At least for the time being "powered by Ford" probably meant propelled by eight-cylinder engines, not four.

Its narrow width, just 61 inches, contributed to its appeal at a time when many show cars were large and boatlike. Troutman & Barnes and California Metal Finishers in southern California fabricated the hand-hammered aluminum body.

However, perceptions change. Misch and Briggs saw a Najjar-Sipple design for a small, mid-engine sports car that showed strong potential for their show car purposes. Misch authorized it and on May 8, he assigned Lunn, who was an executive engineer in research by that time, to make it work. After all, "powered by Ford" did not mean "pushed around by Ford employees." Lunn picked his own crew to accomplish the feat. And feat it would be: Misch wanted the car ready to dazzle journalists and car enthusiasts at the United States Grand Prix in Watkins Glen, New York, held on October 7, 1962. That was only 22 weeks away, 100 days not counting weekends or the Memorial Day, Independence Day, and Labor Day holidays.

Misch's engineering department had hired a fresh-scrubbed, young engineer from Oregon State University named Bob Negstad in 1956. Working in the same college graduate training program that Lee Iacocca had attended, he became fascinated by front-wheel drive technology and investigated its chassis, steering geometry, and suspensions in the drafting room on his own time. His supervisors noticed his enterprise a year and a half into his two-year program. They made him a full engineer and transferred him to Germany to work on the Cardinal-Taunus front-wheel drive project.

In conjunction with that assignment, other work in Europe and England enlarged his skills. He returned to the United States just in time to join Misch's show car project. Lunn recruited Negstad to be his assistant to handle chassis development while they worked with other engineers, including Norm Postma, Charlie Maddox, Len Bailey, Chuck Mountain, Bud Anderson, and engineer-designer Jim Graham.

On May 9, they began with Najjar's drawings and all of them quickly concluded that there was no time to follow normal procedures. Even if they were willing to work weekends, holidays, and around the clock, the company building shut down each day at 5 P.M. There was no time to ask permission or file requisitions.

During the next two weeks, they tried a variety of configurations, all within the "package" concept. John Najjar drew in an English Ford in-line four-cylinder engine as part of a standard front-engine-rear-wheel-drive version. Though acceptable for a production coupe or sedan, everyone agreed that the cowl height and weight balance this version produced would not lend themselves to a sparkling show car, nor would it advance the state of automotive art. Najjar drew in Frank Theyleg's Cardinal V-4 behind the driver's seat, utilizing the transaxle system he had developed. It fit, and the profile and its measurements suddenly looked appealing. Lunn and his engineers conceived a one-inch steel tube semi-unitized space frame that incorporated the engine and transaxle as partial load-and-stress bearing elements.

On May 23, Lunn visited custom car fabricators Troutman & Barnes in Culver City, California, to arrange for them to fabricate the body. The next day, back in Dearborn, the program began. From the Najjar-Sipple full-size clay model, they now made working drawings that they delivered to Culver City by June 4. Meanwhile, the modelers formed a female plaster mold and created fiberglass and resin body forms from these. Once these hardened, they cleaned up the forms, painted them, and fitted them to a body buck for wind-tunnel tests. The shape worked, and the side-mounted radiators placed in high-pressure areas in the air stream along the car body proved to

Two levels of engine tune were part of the Mustang group's proposal for production. A street version offered 89 horsepower at 6,600 rpm. In racing tune, it developed 109 horsepower at 6,400 rpm. Still, it was a very simple overhead-valve engine meant for an economy car.

Najjar and Sipple included a roll bar in their design since the car would debut at an international Formula One Grand Prix. The cockpit had fixed seats to make maximum use of the car's limited interior space.

have just enough air flow through them to cool the engine. Design and engineering agreed that retractable headlights would improve airflow over and around the car. Immediately after the wind-tunnel sessions, Lunn shipped the body to Troutman & Barnes to be fabricated from welded-together aluminum panels.

Meanwhile design created the interior. They molded two fixed seats in one piece that they mounted rigidly to the car body. This added torsional stiffness to an already tight frame. Because Misch wanted the car to debut at an international road race, Lunn and his staff designed the chassis and built it as a race car. Its roll bar and other features met international rules. Its fully independent suspension used upper and lower A-arms front and rear, adopting current racing technology. They adapted outside vendor front disc brakes and large rear drums. They fitted a rack-and-pinion steering system with a flexible steering shaft. This allowed fore and aft movement of the steering wheel, and the foot pedals adjusted to the driver because the seats were fixed. They shipped much of this to Culver City by August 23, including a mockup of the V-4 engine and transaxle for test fitting.

While engineering finished up chassis and engine development and Troutman & Barnes' craftsmen hand-hammered and assembled the body, the designers went to work again. They pulled a truck and trailer from a corporate motor pool, thoroughly cleaned it and repainted it. They carpeted the trailer that they would use to transport the new car to Watkins Glen and fitted it with toolboxes.

The body and chassis were returned to Dearborn on September 7. Eleven days later, Advance Engine Engineering shipped a modified V-4, similar to the engine being produced in Germany for the Taunus 12M. Transmissions and Drive Train division delivered the transaxle on September 21. On September 23, design brought over the painted and finished Troutman & Barnes body, and from then until October 2, no one in the project rested. Details and finish work kept the team slaving around the clock, with only enough time out for a trip home to shower, change clothes, grab a meal, and return. Sleep, such as it was, often came on the benches and the floor around them.

The car already had a name. Designer John Najjar had long admired World War II fighter airplanes, especially the P-51 Mustang. The lines of his design appealed to him as much as that airplane, and he felt that engineering had produced a car worthy of the name. John Breeden, who handled public relations for design, ran the name past the legal department. Somewhere along the line, someone liked another dictionary definition even more than Najjar's interpretation. The wild American horse fit everyone's concept of this car. Designer Phil Clark drew the galloping horse logo. Design added the name to the side of the white-painted transporter and Breeden teased the population of Detroit with a newspaper ad announcing "a new horse in Ford's corral." On October 2, Misch and Hal Sperlich approved the completed vehicle, and Lunn and company loaded it into its transporter and left for New York that afternoon.

On October 6, Bordinat arrived at Watkins Glen. He was to host the press conference the next day to introduce the new Mustang as an example of the "Total Performance" concept that was "powered by Ford." Dan Gurney drove the car out onto the track and engineer Bob Negstad, there to keep the car running smoothly, remembered hearing lap times that would have been respectable in any sports car race at that track.

Ford printed 20,000 brochures introducing the new Mustang and gave all of them away that weekend. To race fans and journalists, it appeared that Ford had done something remarkable. Automotive artist Peter Helck drove the parade laps with English racer Stirling Moss as his passenger. When Dan Gurney drove pace laps before the race start in the same car, the spectators believed they were seeing the next great thing, and reacted as if it was the most exciting thing any of them had ever seen from an American carmaker.

(previous) *They were both symbols of war and from the same era. Where the Phantoms and Crusaders blazed through the skies of southeast Asia, Carroll Shelby's 427 Cobra, powered by Ford, rampaged over race tracks worldwide. Both examples of American technology humbled their opposition.*

427 Cobras were capable of going from 0 to 100 miles per hour and back to a standstill in just 14 seconds.

(October 1962–April 1964)

MORE GREAT IDEAS AND SLEEPLESS NIGHTS

No one anticipated the clamor the mid-engine car would create. Nobody expected such strong, positive reactions. The Mustang accomplished something for Ford Motor Company that no other Ford division car had done in several years: it provided favorable enthusiast publicity. That recognition went to Iacocca.

Between mid-October and early November, magazine and newspaper writers and photographers kept the car visible. The Mustang got cover play on the December issues of the major and minor auto magazines. The most recent Ford-powered product to garner that kind of attention had been just nine months earlier when Carroll Shelby's Cobras had caught the eyes and the hearts of the car magazine writers and editors. But that, Iacocca knew, was Shelby's car, not his. Now he had an accomplishment he could point to that was achieved under his tenure. However, it was exactly what he didn't want: a wildly favorable reaction to a two-seater.

Misch freed up several of the engineers involved in the project, and they took the Mustang on tour across the United States. It starred in major auto shows from New York to Los Angeles. After the big shows, it began a college tour. On one run alone, they visited 17 universities where there were mechanical or automotive engineering schools and student chapters of the Society of Automotive Engineers (SAE). Ford printed another 30,000 brochures and its engineers gave every one away. On occasion they showed up with the car unannounced, just to

It gathers a crowd wherever it goes. With 490 horsepower under the hood, Carroll Shelby's 427 Cobra, in competition trim, is still one of the most potent performance automobiles ever assembled.

gauge spontaneous reaction, driving it onto college campuses from coast to coast. It created traffic jams. Crowds constantly, and sometimes instantly, mobbed the car. Ford engineering took advantage of the frenzy and used the Mustang to recruit top engineering candidates to come to work for Ford. Everywhere the engineers traveled with the Mustang, people wanted to know when it would be available and how much it would cost.

Roy Lunn commissioned a detailed analysis of the specifications and features of the sports car competition from around the world as part of his vigorous campaign to put the two-seater into production. The Mustang compared favorably in most ways. In terms of its engineering features and design, it was far ahead of the field. Charlie Maddox and Norm Postma prepared a paper, "The Mustang–Ford's Experimental Sports Car," for Lunn to present to the SAE during its national convention held in Detroit in mid-January 1963. By that time, however, Iacocca had begun making it clear the car would not be produced. He recognized its image value, though, and in public he characterized it as something "to show the kids that they should wait for us because we had some good, hot stuff coming."

"The *corporation* never did decide to build *that* car," the late Bob Negstad recalled nearly 30 years after the Watkins Glen showing. "That was done by the guys over in Research and Advanced Vehicles, who had this task of showing a car, 'powered by Ford.' That Ford engineering had new engines and the engines were exciting, that just got completely pushed to the sidelines. We took the 'engine' engineering and we moved it right out onto wheels and tires and brakes and suspension. Most styling cars are just push-arounds, they're good for photography, but not functional. That Mustang was completely, totally functional."

Because the Mustang functioned so well, it thrilled the magazine writers and photographers. During the same Grand Prix weekend, Chevrolet introduced its Corvair Monza GT. While GM employees pushed their show car from one display area to the next, the Mustang ran laps as the official pace car for the race. Lunn's group later assembled a second Mustang made

On its best days, the Cobra was never an aerodynamic package. In fact, wind resistance of the open body 289 models forced Shelby to "get a bigger hammer" and install a bigger engine to win against sleeker European coupes.

From any angle its aggressive lines and squat stance suggest the power it offers. The large filler cap covers a 42-gallon, competition-size fuel cell. Gas mileage is never discussed.

This is the office. With its competition shoulder harnesses stuffed behind the seat backs, it looks like any ordinary English two-seater sports car. In fact, this model was a street model and converted to competition specs in 1977.

Shelby and ace engineer Phil Remington were serious about cooling these brutes. While the radiator held 20 quarts of coolant, its dry sump oil system required 14 quarts and was fed by hoses in and out of the cooler below the larger air intake.

of fiberglass. It did not have an engine/transaxle and it was only a push-around model for auto-show static displays.

While the mid-engine Mustang had been in the works, around mid-1962, Iacocca had proposed to Henry Ford II a new car program that would produce a four-seater based on what he'd seen in Bordinat's studios. He had received a cool reception. Iacocca's Falcon Sprint had failed to meet its sales expectations, in part because its sale price came in about $600 higher than the Corvair Monza, even though it had fewer standard features. Ford dealers couldn't give them away, nor would they stop screaming about it. For Henry Ford II, the idea of committing corporate funds now to a new four-passenger sporty-car seemed ill-advised.

Design seemed to be moving along slowly, too. Iacocca grew impatient. He wanted this four-seat car and had come to believe in it, whatever it might look like. Corvair's Monza continued to sell, and his old friends in dealerships called him personally to complain. The mid-engine Mustang show car was out promoting a car that, as of yet, no one had even designed, let alone approved for production! He told Bordinat that he wanted a design contest, as a way to challenge the designers from Ford, Lincoln-Mercury, and the Corporate Advanced Studio. Bordinat alerted Don DeLaRossa, now head of Corporate Advance Studio after his success on

McNamara's Falcon. He visited Ford Studio chief Joe Oros and asked him to spread the word. Oros stopped at Gale Halderman's drawing board and, as he recalled in an interview with Jim Farrell in *Collectible Automobile*, Oros said, "We've just been given an assignment by Bordinat to do a proposal for a small car that Lee wants to build." Halderman, a Ford designer since 1954, had worked with Don DeLaRossa on the successful proposal for the Falcon, but now Halderman was up to his neck in 1965 Ford design assignments. Still Oros asked him and three others to sketch a few concepts. Halderman did half a dozen ideas at home that night, and posted them on the board the next morning for Oros to review. Of the more than two dozen drawings on display, Oros picked one of Halderman's.

Oros immediately commissioned a full-size clay, assigning to George Schumacher in the advanced studio the task of creating it. Halderman went back to work sketching 1965 production cars but, working just across the hall, he came in regularly to monitor progress. He and Schumacher completed the rear end while Oros and Charlie Phaneuf did the front. Modeler Dave Ash started work on a four-door model based on Halderman's concept, but it got little consideration. Stretching the passenger cockpit and adding rear doors created proportions that recalled the Falcon. Ash and John Najjar made subtle improvements to Halderman's design as it progressed into the full-size model. During the process, Ash named the car the Cougar. When Bordinat announced the winner of Iacocca's inter-studio design contest, the Cougar team had won.

The car was striking and simple. Halderman and the others slightly exaggerated the opposite perspective of the short-hood, long rear-deck motif that characterized the Falcon and the Fairlane. Najjar carried over his long sculpted scoop that had led cooling air into the radiators on the mid-engine car he had developed with Jim Sipple.

Even these fat Goodyear Blue Streaks could not hold the power on the ground. It is possible to break the rear tires loose at 100 miles per hour.

On September 10, 1962, Iacocca pitched the Oros team Cougar design for full production. Iacocca had asked Hal Sperlich to identify which markets and product lines Ford was missing. Sperlich concluded that Ford lacked an exciting, fun-to-drive entry-level car for young people and young married couples. Corporate president Arjay Miller, another one of the Tex Thornton "Whiz Kids" hired with McNamara, had commissioned an estimate of how many cars the company would sell. The report took into account the numbers of customers switching from Falcon, Fairlane, and other Ford models to this new car, but its goal was to find the number of additional cars that would be sold. Corporate research head George Brown produced a figure of 86,000, not really enough to justify the cost. But for months now, Iacocca had done his homework, and he did his salesman's-best attempting to sell this car to Henry Ford II. He emphasized that, by using mostly Falcon pieces, the car could go into production quickly and at reasonable cost. The chairman had come to like the idea of the car. After seeing the "Cougar" clay model in the Design Center courtyard, Iacocca got excited and called the chairman to come see it. Henry Ford II came down, approved it on the spot, and told Iacocca to go ahead with the car. They set production at 150,000 units for the first year. Henry Ford II assigned $40 million and a target date of March 9, 1964, for Job One, the first cars to drive off the assembly line. Public introduction would be five weeks later. This meant

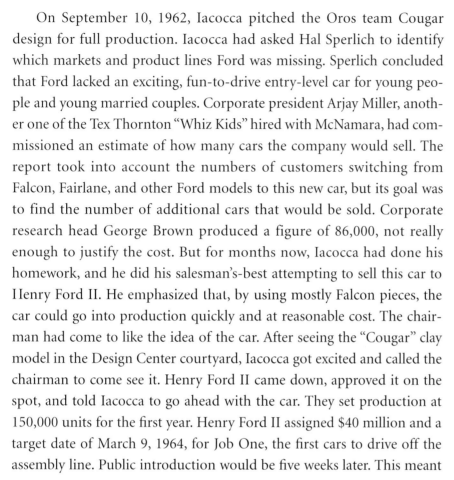

A sense of perspective is valuable. This road rocket sits on a 90-inch wheelbase just as the tiny Mustang I did. It is 156 inches long, just 1.6 inches more than the Mustang. At 2,150 pounds, it weighs 500 pounds more than a Mustang I and has 380 more horsepower.

Iacocca had barely 18 months, about half as long as usual, to reach Job One. Now that the car had the go-ahead, the thousands of small details that previously had been just variables in a prototype needed to be nailed down, not to mention making the car move and turn and stop.

The foundation of the production car, still called the Cougar or referred to by its in-house code designation as the T-5, basically was the Falcon Sprint. Nothing invented for Roy Lunn's Mustang would be carried over into production. That technology would go elsewhere with Lunn, and later with Negstad and others to England and on into racing.

To produce a working, running Mustang in such a short time period meant borrowing parts and ideas from somewhere else. For years, Detroit Steel Tube (DST) had done custom fabrication and modification for Ford Motor Company to prepare prototype cars for evaluation and modeling purposes. Ford engineering had already asked them to put the new Fairlane 221-ci V-8 into the Falcon. It became the Falcon Sprint, an evolution that had required countless other modifications. Ford chassis engineer Bob Negstad was involved from the start.

"Jim White and Andy Hotten and their guys at DST," Negstad explained, "came back in nothing flat with a V-8 stuffed into a Falcon. Along the way, we adapted a lot of Fairlane parts

Exhaust noise inspired thrills among spectators and heart palpitations among competitors. The tuned steel tube headers were deafening.

(opposite) This is "power by Ford". The competition 427 bore and stroke measured 4.24x3.788 inches. It sucked fuel (and perhaps even airplanes from the sky) with its 780 cfm Holley four-barrel carburetor.

This was Carroll Shelby's dream come true. He took an English sports car with pretty good handling and installed an American V-8 with exceptional reliability and power. It helped launch the new image of Ford Motor Company.

(opposite) For street versions, Shelby used Ford's 271 horsepower engine. In a car weighing just 2,100 pounds, performance was quick and top speeds of 140 miles per hour were routine. The chrome "tuned" air cleaner was a $4 option.

to the Sprint. We borrowed the front spindle so we could borrow the front brakes. The Falcon was designed for six-by-thirteen inch tires and it had nine-inch brake drums. And those were just totally inadequate for anything other than, say, parking it when you were shopping. None of that was going to work with a V-8 in the car.

"So more Fairlane parts kept going into the Falcon; a bigger sector shaft on the steering. It picked up the axle out of the Fairlane, the transmission and clutch parts, the radiator, and on and on. When they got all done, the Falcon Sprint was nothing like a Falcon. It was a re-mix of parts off the shelf from other car lines, mainly Fairlane. To share components made the Falcon into a viable alternative. It came out too expensive but....

"Then Hal Sperlich saw this Falcon Sprint," Negstad continued, "and knew that Ford had spent a fortune tooling and modifying it and couldn't give it away. The tools were there, bought and paid for." Don Frey had brought in Sperlich to develop the idea of Product Planning. "He saw the success of the small sporty, two-passenger Mustang and said, 'Whoa, here's an opportunity.... Take this Falcon Sprint, re-skin it, re-do it, re-trim it, and re-present it as a sporty car.'" Sperlich put together a think tank, including Negstad, to conceive of new packages for the Falcon Sprint.

"Everybody was given a different scheme," Negstad explained. "My assignment was to try to put the six-cylinder engine behind the seat, transversely mounted, and make a rear-engine/rear-wheel drive Falcon. Really! The only one that made any sense at all was to take a Falcon Sprint just like it was; take everything off that Sprint and throw it away. Peel off the fenders, the doors. Put on a body that didn't look anything like a Falcon Sprint.

"The Falcon Sprint had a short nose and a long tail. Fine, we'll make a short tail and a long nose. Gene Bordinat and DeLaRossa's people did that. Turns out, it looked pretty good. When they 'costed' it—calculated what it cost to build it—it was peanuts. The Mustang was born. It borrowed the emblem and the name."

That was mid-September 1962. In less than a week after selling the Cougar to Henry Ford II for nothing down and $40 million over 18 months, the biggest sale of Lee Iacocca's career, Bordinat's designers had made full-size drawings off George Schumacher's clay model of Gale Halderman's concept. When the car appeared 18 months later, it was closer to Halderman's original idea than any car that had come before it. Everyone involved with the project, from Henry Ford II down to the newest engineering trainee, came to like the car so much that many of the usual conflicts didn't happen. There were still glitches and problems, arguments over pedal placement, front and rear suspension travel, the typeface to be used for the car's name, the car's name itself, battery placement, roll-up rear quarter windows, the direction of the logo, and the stitching style to be used on the upholstery. There was a feeling about this car, though: that it was right, that it had possibilities and that those possibilities could make for an exciting future at Ford.

Surveys, market research, and viewer tests went on at an accelerated pace. Trends that Chase Morsey, Bob Eggert, and Frank Zimmerman had cited in Fairlane Committee dinner meetings with Iacocca were reinforced with further studies and through practical observation. The buyers coming into dealerships *were* younger. The gross national product was rising. Wages also were rising, and starting salaries for new college graduates entering their first jobs were higher than ever.

The 289-ci Cobra is a car that encourages road trips. It inspires its owners to find twisty roads and take the long way home.

Carroll Shelby's goal was a reliable car that racers like him could afford. For the street, dress-up options such as the front grille guard ($39.50) and the wind wings ($22.50) appeared on top of its $5,995 base price.

New product surveys gave groups a chance to see a mock-up of the new car and estimate its price based on the features that were listed. Consistently, people overestimated this figure, in some cases by as much as three times its projected introductory price. When they made this assessment, they looked longingly but distantly at the car. When they learned it could be sold for less than $2,500, they immediately began to think of ways they *could* afford it and reasons they *should* have it. At less than $2,500, this car was not an unapproachable luxury; it became a practical form of transportation that offered unmatched style and flair.

This encouragement provoked Ford division management to rethink initial sales projections. With the Edsel and the Falcon Sprint, there had been optimism and there were mistakes. It was one thing to produce a failure of a car that didn't sell up to expectations and be stuck with unwanted inventory. It was another to fail because the product exceeded expectations, but it had insufficient inventory. By the summer of 1963, Iacocca believed that Ford would sell more than 200,000 of them. As the educated predictions continued, Iacocca went to the board to ask for more production capacity for what he believed might be a first-year sale of 360,000 cars. They accepted his judgment and manufacturing prepared the San Jose plant for conversion. Just before spring of 1964, manufacturing retooled the Metuchen plant in New Jersey as well.

The question of the car's name kept coming up. Dave Ash's boss, Joe Oros, sent notes to Iacocca throughout the fall of 1962 supporting Ash's candidate for the car's permanent name and reasoning with the general manager to keep it "Cougar." But historically, Ford Motor Company's ad agency proposed the automobile names after clearing their availability. In their thoroughness, the J. Walter Thompson agency sent its researcher, John Conley, to the Detroit Public Library. Conley submitted a list containing 6,000 possibilities for this new car. Through

its usual processes, Ford's account executives narrowed it to a final six: Cougar, Bronco, Puma, Cheetah, Colt, and Mustang. By November 1962, Henry Ford II and Iacocca had settled on Mustang due to the word's suggestion of moving fast through the open country.

Oddly, as late as January 1964, people within the division still called the car the Special Falcon, the Cougar, T-5, the Mustang, and even the Torino, a name someone introduced to honor Iacocca's heritage. Though the J. Walter Thompson agency began preparing advertising copy, shooting brochure photographs, writing press releases and television advertising scripts, some in management continued playing with the name.

The flood of publicity surrounding the mid-engine Mustang still swirled around Ford. While survey groups had seen, without being told specifically, what the 1964? car would look

like, public affairs, design, engineering, and even Ford World Headquarters still got letters asking for the two-seater.

Iacocca felt it was necessary to put out the fire that boiled under the two-seat enthusiasts as well as redirect the publicity toward what was coming. Gene Bordinat delivered a pre-production prototype to DST for modification. Called the Mustang II, the modified car clearly would retain its true four-seat identity, but it also would carry some of the styling cues of the two-seater, now known as Mustang I. Bordinat had the new show car painted white with a blue racing stripe and a blue interior, the same color combination used on the Mustang I. DST added fiberglass bodywork to the front and rear to restyle the nose and tail, and its slightly modified roof line gave the impression that this car was much longer and lower than the actual 5 inches it was lengthened.

Ford introduced Mustang II on the October 6, 1963, Watkins Glen Grand Prix weekend. Iacocca's objective of cooling the passion for a two-seater succeeded, but it did little to dampen the enthusiasm that had grown for Ford's "Total Performance" program. The race weekend crowd picked up brochures, and many asked "When?" with the same anxious interest they had the previous year for Mustang I. Then a serious problem had appeared late in 1963. The early drivable prototypes were breaking.

"The first Mustangs," Bob Negstad explained, "were put together and sent out on 'durability'— potholes. And they destroyed themselves. The body structure was terrible. There was a relatively small group of people who did this development part, the Make-a-Mustang-Out-of-the-Falcon-Sprint group. When the car started to have trouble, everybody scattered, disappeared. They said, 'Oh my God. Here's a disaster.'" (This had happened before with the Edsel. Chief designer Roy Brown remembered those involved fleeing and denying any past support of the project. When the corporation pulled the plug on it, many of those who had hung on found themselves exiled to meaningless jobs or into early retirement.)

"The few people who were the real movers and shakers behind the car, Hal Sperlich and Lee Iacocca, and the people who were stuck with this Mustang, we knew we had to fix it, do the development work. The plan was very simple. We would *make* a convertible.

"We added the structure to make a convertible, did all the testing, evaluating, twisting, and the durability. We fixed the convertible. When it came down to the coupe?… Piece of cake, put a top on a convertible and you've got even more stiffness. The Mustang coupe was too stiff," Negstad chuckled. "And that was a cost reduction from '64 ½ to the '65. Remove some parts."

Months earlier, Ford studio chief Joe Oros had ordered clay modeler Charlie Phaneuf to start on a fastback design even before the concept got approved. However, Oros believed in the design

While it shared the 90-inch wheelbase of its hairy big brother, the 289 model stretched 11 inches longer out to 167 inches. This 289 model is nearly 10 inches narrower than the 427. The rear bumper guard was a $42.50 option.

Shelby offered a "custom" AM radio and antenna for an additional $58.50. A heater was another $95 optional decision.

and the idea, arguing, as Halderman recalled, "if we really wanted to make this a sporty car, it had to have a fastback model." Phaneuf did it in complete secret, not allowing even Hal Sperlich or Iacocca a preview until Oros had it cast in fiberglass and painted bright red. When Iacocca did finally see it, just as the coupe and convertible began production, Halderman remembered he said, "We've got to do it!"

As the car approached Job One, Iacocca and his Mustang team enjoyed some other pleasant surprises. The efforts to keep costs down had succeeded. From their experience with the Edsel, they learned they needed to simplify rather than complicate a new product line. The Edsel lineup featured entry-level, mid-range, and luxury models. For the Mustang, they settled on a coupe and convertible, followed by the fastback. This saved Ford the costs of different names, badges, sales brochures, promotion and advertising expenses; money the division could put to other uses for the new car.

Ford announced a selling price of $2,368, an odd figure with a curious and easily remembered ring to it. Ford used the extra money it had saved on development costs to provide the new Mustang with a long list of standard features. Each car received: full-size hubcaps, full carpeting, bucket seats, front armrests, a cigarette lighter, padded dash, self-adjusting brakes, a sport steering wheel, a three-speed floor-mounted gear shift, bumper guards front and rear, automatic door courtesy lights, and a glove box light. Many buyers would remember April 17 as the first time they ever saw an affordable car so thoroughly equipped at no extra cost.

To this, Ford added an options list offering 40 more factory choices with which to personalize their new car, as well as nearly two dozen other accessories available from the dealer. A buyer could upgrade the standard in-line 170-ci 101 horsepower six-cylinder engine to a 260 or 289-ci V-8 and replace the three-speed with a four-speed stick shift or a T-bar Cruise-O-Matic automatic transmission. There were: power brakes, steering, and top for the convertible, air conditioning, tinted glass, vinyl roof covering, 14-inch wire wheel covers or 15-inch sport wheels and tires, and dozens of other possibilities before the buyer ever saw the color chart.

However, throughout the winter of 1963 and into the early spring of 1964, leading up to the introduction, one more concern crept into management, engineering, and design's minds. The recent, undesirable experience with a product that had received so much pre-production interest was beginning to worry some of the participants. Few people even were willing to mention the "E" car, but the similarities alarmed many people.

Ford management had learned a great deal after the disaster of the Edsel. Now, seven years later, after all the buildup for this new Mustang, all the publicity, all the research done to confirm the buying public's hunger for such a vehicle, would this new four-seater become known as the M-car?

Between 1962 and 1965, Shelby manufactured 654 Cobras. Competition cars started at $6,275 and went up to $12,405 for a car equipped with the 370 horsepower, full competition engine. These models humbled Corvettes and inaugurated the Cobra legend.

1964½–1966

(1 9 6 4 ¹/₂ – 1 9 6 6)

AN OVERNIGHT SUCCESS...AFTER YEARS OF HARD WORK

Ford registered 22,000 Mustang sales the first day. By the close of business, December 31, 1964, the division had sold 263,434 of the cars, and when the sun rose in Dearborn on April 17, 1965, the sporty four-seater had accumulated 418,812 sales during its first calendar year. Mustang beat the Falcon sales record by 1,638 cars.

The introduction was carefully orchestrated. On March 2, a week before Job One and 45 days before the official launch date, William B. Ford III snuck out from Dearborn to lunch in downtown Detroit in a black Mustang convertible, one of the 150 pre-release cars built to de-bug production lines. *Detroit Free Press* staffer Fred Olmsted noticed the car and called a staff photographer. The pictures moved over the wire services. Newspapers and magazines nation-wide published an advanced look.

The previous fall, Ford public affairs invited magazine writers to Dearborn for a day-long briefing. Hal Sperlich outlined the influences and studies that had dictated and shaped the new car. Lee Iacocca emphasized the car's sporty nature as well as how economical it would be. The following January, Ford division invited back many of the same writers for "ride and drive" sessions around the Dearborn handling track in pre-production models. Then dealers in 13 major North American cities saw live musical stage shows that introduced the car and built support and excitement. Months later, just before the official introduction, Ford mailed

(previous) The short trunk and long hood of the first-generation Mustang helped define the entire "pony car" genre. In 1966, almost half a million hardtop Mustangs were sold, compared to 35,698 fastbacks and 72,119 convertibles.

Optional styled steel wheels were $93.84 and only available on V-8-powered cars.

72

Triple vertical taillights have been a Mustang hallmark since day one.

(opposite main) Recent documentation suggests that this unassuming coupe is the first production Mustang sold. Equipped with a 170-ci, straight six-cylinder engine with manual transmission, it was fitted with a generator, unlike later Mustangs that had alternators.

11,000 press kits to newspapers and magazines in Canada, the United States, Puerto Rico, and Mexico.

On Monday, April 13, four days before the public introduction, Ford hosted 150 journalists at the New York World's Fair. After leading them on a tour of Ford's Pavilion, Iacocca again explained the nature and the history of the car they would be seeing, though not for several more days, he said. They all adjourned to a luncheon whereupon the startled writers were handed keys to 75 new Mustangs and released to drive themselves back to Dearborn. Later that evening, Walter Hoving, chairman of Tiffany and Company, presented Henry Ford II with Tiffany's Gold Medal Award "for excellence in American design."

At 9:30 P.M., Thursday, April 16, Ford aired what many suggest was some of television's first infomercials unveiling the new Mustang simultaneously on ABC, CBS, and NBC. Ford had bought exclusive time on the three networks, and Neilsen ratings indicated that nearly 29 million viewers first saw the car in their own living rooms.

The media blitz continued Friday morning and throughout the weekend in 2,600 newspapers with stories and paid advertisements, more than 100 of those in women's sections of major metropolitan area newspapers. By the time most Ford dealers opened their doors on Friday morning, April 17, crowds surrounded their stores. A dealer in Pittsburgh had his only

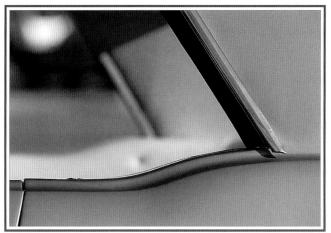

Mustang up on the wash rack when the crowd found it. It remained there all day because the crowd never thinned out enough for him to remove it and drive it into the showroom. A Texas dealer sold his last floor sample to the highest bidder who insisted on sleeping in the car overnight while the bank cleared his check. Mustangs went on display in banks, airports, hotels, and shopping centers. Ford provided convertibles in Wimbledon White as official pace cars (some sources report two, others say three were built) for the 48th annual Indianapolis 500 mile race, equipping them with performance and handling modifications in addition to what was provided in the 289-ci engine's "Hi-Po" high-performance option. Ford division also provided another 190 coupes and 35 convertibles—also in Wimbledon White—as pace-car replicas to the 1964 race officials. The replicas, however, came with the 260 V-8s.

Iacocca's idea with the publicity and media blitz was to put the car in front of everyone in North America. He was sure that once they saw it and discovered its price, they would want it and buy it. Because participants in marketing tests done before the introduction had expected a much higher price tag when they saw the prototypes, all the advertising and even its luxurious

74

Simulated air vents were inspired by the vents on the Mustang II, which were stylistic interpretations of the functional vents on the Mustang sports car from 1962. The body line highlighted by the chrome trim has been an on-again, off-again styling cue throughout the Mustang's career.

Far from Indiana's fields, this 1964-1/2 Pace Car Coupe displays the interior that helped make the Mustang so popular from day one. Simulated holes in the steering wheel spokes cast a sporty air to the compact interior.

Although technically a 1965 model, most refer to the Pace Car replicas as 1964-1/2s. With a 108-inch wheelbase, the Mustang had trim proportions that reflected its economy car roots.

77

The fastback model was one of three body configurations offered when the Mustang debuted in April 1964. The styled steel wheels were only available with a V-8 engine and cost $119.71.

Functional extractor vents on the C-pillars helped pull air from the interior. A manually operated control that was mounted on the inside of the C-pillar opened and shut the vent.

One of 190 Pace Car replicas built to commemorate the 1964 Indianapolis 500, this vehicle was assembled on April 20, 1964. All the Pace Cars for sale to the public were sprayed with paint code C, Pace Car White. The actual pace cars were painted Wimbledon White, paint code M.

The K-code 289-ci V-8 was the strongest Mustang on the menu for 1965, and generated 271 horsepower from the solid-lifter engine. Ford spent considerable effort to ensure the folded convertible stack was low enough to allow a snap-on cover to hide the top.

The vast majority of 1965 Mustang GTs were equipped with a 225-horsepower, 289-ci V-8. Rocker stripes were part of the $165.03 GT package.

full-color sales brochure presented its "Unexpected Look! Unexpected Price! Unexpected Choice!" of options and its "Unexpected Versatility!" Television commercials made it clear that radical personality changes would occur in Mustang buyers, turning them from shy, retiring individuals into lively, interesting, and exciting people.

In the ten years since Chevrolet introduced its Corvette to enthusiastic reaction but poor sales, America had changed, growing wiser and more worldly. Scientists had discovered the double helical molecular chain, DNA, that contained the "blueprint" of each individual life. Crooner-singer Elvis Presley brought African-American music, now labeled "rock-and-roll," to a white audience. In Montgomery, Alabama, Rosa Parks lifted an entire nation's awareness of racial inequality. The Soviet Union launched Sputnik and inaugurated a decades-long space race beginning in 1957, while Mary Leakey unearthed the 1.75 million-year-old skeleton of a man in the Olduvai Gorge in Tanzania in 1959. Retired chemist Margaret Sanger saw the fulfillment of her lifelong efforts to help women achieve reproductive freedom with the introduction of the birth control pill. In 1962, President John F. Kennedy agonized over launching a missile attack against 162 warheads stockpiled on Cuba. Just 13 months after that, on November 22, 1963, Kennedy was dead, assassinated in Dallas. Then, barely two months before Ford introduced the Mustang in New York City, newspaper columnist and TV host Ed Sullivan introduced the Beatles—Paul McCartney, John Lennon, George Harrison, and Ringo Starr—to a screaming, squealing audience in his Studio 50 at CBS and to the nation at large.

Disc brakes were standard with the GT Equipment Package.

Grille-mounted fog lamps were part of the GT Equipment Package option. The honeycomb grille has returned on contemporary Mustangs.

Embossed seat backs were part of the Interior Décor Group, a $107.08 option that included a five-dial instrument panel that replaced the horizontal speedometer. This option is popularly called the Pony Interior.

Thirty years after the Mustang's introduction, in the October 1994 issue of England's *CAR* magazine, writer Stephen Bayley recaptured the car's appearance better than any who had come before him:

> There was the air intake, a perfectly judged oblong slot with pretend lateral louvers which would irritate were they not executed with such conviction. American designers have a genius with orifices. Then there were the kicked-up haunches, the most winning interpretation of the Coke bottle look. And lastly there was the turned-up back bumper which gave the rear end a pick-up-your-skirts-and-run aspect.

The concept, design, and promotion all worked nearly too well. Ford division had produced about 16,000 Mustangs during the six weeks before the official introduction date—around 535 per day from the River Rouge plant, beginning March 9. And by the end of the first day of sales, Ford Motor Company was already about 6,000 cars behind. (The San Jose plant

Two-tone interiors, such as this parchment with aqua, were popular in 1966. This hardtop, a 200-ci Sprint model, changed little from the 1965 design.

Only 9.5 percent of 1966 Mustang buyers spent the extra $310.90 for underdash air conditioning. On the other hand, 62.8 percent of Mustangs built in 1966 came with the $175.80 Cruise-O-Matic transmission.

With a 9.2:1 compression ratio and hydraulic lifters, the 200-ci, straight six found in the 1966 Mustang Sprint developed 120 horsepower at 4,400 rpm. Carburetion was an Autolite single-barrel Model C6OF-9510-AD. A chrome air cleaner was standard with the Sprint package.

84

wasn't up and running until early July, according to the *Mustang Production Guide, Vol 1, '65-'66,* and San Jose then quickly changed over to 1965-model year production. Metuchen would not be in operation until February 1965.)

Supply was always slightly behind demand, which was almost a problem, but as far as problems went, this was the best kind to Henry Ford II and Iacocca. Dealers sold every car they got. Delays stretched as long as eight weeks, yet customers waited. Ford division met the Financial Production Volume, the number of cars they need to sell to pay for the tooling, within the first six months. This meant that the Mustang was profitable shortly after its 1965 models were introduced (officially, all the first year-and-a-half of production are known as 1965 models). While Ford base-priced the hardtop at $2,320.96, most cars sold with options that ran delivery prices up to around $3,000. As McNamara predicted, dealers and Ford division were making even more money off the options.

The new owners treated each other on the roads as traditional sports car owners had done in the days before Mustang, honking and waving, as if they alone understood a secret or had joined a club. There were clubs to join, too. Outside the company, an organization called the National Council of Mustang sprung up, and when they held their first Rally Day U.S.A. on April 16, 1965, a year after the launch, more than 12,500 Mustangs and owners representing 250 clubs showed up. The owners wore Mustang logo jackets, T-shirts, hats, and pants.

The late Ken Purdy, one of America's most-accomplished automotive journalists, once wrote: "Great cars are designed by small groups of dedicated people." That was especially true with the mid-engine Mustang I sports car prototype, and it held true with the 1964 ½ production car. Gary Witzenburg quoted development engineer C.N. Reuter recalling the trouble he had obtaining cooperation from the other divisions that were supposed to supply parts to the Mustang program. As Lunn, Negstad, and others had experienced on the Mustang I, there was a forced-march mentality among those involved with the Cougar/T-5 program. Yet among all the outside divisions and suppliers, things still had to be done through channels with requisitions providing the proper number of copies signed off with authorization. So instead, design and engineering personnel called in favors to finish making the car. Just as it had been with Mustang I, once decisions were made, there was no time for second guessing.

"It was an interesting program," Reutter told Witzenberg, "and if it hadn't been so short, I think we would have made more mistakes." Once the Mustang succeeded, product planners and marketing staff launched an effort to move the car upscale.

The wood-grained steering wheel was a rare option, as was air conditioning. A center console with air conditioning went for $31.52.

"A planning paper came along," Bob Negstad recalled, "where they said 'We want to do a super-deluxe interior, with leather and built-in air-conditioning in the dash, not a hang-on. We want to do higher series wheels and tires. They had a whole long list of items to move the car toward what would be an upscale, more personalized, popular car, a Thunderbird. They produced a dollar figure and an investment figure to accomplish this.

"We offered an alternate proposal. 'If you want to upscale the car, let's upscale in two directions,' we said. 'Yes, a luxury car, that's fine. But we ought to take the Mustang towards some of its original concept because we've said all along there's a market out there for the enthusiasts' point of view.' They said okay!"

Negstad's proposal included disc brakes. Ford had become an industry leader with its disc brakes after Holman-Moody built the Falcons for the Monte Carlo rally. These cars couldn't race with their small drum brakes. To satisfy the Federation Internationale de l'Automobile (FIA) sanctioning body's rules for the Falcon Futuras for Monte Carlo, Ford division had to complete a thousand cars with matching specification. Ford ordered 10,000 sets of disc brakes. Falcon won its

Taking advantage of cool morning air, this 1966 Mustang "Old Muscle" prepares to better its record 236.5-mile-per-hour run. Powered by a Ford SVO 351-ci V-8 de-stroked to 302 cubic inches, it's fed by a pair of turbochargers with liquid-to-air intercoolers to generate 876 horsepower at the rear wheels.

For 1966, the side trim behind the doors was changed. It was an inexpensive way to freshen a new model. Horizontal bars in the grille replaced the honeycomb pattern for 1966.

class in 1963, completing every stage in the best time (but regulations used a mathematical formula that favored smaller displacement engines, giving the overall victory to a Mini-Cooper). All the engineers wanted to use those brakes on the performance-version Mustang. Negstad and others also wanted an independent rear suspension (IRS). They got permission, but with it came the understanding that they could not change the body.

The chassis engineers set out to design a major subassembly so the production line assemblers could just bolt it onto the car the same way they put in the solid rear axle. When the engineers had invented and assembled it with its rear disc brakes, the entire structure fit into existing bolt locations with only three additional holes.

Ford division killed the IRS for several reasons. Other projects with greater perceived benefit could better use the money. In addition, times were changing: projects had to come from larger groups, and preferably those groups would incorporate a few other departments besides engineering and design alone. The two fastback prototypes with the independent rear suspensions and four-wheel disc brakes still are preserved in storage in suburban Detroit.

The engineers intended to turn the fastback 2+2 into a true European-style GT car by using independent rear suspension. When the division introduced the fastback as a 1965 model on September 25, 1964, magazines that had praised the coupe and convertible fell in love all over again. Their rekindled passion was justified. Even without the IRS, the fastback handled better due to the extra weight of the sheet metal and the vast back window weighing

The extended C-pillar of the 1965 fastback Mustang resulted in a graceful balance, but rearward visibility was restricted.

A quick twist-off gas cap lent some sports car flavor to the Mustang. Dual exhaust pipes were standard with the 271-horsepower, K-code, 289-ci option.

In 1966, only 9.5 percent of Mustangs were fitted with a $74.36 vinyl roof. The small emblem on the front of the fender denoted a 289-ci V-8 engine.

The Interior Décor Group option included a deluxe woodgrain steering wheel and dash inserts. For 1966, the factory underdash air conditioning unit was painted black. Padded sun visors became standard in 1966.

down the rear wheels. While one or two hard-noses chastised design for the non-functional side scoops behind the doors, the louvers in the fastback side panels that brought air into the rear seating area silenced them. The designers also created an innovative fold-down rear seat that increased storage room greatly. It turned the 2+2 back into a two-seater with enough luggage capacity for a month on the road. Other suspension, handling, and powertrain options furthered Iacocca's claim to "Total Performance."

Coupled with the high-performance 289-ci engine that produced 271 horsepower, buyers could order the GT Equipment Group introduced on April 17, 1965. Available at first only for the coupe or convertible, it specified either the 271-horsepower or 225-horsepower

engines and provided the Special Handling Package. This included stiffer front and rear springs and larger diameter shock absorbers, a larger front anti-sway bar, and 16:1 steering instead of the stock 19:1 gear. Within the grille, a pair of fog lights set the front end off noticeably and stripes below the door sill clearly announced sportier intentions. It also provided front disc brakes and brought the engine exhaust out through rear bodywork, a design cue picked up from the Mustang I. Inside, the GT's round 140-miles-per-hour speedometer anchored its five-instrument cluster, replacing the long horizontal 120-miles-per-hour version used in the non-GT models. Instead of a separate luxury model, the product planners developed options sets such as the Interior Decor Group (providing an 8,000-rpm tachometer and a 12-hour clock on separate pods straddling the steering column and a full-length console), accent groups, a full-width bench seat with center armrest, air conditioning, a deluxe steering wheel, and even a vinyl roof to suit those buyers more interested in getting to the golf course in style than getting around a race course in record time.

By now, Jacque Passino and Ford's racing effort had begun taking back the tracks. Because a European heavy truck maker owned the copyright on the name Mustang, Ford's cars had to be called T-5 for export, and these cars replaced the Falcon in international competition. Two

A very small percentage (1.3) of Mustang owners ordered the high-performance K-code engine in 1965. The Dual Red Band nylon tires were standard with the K-code option, while the fog lamps were part of the GT Equipment Group.

(opposite) The small badge on the fender spoke volumes. Fitted to Mustangs equipped with the $442 K-code option, it denoted the solid lifter 271-horsepower small block.

With a factory steel body and a 427-ci SOHC V-8 engine, the Larsen Ford A/FX Mustang, driven by Bill Lawton, was brutal on the drag strip. It won its class at the 1965 Winternationals with a run of 10.92 seconds at 128.2 miles per hour. Robert Genat/Zone Five Photo

of Ford's hardtops, entered by Alan Mann Racing in England, won the Touring Class of the 1964 Tour de France. This brutal flog covered nearly 5,000 miles over 10 days and included eight hill climbs and a total of 12 hours of flat-out racing spread over eight race courses. The rules allowed no repairs overnight, only during event hours, thereby taking time from competition. Then Jim Clark drove Colin Chapman's Lotus-Ford to victory at the 1965 Indy 500. Shelby's Ford-engined Cobras had begun teaching Ferrari how to be graceful in defeat, and Holman-Moody began convincing other competitors that the Blue Oval might own the super oval championship by year's end.

The Tour de France helped the T-5 Mustang earn its first motion picture role in 1965. Ford of Britain had hired Walter Hayes in 1962 as its director of public affairs, putting him in charge of all United Kingdom and European media relations and promotion. When Hayes heard that French filmmaker Claude Lelouche was preparing a film involving a race car driver who falls in love with a Parisian school teacher, Hayes seized the opportunity to promote Ford's motorsports products. When the film *Un Homme et Une Femme (A Man and a Woman)* appeared, lead actor Jean-Louis Trintignant costarred with a rally-prepared white T-5 Mustang notchback. Lelouche's budget only would cover black-and-white film and so Hayes hired him to shoot commercials in color, telling the director-producer he could keep any leftover color film stock. The film drifts dreamily from black-and-white to color and back, and features spectacular images of a yellow, headlight-equipped T-5 Mustang flying through the French countryside, as well as some testing scenes with a very early GT40 and a prototype Ford Formula One car. The film created a huge demand for the T-5 in France, and it became Ford's biggest export market for the cars. (The same baby boom that arrived in the United States also reached France and England, creating a market for Ford's more exciting cars worldwide.)

France and Europe were not the only export destinations for Ford and its Mustangs. Ford of Australia brought in 200 Mustangs in late 1965 and had the cars converted to right-hand drive there. English customers could order a new Mustang almost from the beginning from Lincoln Cars of Great West Road, a subsidiary of Ford UK. The cars came into England as left-hand–drive, and Rudds of Worthing did the conversion. A fastback with the 289 V-8, four-speed transmission, and disc brakes set the owner back £1627 with purchase tax of another £327, or roughly $5,000 in U.S. dollars at the time. Engineering fitted the heavy duty suspension and the "export brace," a tube that tied the tops of the front shocks to the firewall.

The first five regular production Mustangs assembled all had been shipped to eastern Canada for display. The very first production car, a Wimbledon White convertible with black interior, caught Captain Stanley Tucker's eye as he drove past the Ford dealer in St. Johns, New Foundland. The dealer, either unaware the car was meant for show only, or unwilling to pass up a sale to a local customer, let the car go. Ford of Canada was supposed to return the car to Dearborn for display, but the 33-year old pilot for Eastern Provincial Airlines refused to let it go.

Ford introduced the 1966 model on September 16, 1965, with very few changes. Five months later, 676 days after Job One, the Rouge plant produced Mustang number 1,000,000. In the late fall of 1966, Captain Tucker relented and in a ceremony back in Dearborn, he traded his 10,000+ mile convertible, car number 1, for a new Silver Frost convertible, car number 1,000,001.

Originally designed for use in NASCAR, the 427-ci SOHC V-8 was known as the Cammer. Due to NASCAR rules, the engine was banned from stock cars, but settled into drag racing history. Robert Genat/Zone Five Photo

chapter five

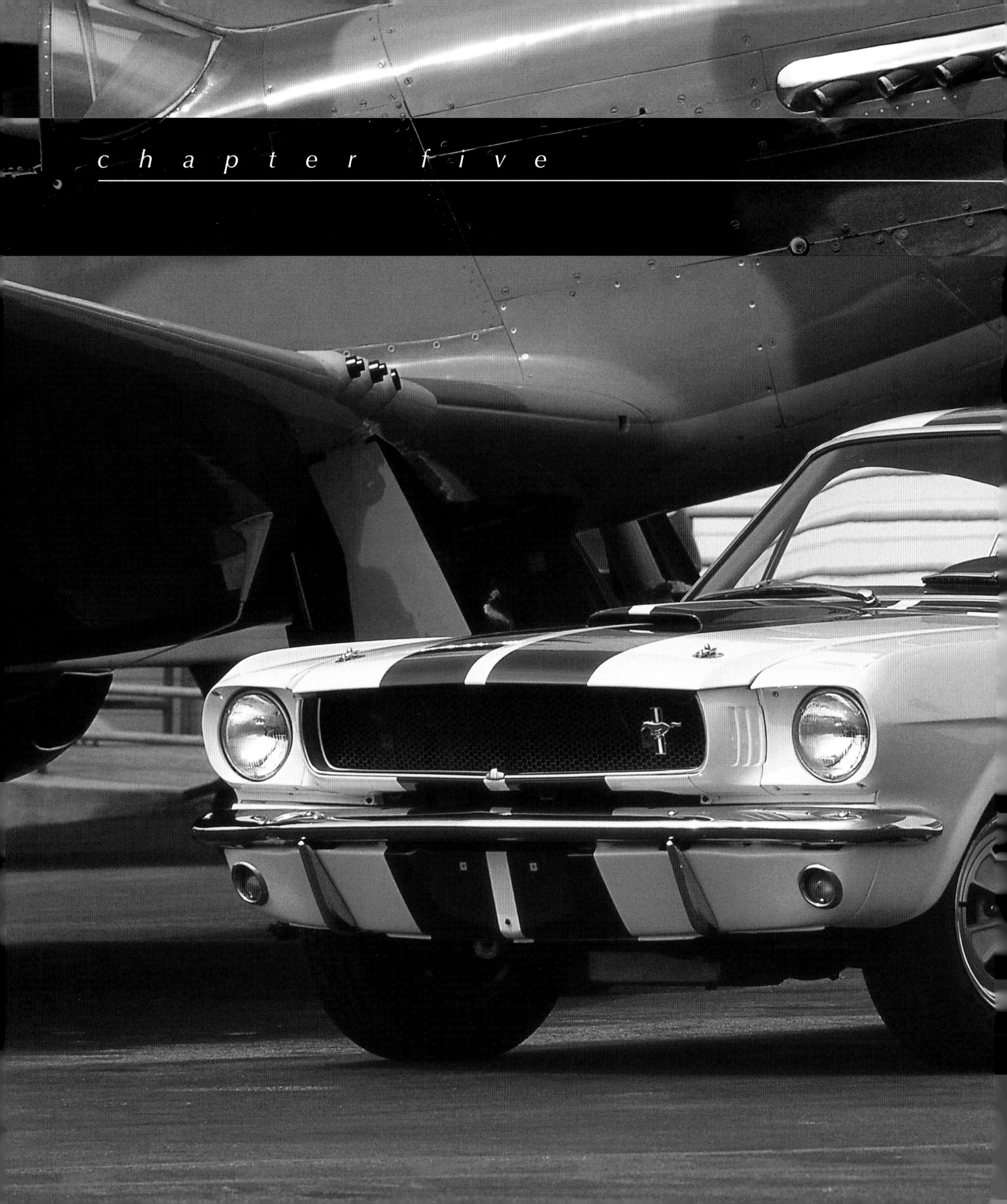

(previous) The galloping horse in the stock Mustang's grille was removed on the 1965 Shelby GT350 and replaced with the small Mustang badge. Suspension modifications relocated the mounting points to lower the car.

Race-inspired locking pins restrained the fiberglass hood, which sported a functional scoop. Talbot-type, bullet-shaped exterior mirrors were a competition touch.

(S h e l b y   M u s t a n g s   1 9 6 5 – 1 9 6 6)

VARIATIONS ON THE THEME

By August 1964, Ford division management knew that both General Motors and Chrysler were taking the Mustang seriously. Rumors drifted over from GM's Technical Center that Chevrolet had a challenger to the Mustang to be release for 1967. Plymouth had introduced its Valiant-based Barracuda on April 1, two weeks before the Mustang. Not only did the Barracuda arrive first, but at $2,365 for the six-cylinder base version, Chrysler priced its car $3 less than Ford. Through 1964 and 1965, Plymouth sold barely 85,000 units even after Chrysler engineer Scott Harvey created, for 1965, the Formula S package that provided a 235-horsepower, 273-ci V-8 and a more sporting suspension. Ford product planners also knew that while Plymouth's car would be mildly updated for 1966, it would be partially re-skinned the next year, and designer Milt Antonick's new lines would transform the car from the fastback Valiant it had been.

Mustang's most serious threat came from Chevrolet's Corvette. GM's two-seater offered a 360-horsepower fuel-injected engine in 1963 and would have 375 horsepower for 1964. The 1963 Stingray design, originated and developed by designers Peter Brock and Chuck Pohlmann and made production-ready by Larry Shinoda, had caused a clamor. Ford could bet that the second- and third-year updates would further improve the car's appearance. Worse, Pontiac had a new option for its compact Tempest in 1964 named the G.T.O., after an exotic racing Ferrari. This option would offer a "tri-power" 389-ci V-8 producing 348 horsepower. In an era *(opposite) It took a few external changes to turn a Mustang fastback into a Shelby GT350. Most of Shelby's efforts went under the sheetmetal to transform the Mustang into a genuine race car that could be driven on the street.*

Shelby knew that race cars didn't have rear seats, so he mounted the spare tire under the large rear window to improve weight distribution. The list price for the 1965 GT350 was $4,547.

of 30¢-per-gallon gasoline, these were the first shots fired in the performance war. Ford seemed to be selling Mustangs as rapidly as its factories could produce them, but no one at Ford expected this to last forever.

The broad reach of Ford's "Total Performance" program took Mustangs to France. In January 1962, it sent Ford engines to England to help create the Shelby A.C. Cobra. These hybrid Cobras led struggling A.C. Cars to a healthy comeback while capturing the hearts and minds of journalists and performance car fans when these cars seized nearly every checkered flag they sought. In late 1963, attempting to overcome the aerodynamic drag limitations of open roadsters, Brock, who had left Chevrolet and joined Shelby, designed the equally beautiful and devastatingly effective Shelby Daytona Cobra coupe. At that point, Shelby needed more space and found a facility available in Venice, California, north of Los Angeles International Airport (LAX). Here Shelby and his staff produced racing and street Cobras. Throughout 1964, Shelby American continued taking on Ferraris and all other comers.

By summer, a consensus grew among Ford division personnel confirming it was time to bring some of Shelby's imagination and skill back home. In a meeting with Lee Iacocca, Shelby learned that Ford's Ray Geddes had gotten nowhere trying to get the Mustang recognized as a "production race car" for Sports Car Club of America (SCCA) competition in the United States. Shelby had first met Geddes, who held a masters degree in business and a law degree, when Frey had brought him in to help Shelby manage the business end of the Cobra project in mid-1962. As car-designer-cum-journalist Peter Brock recalled, Shelby initially resisted getting

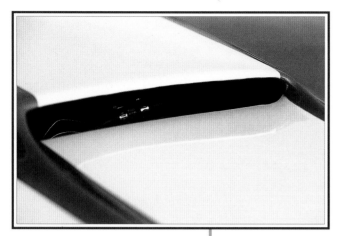

involved with production Mustangs. He had Cobra roadsters racing throughout the world, and, for months now, his new six-car Daytona Cobra Coupe program was vigorously fighting against Henry Ford II's arch racing enemy, Enzo Ferrari, for the world manufacturers' championship. This was in addition to Ford's other program with Holman-Moody campaigning GT40s against Ferrari as well. However, Shelby knew John Bishop, the executive director of the SCCA, and, after some delay, the Texan agreed to get involved. He told Iacocca he believed he knew what it would take to run the Mustang in Bishop's events.

Bishop told Shelby that to qualify for production classes, the car had to be a two-seater, and either the suspension or the engine could be modified for racing, but not both. The major hurdle was that Shelby had to have 100 cars manufactured by January 1, 1965, to be eligible to race that year. Bishop hinted that he thought this was impossible to accomplish in less than five months, but he didn't know how Ford had been working lately.

Shelby, still with unsold 427 Cobra racers sitting parked behind his shops, understood that he could never sell 100 pure race Mustangs. Rick Kopec, editor of the 1987 second edition of the *Shelby American World Registry*, reported that Shelby figured he could produce two models, one of them for racing and another for the street. Racing suspensions were something that Shelby could put a warranty on, while racing engines were another matter altogether. Shelby returned to Iacocca and told him that all they needed to do was build 100 and he knew how to do it. Iacocca approved the "Mustang-Cobra" program, and Ford launched it immediately.

Back in California, Ken Miles, an erudite Englishman with a wry wit, was Shelby American's competition director, staff racer, and development driver. Late in the summer of 1964, he headed up to Willow Springs Raceway near Mojave, California, with two notchback Mustang coupes and some Ford parts books. Shelby assigned him to produce a car that would hang onto the race track without being unmanageable on the street. What's more, it had to be cost effective, modified with parts readily available to keep the selling price reasonable.

Dearborn engineering sent out chassis specialist Klaus Arning, and together with Miles and Bob Bondurant, Shelby team co-driver, they dialed in the cars and returned with what became the street Shelby Mustang-Cobra suspension. Near the end of testing, Ford shipped out one of the two prototype independent rear suspension cars for comparison. However, by the time Miles had finished with the first two notchbacks, he had them handling as well as the IRS cars. (This was another factor contributing toward that experimental suspension never seeing production. Shelby and Miles simply said it wasn't necessary.) Then Shelby ordered three stock white fastbacks. These San Jose-produced cars became the first prototype street car and the first two race cars. More testing time at Willow Springs sorted these cars out, and Shelby was ready to work. He ordered another 100 cars from the San Jose plant, which shipped these cars "knocked down," the terminology used for incomplete cars. Shelby's cars would arrive as virtually identical all-white fastbacks with black interiors and be equipped with the 289-ci 271-horsepower engine, four-speed transmission, and nine-inch rear end, but with no hood or latches, grille, radio, seat belts, rear seats, exhaust system, or emblems of any kind.

C-pillar vents remained functional in the 1965 Shelby GT350 street cars. Stock glass was used throughout the car.

Minimal but comfortable, the interior of the 1965 GT350 used stock parts, but added a dash-mounted tachometer and competition seat belts. The wooden steering wheel was a Shelby piece.

Bred for the racetrack, Shelby's 1965 GT350 used a warmed-over K-code 289-ci V-8 rated at 306 horsepower. Exhaust pipes dumped burnt gases directly in front of the rear tires, which filled the interior with noise.

Shelby only built 36 R-Models, purpose-built racers not intended for the street. Removing the rear bumper was a legal way to reduce weight.

In its element, a 1965 Shelby GT350R is hard on the brakes as it approaches the famed Corkscrew turn at Laguna Seca Raceway during the annual Monterey Historic Races. A considerable number of GT350s are still raced at vintage race events.

Aided by Chuck Cantwell, Ford division's Mustang-Cobra project engineer, they found and fit other odd parts onto the car. One of these was the "export brace," the stiff single-piece stamping that Ford placed on all T-5 Mustangs shipped to Europe. To this they added the "Monte Carlo bar," a cross engine-compartment rod that linked left and right front fenders, further tightening the body and chassis. Arning and Cantwell added larger disc brakes and oversize Fairlane station-wagon rear drums along with an aluminum-case Borg-Warner close-ratio, four-speed type T-10 transmission. The 100 cars represented just about two days production from San Jose, something Bishop could not have known. As soon as the plant completed assembly, it shipped them, six to a carrier, down the coast, not to Shelby's shops in Venice, but to two huge, leased airplane hangars, part of the former North American Aviation airplane assembly facilities stretched over 12½ acres of LAX's south side.

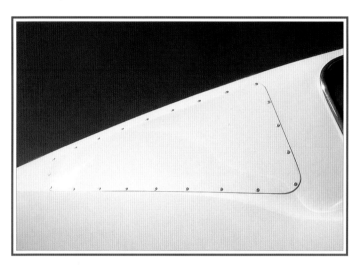

Once the cars got to Shelby, his crews modified the front and rear suspensions substantially. They lowered the front, upper A-arms, a revision that necessitated new locating holes. They replaced the stock ⅝-inch anti-sway bars with beefier one-inch-diameter pieces. They removed the entire rear end assemblies, the differentials, half-shafts, and suspensions in order to cut holes through the floor pans so they could weld in brackets on which to mount over-ride traction bars. This was the Miles-modification that contributed to handling that matched the IRS. Miles dictated Koni shocks all around. Inside the cars, Shelby's staff bolted three-inch-wide competition lap belts through the side frame rails and the transmission tunnels. The other end of these tunnel bolts held straps to keep the driveshafts in place. They relocated the batteries to the trunks to improve weight balance, but for the first 100 cars only. Buyers complained of battery acid fumes corroding inside the rear deck lids and seeping through to the passenger compartments. From mid-1965 on, the batteries were up front.

Shelby and Ford's Ray Geddes asked Peter Brock to "work on the look of the Shelby Mustang." Back in 1961, after Carroll; Joan Cole, his office and business manager; and Brock had moved the shop to Venice, Shelby had promoted Brock to manager of special projects. Now for the Mustang-Cobra, Brock and his assistant Alex "Skeet" Kerr modeled the new hood, wheels, the side scoops, and the small instrument pod that Shelby attached to the original dash panel. Among Brock's other tasks was designing of the exterior graphics (the two bold stripes motif first appeared on his 1946 Ford convertible hot rod); he also designed and produced Shelby's brochures, posters, and advertising. Brock was responsible for the creation of Shelby's CS logo and the Cobra logo and badge; now Shelby and Ford needed one for this Mustang. Again, the name issue came back to haunt everyone. Names needed legal approval. Engine designations were fine except that when the engines changed, badges and printed material already

The air plenum surrounding the 715-cfm center-pivot Holley carburetor fit against the inside of the hood, directly under the scoop. The 289-ci V-8 sat under a Monte Carlo bar attached to the shock towers to stiffen the front suspension.

Touted as a fireproof interior, the GT350R attained that level of safety by eliminating anything flammable. Pulling a strap on the door raised the Plexiglas side windows because the regulators were removed to save weight.

Plexiglas windows replaced the C-pillar extractor vents in 1966 and removed the large blind spot that affected GT350s in their first year of production. Ivy Green, color code R, was one of five hues offered for 1966.

made were useless. Most race cars, excluding Shelby's own Cobra and a few others, went for just numbers. The best solution was some designation that meant nothing but *seemed* to represent something. For the cagey Shelby, it had to be a number also that suggested more than it revealed. That way, the model could continue for several years and receive updates constantly without alerting sanctioning bodies.

The story goes that Shelby looked across the street and asked his chief engineer Phil Remington how far away he thought a building was from where they sat. Remington had worked as an engineer for Scarab race car builder Lance Reventlow in the Venice shops Shelby now leased. Remington stayed with the shops when Reventlow vacated, adopting Shelby and the new operation. They each made guesses and then Remington paced it off. It came to 350 feet. "Fine," Shelby said, "let's call the little car the GT-350. If the car's good, the name won't matter, and if it's no good, the name won't matter." Of course, it didn't hurt that this new name coincided with the recent trend, such as Chevrolet's 327s and Ferrari's 250s, 275s, and 330s.

Shelby used the 1966 Mustang grille in the 1966 GT350, except for the "pony and corral" brightwork. For the first time, the GT350 came with back seats. The AM radio was a factory-installed option offered mid-year.

Side scoops made their first appearance in 1966 and directed air to the rear brakes. For 1966, exhaust pipes were routed to the rear of the car to quiet the interior.

While the GT350 gas cap was used throughout the entire 1966 production run, the panel emblem was not installed until the first 300 or so were built. Standard Mustang taillights were used.

The vast majority of 1966 GT350s sported twin stripes that extended the full length of the body. Unlike the previous year, the side stripes were now a 3M tape appliqué.

Shelby ordered an additional 15 cars from San Jose, which were stripped further than the first 100 cars. Ford delivered these without side or rear window glass, interiors, insulation, or head liners, heaters, defrosters, or gas tanks. Work continued at a more accelerated pace on the other 100 cars. These 15 were to be the first racers, and work proceeded more deliberately.

For two years, Shelby had raced the 289-ci V-8s. Remington and the rest of Shelby's wizards could charm a reliable 385 horsepower out of the Cobra engine for racing purposes, even when detuned somewhat for longer endurance events. For the GT350 race cars, they dismantled the engines and sent out the heads to have intake and exhaust valve ports enlarged and polished. Remington and the others balanced all the reciprocating pieces, pistons, connecting rods, and crankshafts, and they reassembled each engine to "blueprint" tolerances. New specifications called for a high-capacity Holley 715-cubic-feet-of-air-per-minute (CFM) carburetor that had a center-pivot float which kept the float from hanging up against its bowl and flooding out the engine during hard cornering. Tubular steel exhaust headers led back to glass pack mufflers, and most states allowed the exhaust tailpipe to flare out just ahead of the rear tires. (Both California and New York mandated running tailpipes to the rear.) Street engines produced about 306 horsepower, while the racing cars developed between 350 and 360 horsepower in dynamometer tests.

Race cars weighed some 250 pounds less than the street cars. SCCA rules allowed Shelby to remove front and rear bumpers. They replaced the front bumper with a fiberglass piece into which they had cut a large lip to better direct airflow through the oil cooler and radiator. Another hole on both sides of the lip led air to cool the front brakes. Brock covered the vents on the side of the fastback roof to improve airflow. His one-piece fiberglass clip-on hood with functioning air scoop saw use on both street and racing models.

When SCCA inspectors arrived at Shelby American shops they were stunned to see more than 100 Mustang GT350s. Some of the full race cars still were in preparation. Completed cars sat parked outside in tidy rows. In a November 7, 1964, story in *Competition Press & AutoWeek* magazine, SCCA announced that it had homologated the "Mustang-Cobra" for Class B Production for 1965. There was no photo, so Corvette racers could only read it and wonder what Shelby had done now.

Shelby's crew had completed the first two GT350R race cars in time for the February 1965 Daytona debut, having had all 15 ready by spring. Because they had assembled 100 street models, each with identical suspensions, they became the production base. From that, he or others could modify racing engines as much as they pleased. After a track test, published in the March 1965 *Sports Car Graphic* by Jerry Titus, orders began to arrive. The first two race cars became

Topped with an owner-installed dual-carb induction system, the 289-ci V-8 was virtually identical to the 1965 GT350 and factory rated at 306 horsepower at a lofty 6,000 rpm.

Shelby GT350Hs did not come equipped with the Plexiglas rear window and fiberglass front apron used in the 1965 R-model. This example was installed by the owner.

Shelby's factory entries. The other 13 went out quickly. Shelby shipped meticulously gathered information updates and tips to his customers. He wanted none of the ill will that he knew existed between other official teams and customers who knew they could never win against the "factory." For Shelby and Ford what was important was that a Mustang won; and win they did. Shelby's GT350Rs established the same kind of near invincibility as his Cobras had achieved. The Mustang Rs grabbed the SCCA B-production class championship in 1965 and again in 1966, though most of the victories and entries were with year-old 1965 Rs.

For 1966, Shelby withdrew his Mustang team from racing. The factory effort had proved its promotional value and Ford division now needed Shelby's help on the so-far unsuccessful GT40 program. Shelby began paying incentives to his privateers; each time a Shelby Mustang won, its owner got a check for $150, and second place received $75. Shelby American completed the remaining R-model Mustangs during 1966, 20 in all, five of which they shipped to Australia, and they got 1966-style grilles (even though the staff had begun preparing a number of them in late 1965).

The 1965 racers sold for $5,995, while street models went for $4,547. In 1965, Shelby produced 515 street models, 35 competition cars, and nine "drag cars," not including the first three prototypes. As the 1966 model year approached, Shelby looked into ways he could make his cars different from the 1965 car. He installed a Paxton supercharger on one prototype to evaluate performance differences, and on another car he fitted the long narrow sequential turn signals taken from the 1965

Although discouraged by Hertz, many GT350Hs found their way onto racetracks. With an ad campaign that touted how the public could "rent-a-racer," some drivers took Hertz at their word.

The majority of 1966 GT350Hs were painted black with Metallic Bronze stripes. In the May 1966 issue of Car and Driver, a GT350H took only 6.6 seconds to reach 60 miles per hour.

Except for the special gas cap and GT350 badge, the rear of the GT350H was standard Mustang.

The functional hood scoop directed outside air into the engine compartment. Shelby did not believe in fitting aerodynamic aids for appearance.

Thunderbird. Shelby liked both these ideas and planned to use them further down the road.

Shelby dealers (meaning Ford dealers) had received feedback from buyers and potential customers. It was the first time Shelby heard a litany that became too familiar later on: two-seat-only configuration; limited color choice of white only; loud exhaust; loud rear differential; hard suspension; four-speed floor-shift manual only. These were comments dealers relayed to Shelby and to Ford division. Shelby's was a rough and raucous Mustang, something uncompromised and possible only because Ford's "Total Performance" program not only permitted it, but demanded it. Still, even auto writers noticed its unpolished edges. *Car & Driver*'s Steve Smith described the 1965 Shelby Mustang as "a brand new, clapped-out race car."

When Ford division prepared its factories for model year change-over, an early burst of 252 of the 1965 models emerged from San Jose. Ford shipped these to Shelby to become the first of the 1966s. To soften the ride, Shelby engineers eliminated the most time-consuming and costly suspension and chassis modifications from the 1965 cars. They no longer lowered the front upper A-arms, nor did they change the rear end or add rear over-ride traction bars. Sadly, this negated Ken Miles' success in improving the handling without the IRS option. After Shelby sold the first 252 cars, the rest of the 1966 models were kinder and gentler.

For 1966, Shelby himself offered subtle changes in the street cars, including a clear Plexiglas rear quarter window in place of the functional vent and a functional side scoop to

Peter Brock, automotive stylist and Carroll Shelby's first employee, designed the GT350H's rocker stripes.

117

In 1966, this was a great way to test drive a Shelby GT350. For $17 a day and 17 cents a mile, Walter Mitty could get his fix.

cool the rear brakes. This replaced the nonfunctional decoration on previous cars for which he had been criticized. Engineers permanently reset the battery in the engine compartment and moved the spare tire, which had taken up the back seat area for better weight balance, back in the trunk. They restored the rear seat, offered an automatic transmission, and expanded the color chart to include Raven Black, Guardsman Blue, Sapphire Blue, Candy Apple Red, or Ivy Green. Shelby, who had offered the Paxton supercharger as a "parts list" item at $485 complete for owner installation on his 289 Cobras, offered it as a Shelby "factory only" option for 289-engine GT350s. Apparently, Shelby delivered fewer than 12 supercharged 1966 cars. He published a list price of $4,428 for the cars equipped with either automatic or four-speed transmissions.

One of the most remarkable promotions of Shelby's Mustang program came on November 23, 1965, when Hertz Rent-A-Car Corporation ordered 200 GT350s. This order and what followed it have made up a huge part of the Shelby Mustang legacy. However, Greg Kolasa and Carol Padden straightened it out in recent years, in the *Shelby American World Registry*.

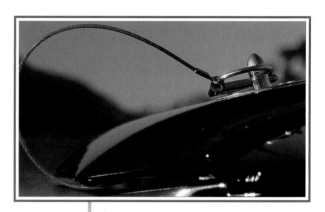

Essentially a stock Mustang interior with wide competition seatbelts and a Shelby logo on the horn button, the 1966 GT350H was a capable long-distance cruiser. Hertz paid $3,547 for each GT350H, plus $45.45 for a Shelby-installed AM radio.

When Shelby American General Manager Peyton Cramer presented Hertz executives with a prototype GT350H, he had painted it the same color Mr. Hertz had used in his early rental fleet. Cramer did his homework and took home a contract for 1,000 vehicles.

Triple-lens taillights were a Mustang staple, and Shelby saw no need to change them.

The 1966 Shelby GT350H brought a youthful excitement to the staid world of rental cars. Most were thrashed to within an inch of the wrecking yard, but many have been restored to better than new.

Ivy Green was one of the colors GT350Hs were painted toward the end of the production run. While most Hertz Shelbys used chromed 14-inch Magnum 500 steel wheels, a number of cars had 10-spoke cast aluminum wheels.

Magnum 500 steel wheels were one of the styles available for the 1966 Shelby GT350. This wheel became standard in the latter days of 1966 production.

With the adoption of the five-gauge Mustang instrument panel in the 1966 GT350H, an additional oil pressure gauge was not necessary.

122

Under the hood of a 1966 GT350H, it was business as usual. That meant a 306-horsepower 289-ci V-8 with solid valve lifters.

In 1965, Hertz operated an exclusive program for executive and business travelers who had good credit and clean driving records. This occurred during a period when "number-2" Avis aggressively hounded Hertz for the number 1 rental-car position. Hertz offered a generous handful of Corvettes for rent to its "Hertz Sports Car Club" members. Shelby had heard about the club and asked Peyton Cramer, the friend who had arranged the lease of the airplane hangars, to contact Hertz in New York. Cramer researched Hertz and learned that John Hertz started his business career in 1925 by buying an existing livery service in Chicago that manufactured its own cars. Hertz's plan then was to rent out self-drive cars to encourage sales. To identify the livery and promote the self-drive idea, he had all the cars painted black and gold. Cramer prepared a black-and-gold prototype GT350 and had it flown to New York. When he met with Hertz executives, they were impressed. They proposed adding an "H" to the rocker

The 6-quart cast-aluminum oil pan hanging down from the 306-horsepower, 289-ci V-8 wasn't there for show. As a vehicle meant for street and track duty, sufficient oil was always a racer's concern.

panel tape logo and placed their order. Then Hertz began a promotional blitz, announcing the availability of the cars at airports in certain cities. With the ad campaign underway, Hertz ordered an additional 800 cars on December 21.

Hertz wanted all 1,000 cars to have automatic transmissions (though the first 85 did not) and radios. Shelby delivered the final 15 in late 1966. The first 200 were black-with-gold stripes and, according to Kolaso and Padden's research, because Hertz had not specified differently, the next 230 cars ended up in a mix of the red, green, blue, and white, all with gold stripes. At that point, Hertz spoke up. Shelby delivered the rest in black and gold. All interiors were black and had rear seats with standard Ford rear seatbelts. Hertz charged $17 per day (or $70 a week) and $0.17 a mile, but only to drivers over 25 years old.

As many misconceptions as Kolasa and Padden cleared up, there are still many stories that may be unfounded and capricious about Hertz rental Mustangs, such as renters going to the races *and racing* while they were there. While the Hertz cars had standard Shelby brakes with metallic linings, which worked best when warm but caused some concern to first-time renters on cold days, they had no roll bars. What's more, while the first 85 cars went out with stick shifts (and bolt-in roll bars certainly were available), few racers had faith in

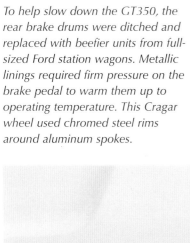

To help slow down the GT350, the rear brake drums were ditched and replaced with beefier units from full-sized Ford station wagons. Metallic linings required firm pressure on the brake pedal to warm them up to operating temperature. This Cragar wheel used chromed steel rims around aluminum spokes.

automatic transmissions. Still, stories such as these have added greatly to the legends and myths surrounding the Shelby Mustangs.

At the end of the 1966 production run, the last 16 or so Shelby cars assembled were convertibles. Several of these had automatic transmissions and were air conditioned, and eventually Shelby gave them to individuals who helped him and the Mustang GT350 project above-and-beyond the call of duty. Each had black interiors, though the exteriors were white, yellow, red, green, and blue, with one pink one reportedly made as a gift to Shelby's secretary.

In all, Shelby American produced 1,370 regular production fastbacks in addition to the 1,000 Hertz cars in 1966. They turned out another four drag cars as well as the convertibles. Between the 2,380 cars in 1966 and the 562 manufactured in 1965, there was only one complaint that Carroll Shelby and Ford division heard loudly. It was true that his street cars sold for nearly twice as much as regular production Mustangs. But as early as 1965, some people who *didn't* buy one expressed aloud their belief that GT350s should look like they cost twice as much.

When Peter Brock returned from England in the middle of 1965, he found Ford had taken over Shelby's shops. He had gone to develop a 427 version of the Cobra coupe and now he found Ford had dropped the Cobra program in favor of the GT40s they had brought to Shelby from Holman-Moody. Soon after he returned, Brock learned his "services would no longer be needed." At that point, Ford moved Shelby Mustang production back to Dearborn.

Fitting a fiberglass apron to the front of the GT350R reduced weight, and the large openings allowed cool air to flow into the radiator, oil cooler, and front brake ducts. Headlights were taped during races to minimize the chance of glass on the track.

1967–1968 ½

(1967–1968¹/₂)

LOOKING INTO A CRYSTAL BALL

E ngines drove Ford division by this time. Ford had designed and manufactured the thin-wall 221-ci block for the new Fairlane. To compete, the Fairlane had to offer higher performance, yet big-block engines could not fit into its engine bay, for it was conceived and planned before the birth of muscle cars. "Thin-wall" casting required meticulous attention to designing the block and pouring the castings. Foundry workers had to place cores representing cylinders and other essential passages precisely within the molds. This careful craftsmanship yielded a weight savings of as much as one-third over the big blocks.

There was another benefit of this critical core placement. It left enough iron surrounding the initial cylinders so that overboring was easy. Ford engineering quickly increased the displacement to 260-ci and pulled 164 horsepower out of the same block. This was the version that Jacque Passino first shipped to Shelby when he was at A.C. Cars of England. Soon after, engineering had a 289-ci version producing 271 horsepower called the "High-Performance 289," which was to become the foundation for the "powered by Ford" legend. They quickly delivered these to Shelby to replace the 260s in his Cobras. In production dress, it became the famous K-code standard option in the Mustangs. It also provided the basis of the powerplant for Ford's first GT40 race cars.

(previous) *Los Angeles sales district manager Lee S. Grey saw an experimental Mustang, "Little Red," in 1967 and approached Lee Iacocca about developing a version for sale on the West Coast. Shelby American put together two prototypes that were approved.*

One of a myriad of dealer-installed options was the illuminated pony in the grille. It would light up from an internal bulb when the headlights were used.

Eventually, with still larger bores and longer strokes, the thin-wall 221-ci 145 horsepower engine grew to reach 351 ci. Ford manufactured these engines both in its Cleveland engine plant in Ohio and at the Windsor, Ontario, factory. The Windsor engine facility launched the engine, known as the 351W, in 1969, but this engine was destined mainly for station wagons and light trucks. The 351C, the Cleveland plant high-performance version, matched its bore, stroke, and overall displacement, but little else. The "Cleveland" used substantially different cylinder heads to obtain the kind of power output the Windsor engine never sought. While Ford offered two- and four-barrel carburetors on both engines, the later model 351HO (high output), introduced from Cleveland in May 1971 and produced only through 1973, became the engine to want (or avoid if you were driving a 350 V-8 Camaro, 360 V-8 Plymouth Barracuda, or Dodge Challenger).

Ford's other engines were its big blocks. The huge 390-ci V-8 that product planners offered in the regular production-run 1967 Mustangs was Ford's shot fired in response to the horsepower war declared by Dodge, with its 426 Hemis, and Pontiac, with its tri-power 389s. The dimensions of these big blocks forced Ford designers and engineers to widen the Mustang more than 2.5 inches. As a result, they increased front and rear track by 2 inches. This change did yield better handling for the small block 289-engine cars. Ford division had overruled a few of the tricks that Carroll Shelby had used on his 1965 GT350 as being too costly for 1966 regular production. Ironically, however, some of these showed up on the Dearborn-, San Jose-, and Metuchen-built cars in 1967, hidden from view by the fatter tires. Ken Miles' most significant improvement to the car's handling was lowering the pivot point for the front suspension upper A-arm. In addition, engineering moved the front spring to a new location above the top of the frame front cross member, an idea adapted from the Fairlane. This meant that instead of causing camber loss in the turn, giving the driver the sensation that the front tires were rolling under the car while cornering, the front tires on the 1967 and later cars remained perpendicular. Normally, improving cornering and handling required stiffer springs and larger front anti-sway bars; those additions would meet those goals, but stiffen up ride as well. However, all the modifications in this configuration benefited both handling and ride comfort.

Ford's big blocks ranged from 332 cubic inches up to 428 cubic inches. They produced a third series of 429- and 460-ci blocks as well. By the mid-1960s, engineering had thoroughly developed the 390, which was originally introduced in 1961. With hydraulic cams and a Holley four-barrel carburetor, it

Dual tailpipes identify this 1967 hardtop as a V-8 model. The concave taillight panel has been fitted with the optional finned trim piece.

developed 320 horsepower. Product planners offered it as a $232 option in the 1967 Mustang. For 1968, marketing renamed the engine the GT390 and engineering endowed it with an additional five horsepower.

In 1962, Pontiac had staked its claim on NASCAR. Competing with its 427-ci V-8s, it ran away from Ford's 406s. Ford knew that by enlarging the bore of the big blocks it could reach 427 cubic inches as well. In late 1963, Ford offered a 427-ci engine in limited quantities for the Galaxy and the Fairlane. Called the Thunderbolt, or T-bolt, this was available officially as a racing engine,

The $60 tilt steering wheel aided in entering and exiting the Deluxe Interior complete with AM/FM radio with Multiplex Stereo.

(opposite) Simulated vents in front of the rear wheels maintained the stylistic tradition started in 1965. Styled steel wheels cost $115 on hardtops and convertibles, and $94 on a fastback model.

The taillights, rear spoiler, and spoiler fender extensions were part of the high-profile California Special package.

with one or two four-barrel carburetors mounted on either medium- or high-rise intake manifolds. Ford's efforts paid off. Fairlane T-bolts won the NHRA 1964 Winternationals in Super Stock category.

Shelby and his engineers had found a way to stuff the 427 into the Cobra, radically changing what had been a well-balanced 289-engined sports car. Racers reported that driving the big block Cobra was like competing in endless drag races that were interrupted by corners. In Shelby's Cobras and in Ford's GT40s, known at this time as the Mark II 427 GT, Ford used a single four-barrel carburetor on a medium-rise intake manifold. Tuned to last through endurance races, running from a few hundred miles up to a few thousand miles, in such events as Le Mans or Daytona, the 427 produced 485 horsepower. This was the engine that fulfilled Henry Ford II's dream of winning Le Mans. He did it first in 1966, and then repeated in 1967, 1968, and 1969.

In 1966, Ford engineers introduced the 428. Derived from the 390, the division offered it as a performance option for the fastback-bodied Galaxies. Using hydraulic cams, engineers had developed the 428 as a lower cost alternative to the technically more sophisticated mechanical-cam 427 engines. Product planners quickly saw the benefits to the Mustang and to its cousin, Mercury division's newborn Cougar, as well as to the Ford Fairlane and Mercury Comet. In 1968, Ford introduced a hydraulic lifter version of the 427 for the street.

Anthony Young, in *Ford Hi-Po V-8 Muscle Cars*, reported that Bob Tasca, the Providence, Rhode Island, Ford and Shelby dealer, obtained some police interceptor 428s early in 1967. Tasca began to modify and install them in Mustangs for drag racing. (It was during this time that Henry Ford II's young son, Edsel, named after his grandfather, was attending a school in Boston. Needing somewhere to get his own Mustang serviced, he also got his initial automobile business education by working for a short while at Tasca Ford.)

Carroll Shelby had received some early 428s, and with them he developed the GT500KR, his "King of the Road" package, for street use. Ford division, Young reported, had been searching for a name for its new performance engine; product planners merged a Shelby name with an airplane. Marketing christened the new performance engine the 428 Cobra Jet.

In downtown Detroit at General Motors' corporate headquarters, GM's board unwittingly fed fresh ammunition to the battle for high performance. In literature, every adage has a variation: In business, hell hath no fury like an executive scorned. In late 1967, GM's directors passed over Semon E. Knudsen, "Bunkie," for the position of corporation president. When Henry Ford II learned this top GM executive was available, he recommended his board promote Ford corporation president, Arjay Miller, to vice-chairman, opening a key spot for Knudsen. Bunkie, an energetic and product-oriented person, was an innovative car enthusiast, and, in his time at GM, he had encouraged the creation of the Camaro and its Trans-Am-race-series-inspired Z/28. He had vigorously pushed Pontiac division's GTO and other John DeLorean-directed inspirations. Now Knudsen, who knew GM's plans for a few years ahead, unleashed the furies of hell onto his former employer.

California Special script was on each rear quarter-panel, in case the rest of the package didn't tip people off. Federal regulations requiring side marker lights went into effect in 1968.

Henry Ford II happily picked up the displaced GM executive, surprising and disappointing many, including Lee Iacocca who had anticipated getting the job following his successful Mustang project. On February 6, 1968, Knudsen arrived at Ford World Headquarters and moved into the president's office there. To him, this was the chance to get as much good-looking, fine-handling Ford horsepower into the marketplace as possible, and to do it fast. He quickly learned that the corporation already had several projects ready that would race toward that goal.

By the time engineering had completed all the necessary engine testing and chassis development, Ford division had the 428 Cobra Jet Mustang ready for introduction as a 1968½ model within months of Knudsen's arrival. This engine essentially replaced the small production run of the 427-ci engine equipped with low-rise intake manifolds and rated at a more impressive 390 horsepower. As a $622 option, the W-code engine had been a rare and potent handful.

The Cobra Jet was a slightly better bargain at $434, but buyers reading the catalogs believed Ford had gone absolutely the wrong direction. With its single 735-cfm four-barrel Holley carburetor, Ford rated its output at just 335 horsepower. Buyers and drivers quickly learned how conservative this number was. *Hot Rod* magazine tested a 428CJ in a Mustang fastback and achieved 0 to 60 miles per hour in 5.9 seconds, and standing start quarter-mile runs at 106.6 miles per hour in 13.56 seconds. From the factory, the engine developed more than 400 actual horsepower, yet its deceptive rating granted it more competitive placement in lower classes for NHRA and AHRA amateur and professional events.

Unlike the exterior, the interior of the 1968 California Special was pure stock Mustang. The padded steering wheel was a concession to new federally mandated safety measures.

139

The Mustang grew for 1968, especially in the nose, as evident by the GT/CS, or California Special. Mainstream Mustangs did not have external twisting hood locks, side stripes, or rectangular fog lamps.

Ford offered it only in the GT package, including a Ram-Air functional cold-air induction hood scoop (the CJ-R) and power front disc brakes. Buyers could order the car with either an automatic three-speed transmission or a four-speed manual. While Ford assembled 654 notchbacks, it produced 2,253 fastbacks, and a handful of convertibles emerged as well. To keep it on the road, Goodyear introduced its wider F70 poly-glass tires for the Cobra Jet.

Some individuals complained that the 1967 Mustang got too big, too heavy, and grew too much too quickly. At the time, when Gene Bordinat, Don Frey, Hal Sperlich, and so many others had been planning its appearance, each of them looked into their own crystal ball, but just as with the "Magic Eightball" toy, what they saw was "outlook hazy."

Bordinat's designers had begun sketching the 1967 body as production released the 1964½ cars to dealers. Everyone hoped the car would receive a Falcon-like response, but no one could put the company at risk by pushing a second-generation model too hard or too far in any one direction before reading verdicts on the first one. They understood that the American car-buying public was a hard audience to read. Detroit automakers had spoiled their customers by introducing a new body style every three years. With development turn-around time running between three and four years, this practice had cast designers and engineers alike into the roles of visionaries.

The nonfunctional side scoops on the 1968 California Special were lifted directly from the Shelby parts bin. Tape graphics set them apart from the products of the man from Texas.

(opposite) Conceived in Southern California, the GT/CS was a popular eye catcher. Both GT and non-GT Mustangs could be ordered with the GT/CS option, but GT wheel covers were placed on genuine GTs only.

Any size V-8 engine on the Mustang option sheet could be installed in the California Special, but the West Coast appearance option was only available in hardtop form.

The public had gone wild over the 1955 Thunderbird and Ford sold 16,000 of them. The same public was even more enthusiastic about the 1958 four-seater, and Ford sold more than 40,000 of them despite its mid-year introduction. This same public, and especially the automotive journalists, went crazy over the Mustang I prototype. Then eighteen months later the public, and especially the automotive journalists, went crazy over the production notchback coupe and convertible.

So what should a designer do? What influences did an engineer trust? Where did marketers and product planners turn for answers? If 60 percent of Ford buyers purchased the base models, how much weight should be given to the other 40 percent? Enthusiast publications tested the performance versions, either making them or dooming them on their printed pages. Ford Motor Company had known for decades that higher level cars enticed buyers into showrooms, even if they bought base models. Therefore, the wise money bet in late 1964 was that horsepower would become a significant factor in car sales. At that moment, big power from Ford meant the big Thunderbird 390. That engine simply could not fit between the wheelwells of the 1965 and 1966 cars.

In southern California, Ford dealers were selling one in five Mustangs that the company produced. Two dealerships in the Los Angeles area sold nearly 9,000 of the cars each year between April 1964 and March 1968—an average of 30 per day on a six-day sales week for four years. While 1964½ and 1965 combined production had been 680,989, it had barely fallen in 1966, with 607,568 produced. Ford division voiced few complaints about 1967 when production ended at 472,121. Though not as impressive as 1966, it still was ahead of the car's first 12 months (and far ahead of Camaro's first year at about 220,000 cars.) However, a Dearborn factory strike in late 1967 cut all Ford car production by nearly half a million units and also affected parts availability to the San Jose factory. Production in 1968 reached only 317,404 cars due to the circumstances. Still, it was a decent number, but it troubled Ford that Camaros passed Mustangs with nearly 400,000 cars.

(above) A pop-open GT gas cap and almost full-width taillights identify this as one of the Mustang specials.

There were plenty of Shelby dress-up parts for the Mustang in 1968, and this California Special made full use of the catalog. Under the long Shelby air cleaner, twin carbs sit atop a 302-ci V-8.

Located on the nonfunctional side scoop, the emblem for the High Country Special package was identical to the previous year's HCS, except the year on the emblem was updated.

From 1966 through 1968, Colorado Ford dealers sold a High Country Special package for the Mustang. For 1968, many of the styling cues from the GT/CS were incorporated. The vents on the hood were nonfunctional, but housed turn-signal indicators.

The contrasting tape stripe on the rear of the spoiler was part of the HCS package.

Goodyear Polyglas tires were state of the art for 1968, and they fit the California Special image perfectly. Palm trees and abundant sunshine are the perfect environment for the GT/CS.

Southern California Ford sales district manager Lee Grey was concerned that Ford was losing its edge to Chevrolet. He visited Shelby American and saw Ford engineer Fred Goodell at work on a prototype 1967 Shelby notchback, a project the company had begun in February. Nicknamed "Little Red" for its vibrant color, Goodell and Shelby had installed a Paxton-supercharged 428 Cobra Jet in the car. Because Grey knew many southern California dealers already offered "dressed up" and one-of-a-kind option packages throughout their entire line, he proposed that if Ford division did not pick up Shelby's version, they could sell parts for dealer installations and modifications. But changing engines and redoing bodywork to resemble Little Red was more complex than most dealers could handle. So Grey arranged to meet Iacocca on a West Coast trip. He showed him Little Red, and proposed the creation of a California regional Mustang.

Iacocca, who launched his career with a regional promotion and was a salesman at heart, took the idea back to Dearborn. There, according to Paul Newitt in *1968½ GT/California Special Recognition Guide and Owners Manual*, marketing vice president John Naughton, car product planning director Don Peterson, and Jim Wright, vice president and general manager of Ford division, looked it over. While they passed on Little Red as a Shelby "GT/SC," or GT Sports Coupe, they approved a 5,500-unit southern California-only product to be manufactured in the San Jose plant. For California dealers, the car would be called the GT/CS, or California Special. The San Jose plant, Shelby's airport facility, A.O. Smith, the outside fabricator in Ionia, Michigan, and a southern California company called A.G. Stearns Co., began producing parts and assembling the cars.

A production run of 42,325 fastback Mustangs were built for the 1968 model year. For comparison, however, 249,447 hardtops rolled out of showrooms that year.

The strictly southern California idea could not be contained. By the time the production ended, Ford had manufactured 4,025 GT/CS models and had distributed them as far from southern California as Kansas City, Missouri; Houston, Texas; and Calgary, Alberta, Canada. Colorado's own version was called the High Country Special, and Ford produced 300 for the dealers there.

Shelby did not abandon the notchback idea, and, in April 1968, Goodell started a new prototype nicknamed "the Green Hornet." Ironically, Goodell based this car on a green GT/CS that Shelby had acquired. However, Ford division ended production of the specials on July 30, 1968, effectively discontinuing the manufacture of 1968 models throughout all the plants barely a week later. Because the body style was to change, as was Shelby's role in the production of his Mustangs, the notchback idea died.

The California Special exemplified the problem facing designers, engineers, and planners. If a custom edition proposed for 5,500 sales barely sold 4,000 units in car-conscious southern California, how should Ford division interpret this result for future endeavors?

Mustang buyers were fortunate that the people in charge were sensitive to proportion; as the car grew two inches in width and length, nothing bulged or bubbled awkwardly. It could have been worse for the risk of bad design was there. Engine and powertrain considerations strained the package again when Ford offered 427-, 428-, and 429-ci engines for 1969 and 1970. Ironically, when engine sizes began to contract during the proceeding years, the next body design literally stretched proportion and taste much further.

Many feel that the real star of the Steve McQueen movie Bullitt *was his 1968 Mustang GT fastback. Equipped with a 390-ci engine, it is one of the most famous movie cars ever.*

(previous) The 1967 Shelbys were the last ones built at the Los Angeles International Airport shops.

Goodyear Polyglas tires might have been the best on the market, but they didn't stand a chance against the 428 Cobra Jet engine. Shelby vehicles were never wallflowers, and the 1968 GT500KR continued the extrovert reputation.

(S h e l b y   M u s t a n g s   1 9 6 7 – 1 9 6 8)

TAMING AND POPULARIZING THE ORIGINAL THEME

Even while Carroll Shelby was involved with his GT350s, he split his time between Los Angeles and England. At Ford's Advanced Vehicles facility in Slough Estates, he helped Ford build its GT40 race cars. Ford division's primary racing and promotional thrust had shifted now to international competition, with its manufacturing presence in Germany, England, and France. Victories in motorsports in Europe had measurable promotional and sales value. Taking along his new bride, Christina Vettore, Henry Ford II's more frequent visits to Europe, especially Italy, had convinced him that a much more serious racing effort would deliver broad benefits to his corporation's European markets. He and dozens of staff members negotiated for months to acquire Ferrari. The purchase had collapsed moments before Ford's representatives expected Enzo Ferrari to sign the agreement.

Henry Ford II quickly found a new goal. He wanted to win the 24-Hours of Le Mans and to beat Ferrari. He wanted to take the 24-Hours of Le Mans title from Ferrari with a car not only "powered by Ford," but actually called "Ford." Depending on where Henry Ford II needed Shelby most, the Texan commuted between England and California with the frequency and regularity of the tides.

Bolting a Paxton Supercharger to the potent 289-ci engine in the 1967 Shelby GT350 created a significant increase in power, from 306 horsepower to 390. A $600 option, it propelled the vehicle from rest to 60 miles per hour in only 6.2 seconds.

In 1964, though Shelby's lone 289 Cobra coupe had placed fourth overall and first in GT class at Le Mans, neither of Ford's two GT40s had completed the 24 hours. During the 1965 Le Mans race, all the GT40s and Cobras broke down due to inadequate budgets prohibiting quality production of the cars. In September 1965, Henry Ford II called Leo Beebe, his manager of public relations and racing, Don Frey, Ray Geddes, and Shelby into his office. Shelby recalled that Henry Ford II wore a lapel pin that said "Ford Wins Le Mans '66." He gestured to the men to take the other four such pins sitting on his desk. After they picked them up, as Shelby remembered, he said, "Don't make me a liar."

As they headed to the door, Frey turned and asked, "What about fiscal restrictions, Mr. Ford?"

"If there were restrictions, I would have let you know," the man said.

With that directive, and no budget limitations specified, Ford, Shelby, and Holman-Moody launched an all-out effort for 1966. They would erase the previous embarrassment of 1965, when Ford's initial $1.7 million budget had proven inadequate. It paid off. Ford GT Mk IIs took first, second, and third place overall, crossing the line in a near-squadron formation. As Carroll Shelby said years later, "Henry Ford II won Le Mans in 1966 single-handedly." After that, he told Shelby his goal for 1967 was to clearly prove that 1966 was no fluke. Shelby knew this would take even more time away from his own efforts.

Shelby received photographs of the 1967 production Mustang as well as its dimensions. Design and engineering, both directed by performance enthusiast Don Peterson's requirements, had enlarged the car. Some of the factory changes in design and chassis would make it difficult to modify the new model for B production racing. With Shelby's growing commitment to the GT40 program, competing in 427 Cobras and GT350R Mustangs clearly would have to be the job of his customers. Shelby already had ended the manufacture of his 427 Cobras. A number of both racing and street versions remained unsold, parked behind the hangars in Los Angeles, and were considered as out-of-date, undesired, and deeply discounted as day-old bread.

Significantly, Ford did offer to Shelby the big block 428-ci Cobra Jet engine for the Mustang, and in some limited cases, he was able to acquire 427-ci engines as well. He renamed the big block the "Cobra Le Mans." While Shelby, his engineers, and Ford's designers and planners figured out uses for these engines, the Texan must have looked out the window once again. Now instead of guessing the distance to an old, familiar building, perhaps he wondered how far he had come from earlier, simpler challenges. More likely, as before, he considered the 409s, 421s, 426s, 427s, and 440s, when he derived the designation GT500 for the 1967 big-block Cobra-Jet versions of his Mustang.

Following the precept that more power through more cubic inches was the cost-effective way to waste a set of tires, the 1968 Shelby GT500KR was meant to travel in a straight line quickly. While the 428-ci V-8 was rated at 335 horsepower, the torque figure of 440 foot-pounds was more indicative of its grunt.

Running the quarter-mile, the GT500KR covered the distance in 14.97 seconds at 99.59 miles per hour. At a list price of $4,473, the buyer received a lot of flash for the money.

Ford product planners suggested to him that he put his effort and investment toward the outside of his Mustangs rather than under the hood and underneath the cars. Though he'd been his own boss in 1964 and 1965, he didn't argue now. Producing thousands of cars was big business that took Shelby far from the pure pleasure of solving racing problems.

According to Wally Wyss in *Shelby's Wildlife*, Ford loaned Dearborn designer Chuck McHose to Shelby. He worked with Pete Stacey and Shelby's in-house designer Peter Brock on the 1967 pre-production prototype body sent by Ford division before his arrival. This body was sent with the intentions that Shelby American would design its own distinct appearance, chassis, and engine modifications. Together, the three created changes that would make the GT350 and GT500 look wilder than regular production fastbacks. They lengthened the hood 3 inches and recessed the grille deeper into the front cavity of the radiator. Mounting the headlight high beams in the center of the grille was Stacey's idea.

They integrated a huge scoop into the hood design more completely than they could for the 1965 and 1966 models, and added side scoops—resembling those on the GT40s—to the

Early 1967 Shelby GT500s had the high beams installed in the center of the grille. Shelby thought they looked good there. The problem was they were illegal in a number of states.

sail area on the side of the roof behind the doors. The designers took a visual cue from the GT40s mounting small, red marker lights in the 1967 Shelby Mustangs' side roof vent exits. Endurance racers mounted lights on their cars' sides or roof to illuminate the racing numbers. Sometimes crews color-coded these lights to make it easier for timing and scoring personnel to spot the car streaking past at night.

Aside from the center-mounted headlights, the Shelby GT's next most notable feature was the large rear spoiler. Ford's designers had extended the 1967 roof line to the end of the body. It was somewhat reminiscent of the tail Brock had designed for the Cobra coupes, and to which he had fitted a large, nearly vertical air spoiler. Brock and McHose adapted the rear spoiler and set it over the Mustang taillight valance. The sequential taillights they had tested on a 1966 prototype now went into the 1967, taken from Cougar's parts bin. These added a stronger visual identity to the 1967 Shelbys.

Shelby is said to have named the big-block version of the GT350 the 500 because it was a bigger number than anyone else's.

They reworked the Mustang suspension again, now to soften the ride. Buyers who had always believed they wanted a race car became far less certain once they drove their 1965 or 1966 street GT350. In response, Shelby's crew reduced the front anti-sway bar diameter very slightly; still it was thicker than Ford's heavy-duty suspension version. Shelby retained his own variable-rate springs. However, they did some of the suspension modification just to reduce production costs. For example, engineers replaced the more expensive Dutch-import Koni adjustable shock absorbers with U.S.-made Gabriel adjustables.

Shelby used the same solid valve-lifter 289-ci, 306-horsepower engine he had used in the 1965 and 1966 models. He carried over its cast aluminum high-rise intake manifold and 715 cfm Holley carburetor, but Federal emissions regulations took away the steel-tube headers. Ford had rated the 428CJ at 335 horsepower; this extremely conservative figure resulted as much from efforts to sneak the engine into a lower class in NHRA drag racing as to deflect growing concerns over performance versus safety from a newly vocal insurance industry. For Shelby's adaptation, his engineers fitted the 428 with two Holley 650-cfm four-barrel carburetors that they mounted on a medium-rise intake manifold. Hydraulic lifters quieted engine noise for the customers who wanted a race car without the noise and harshness of a real race car.

The biggest problem with the 1967 Mustang was that its growth not only in dimensions but also in weight increased demands on the powertrain. Lee Iacocca's original 2,500-pound coupe had grown to about 2,800 pounds as Shelby's 1966 GT350. Weight would increase to 3,286 pounds in the 428-engined GT500 version. While the extra 49 horsepower nearly made up for the extra 500 pounds of weight, nothing compensated for the weight bias that this heavier engine moved to the front: 57 percent versus 43 percent in the rear (the 1967 GT350 was 53/47). Fuel economy, something few people even considered in 1967 when gas still sold for $0.33 per gallon throughout the United States, was another gripe that would pile up against the GT500. The eight-barrel Cobra Jet was good for 6 to 11 miles per gallon, depending on which magazine tested it (*Sports Car Graphic* got 9.4 miles per gallon); the GT350 still would

Center-mounted high beams impaired airflow to the radiator, so when authorities forced Shelby to move the lights to the outside of the grille, the engine ran cooler.

(opposite) *Functional scoops festooned the 1967 Shelby GT500. The lower air inlet fed cool air to the rear drum brakes, while the C-pillar scoop directed air to the ventilation system.*

The fiberglass hood, like all Shelbys, sported a functional scoop. Under the hood, a pair of Holley carburetors sat atop a 428-ci V-8 and delivered about 10 miles per gallon.

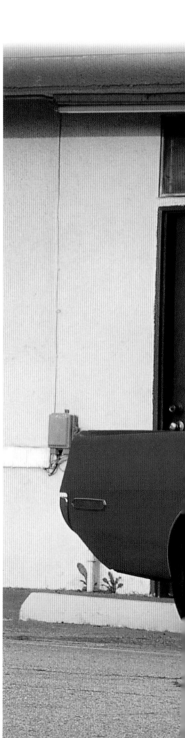

166

squeeze out 15 miles per gallon if drivers were judicious. Shelby reduced the base price of the GT350 to $4,195, and, for the GT500, the buyer paid $4,395 although few dealers delivered either of the models without additional options.

Car & Driver magazine put in context the 1965 and 1966 289-engined Mustangs when it first tested the GT500 for its February 1967 issue.

"The GT500 is an adult sports car," it wrote. "The '65 GT350 was a hot-rodder's idea of a sports car—a rough-riding bronco that was as exciting to drive as a Maserati 300S, and about as marketable a proposition. The traction bars clanked, the side exhausts were deafening, the clutch was better than an advanced Charles Atlas program, and when the ratcheting-type limited-slip differential unlocked, it sounded like the rear axle had cracked in half. It rode like a Conestoga wagon and steered like a 1936 REO coal truck—and we loved it.

"Jumping into the GT500," the reviewer continued, "the most marked difference was in engine noise, which is practically non-existent in the 428-engined car except for a motorboating throb.... All the viciousness had gone out of the car, without any lessening of its animal vitality. It still reacts positively, but to a much lighter touch." *Car & Driver* claimed 0 to 60 miles-per-hour times of 6.5 seconds, but *Road & Track* could do no better than 7.2 seconds. Shelby was able to offer the 427-ci "side oiler" engine as an option later, but they produced fewer than 50 examples.

While Shelby removed race car sensitivity from the new cars, he put in a pair of features that restored the sensation of race cars. In the fastbacks, Shelby welded a roll bar to the floorpan and attached to it a pair of inertia-reel-fed shoulder harnesses that could supplement the standard Ford lap belt. At this time, Federal safety regulations had required over-the-shoulder-across-the-chest clip-in belts, but Shelby replaced these with vertical belts that split behind the driver or front seat passenger's neck and attached at the sides of the seat. This system did make rear seat entry a challenge, however. Shelby found that air conditioning as well as automatic transmissions were options being ordered more often. Buyers' attitudes were beginning to reflect Ford management's thinking of ten and fifteen years before: shifting gears was something they had already done, now they would let a machine do it.

As production increased, Ford division offered Shelby a specialist who could help if glitches occurred. When Fred Goodell moved from Ford's factories to Shelby's hangars, he found nothing like Henry Ford production-line efficiency. The 1967 prototype that Dearborn shipped to Shelby American apparently had suffered some torsional chassis twisting in earlier development work. While McHose, Stacey, and Brock had carefully designed the fiberglass body pieces according to the plans that Ford shipped, they had test fit each prototype piece onto the prototype car body, revised plans accordingly, then ordered production. The result was that many of these pieces didn't fit the San Jose production bodies and therefore required endless hand-sanding to fit them to the factory-correct production cars.

Introduced in mid-1968, the Shelby GT500KR shoehorned the 428-ci Cobra Jet engine into the pony car, which required beefed-up front shock towers and staggered rear shock absorbers. It was ostensibly rated at 335 horsepower, but in real life it generated closer to 400.

David Mathews and Rick Kopec reported in the *Shelby American World Registry* the frustration that Goodell met when he arrived just after the 20th car was complete. No one at Shelby had bothered to clear any of the McHose/Brock styling changes with any state regulatory agencies. But there were other, bigger problems to solve and by the time Goodell got up to California's Department of Motor Vehicles (DMV) in Sacramento, the first stop on his mission, Shelby had completed about 200 of the 1967 model cars. Goodell learned that California (and many other states) had prescribed minimum distances that they permitted between headlights. More seriously, the only vehicles that could operate with red marker lights on their sides were emergency vehicles, such as ambulances and fire trucks. California's DMV didn't understand that Shelby was an independent contractor and, instead, felt Ford was trying to circumvent laws through Shelby. They ordered the center high beams relocated and the red lights removed.

Just as Shelby American was gearing up for the 1968 car run near the end of 1967 production, Shelby's lease expired on the old North American Aviation hangars on Imperial Highway. Another airport-related business wanted the space and zoning regulations gave that use a higher priority. Shelby had to move, yet it proved to be a blessing for him. His production for

The 1968 Shelby GT500KR exhibited a lengthened nose. The car required extended headlight surrounds and a one-piece fiberglass nose. Standard front disc brake rotors measured 11.3 inches.

1967 had increased to 3,227 cars, nearly two-thirds of which were the more luxurious GT500 models. Even with his two huge hangars, he didn't have enough room. Ford Division saw the situation as an opportunity to bring some of the situations that had caused problems with California's DMV (among others) under tighter control. It also knew that it could produce Shelby's cars more efficiently closer to home, with some of the work done through its regular assembly-line process, and save the costs of freight added to each car. Ford relocated production to A.O. Smith's facilities. Ford effectively took assembly and quality control supervision "in house." Shelby used his new-found freedom to concentrate on fulfilling Ford's new efforts in the Trans-Am series, having just accomplished Henry Ford II's goal again at Le Mans.

The GT350 suffered further in 1968, losing its legendary, noisy mechanical valve-lifter 289-ci engine to a quieter hydraulic-lifter 302-ci replacement in the name of "progress." The Holley 715 cfm four-barrel from the 1967 Shelby disappeared as well, replaced with a 600 cfm Holley, which worked better on the lower-speed engine. Still for those who craved the additional power, Ford kept the Paxton-McCullough supercharger option available, which boosted the 302-ci engine output from 250 horsepower at 4,800 rpm, to 335 horsepower at 5,200 rpm.

Stylistically for 1968, Ford's designers changed the headlights back to big singles, then installed Lucas driving lights in the grille, elongated the hood's overbite even further, and widened the twin air scoop nostrils. In addition to the 302-powered GT350s, Ford continued

The new 428-ci Cobra Jet engine was installed in the GT500KR in mid-1968. Available in both fastback and convertible models, a roll bar was installed in both iterations to provide an increased level of safety and stiffen the structure.

The wooden shift knob recalled the halcyon days when blue stripes on white were all a buyer could get on a Shelby Mustang. Virtually any flat surface on the dashboard was covered with woodgrain appliqué.

(oppposite) The instrument panel of the 1968 Shelby GT500KR housed most of the gauges a performance driver needed, but Shelby had an ammeter and oil pressure mounted at the bottom of the center stack. A padded steering wheel was a Mustang unit with a Shelby badge.

Shelby used the introduction of the GT500KR in mid-1968 to debut the new Cobra Jet engine. The taillights were sourced from the 1965 Thunderbird.

Evolutionary lines were evident on the 1967 Shelby GT500. While the gradual growth of the donor Mustang was unavoidable, Shelby did a respectable job and maintained a sporty feel in a car that increasingly leaned away from competition and toward Grand Touring.

to offer the rare 427-ci side-oiler engine as an option for the GT500. They subdued its noise quotient by using hydraulic lifters and fitted the intake with the Holley 600-cfm carburetor. They rated the package at 400 horsepower at 5,600 rpm. However, dealers did their best to talk buyers out of it, and Shelby once again delivered fewer than 50. To replace that, Shelby advertising announced the introduction of a 428-ci option with as much as 390 horsepower. This was the earlier 428-ci version updated with new cylinder heads that provided much larger intake and exhaust ports. For Shelby Mustangs, this "police interceptor" engine again used the Holley 715-cfm carburetors.

The hairiest incarnation of the GT500 was named the King of the Road, the KR. It came complete with the Cobra Jet 335-horsepower-rated engine, and wore special side-tape markings and a large Cobra on each front fender. Unfortunately for enthusiasts hungry for performance, Ford had to delay the introduction of this ground-pounder for two specific causes. First, a Detroit-area labor strike delayed production of many Ford products at the beginning of the model year.

One of one, the 1968 Shelby EXP 500 was nicknamed the "Green Hornet" because of its paint. Ten-spoke cast aluminum wheels were mated with Goodyear Polyglas tires in an attempt to restrain the 428-ci Cobra jet engine.

Built as an engineering exercise, the 1968 Shelby EXP 500 tested the feasibility of Conelec fuel injection and independent rear suspension. The only hardtop made by Shelby was ordered to be destroyed and crushed, but it somehow avoided that fate. This is one of two hardtops Shelby assembled. While he ordered it crushed, somehow it avoided that fate.

Second, the U.S. Environmental Protection Agency (EPA) emission standards testing and certification took longer than expected, moving the KR introduction to 1968½ product. (Emissions testing standards derailed the planned Paxton-supercharged Cobra Jet.) The GT500KR used the 428CJ. To purists, however, the KR reflected much more Ford and less the merchant of Venice.

"Carroll Shelby might not be a prisoner in the Ford works," wrote *Car Life* magazine's reviewer in its October 1968 evaluation of the car, "but every year the Shelby Mustang is a little less Shelby, and a little more Mustang. The first Shelbys, still competitive in road racing and as sports cars at that, were thoroughly revised, with improved front suspension geometry and trailing arms to change and limit movement of the live rear axle. Maybe it wasn't necessary, maybe the customers wouldn't pay for something that didn't show. But now, as mentioned, the Shelby version is Mustang, stiffened."

Steve Kelly, in the November 1968 *Hot Rod* review, expressed similarly guarded enthusiasm. His comments pointed out how, for an auto maker, succeeding at eliminating one customer's complaints evokes another's dissatisfaction.

"Had it not been for Carroll Shelby's 1965–66 series GT350 with its worthwhile features as a sports and performance machine, Ford probably wouldn't be marketing the current breed of GT350's and GT500's. Nor is it likely that such a car would've developed," Kelly wrote.

"Who knows, FoMoCo may not even like perpetuating the brand, but they are, and with greater success than when control was in Shelby's hands. Now the cars are made in Ionia, Michigan, feature bigger powerplants and more closely approach the deluxe appointments of Chevy's Corvette, although lacking the almost complete chassis revision given to the '65–66 machines...."

Performance was better than "deluxe" but, of course, Shelby's enthusiasts and reviewers were jaded. *Hot Rod*, testing the 3,570-pound, $4,857 fastback, could achieve no quicker times than 14.01 seconds in the quarter mile, crossing the line at 102.73 miles per hour. A roll-bar equipped convertible, heavier by 170 pounds and more costly by $500, could only do 97.71 miles per hour in 14.58 seconds.

"They are now much quieter," Kelly added, "and have much more distinctive bodies than before. Although this last item doesn't contribute a great deal to the GT's sports car value, it does separate it appearancewise [sic] from the regular Mustang. When you're marketing a car, this sometimes is more of a sales tool than ultra-strong and competitionlike [sic] underpinnings."

For Carroll Shelby, who would go years before marketing a car of his own again but would much sooner claim still another international victory, words from reviewers such as Dick Kelly stung, but they mattered little. Instead, Shelby listened carefully to the observations and opinions of his boss, Henry Ford II.

(1 9 6 9 – 1 9 7 0)

THE PONY
ON STEROIDS

Mustangs' racing achievements were far down the "Total Performance" spectrum from Ford GT40's international racing victories, but they were no less impressive in their local and regional performances. Mustangs "powered by Ford" began competing in the Sports Car Club of America (SCCA) events in 1966 when new rules in Appendix J, Group 2, from the Federation Internationale de l'Automobile (FIA) welcomed them. This organization sanctioned two parallel race series, the first for amateurs, comprising a total of 50 events across the country. The second series provided seven scheduled events for professionals called the Trans-American Sedan Championship, or Trans-Am. Both series culminated in the American Road Race of Champions (ARRC). There, the regional champions went against the top Trans-Am finishers. This was a road-racing series that, similar to NASCAR ovals and NHRA drag-racing Super Stock classes, was based on production automobiles. The FIA set the sedan class engine-displacement limit at five liters (305 cubic inches). For Ford, that meant its 302-ci V-8. With this engine, heavily developed and strengthened, Ford won the Trans-Am series championship in 1966, its first season, and again in 1967, racing with Shelby American blue fastbacks. By the end of the 1967 season, Chevrolet had challenged Ford furiously with its new Camaro. Ford began work on a new engine for 1968, though this "tunnel port" 302 proved itself unreliable. Chevrolet dialed in its cross-ram induction Z/28 for 1968, and GM's bow-tie division took the

(previous) The huge front spoiler was part of the 1970 Twister Special, a regional offering from the Kansas City sales district. Ninety-six Mach 1s were converted into high-profile sales tools, with a heavy emphasis on performance. They came with either a 351 Cleveland or a 428 Super Cobra jet engine.

Unlike the 1969 models, the 1970 Boss 429 came with a black hood scoop. Vivid colors hit the order sheet, such as this Grabber Orange. Specialty vehicle fabricator Kar Kraft assembled Mustang bodies in white into Boss 429s in their Livonia, Michigan, plant, and charged Ford $4,444 for the conversion work.

The 1970 Twister Special could be ordered in any color a buyer wanted—as long as it was Grabber Orange. The initial order for the Twisters was to be all 428 Super Cobra Jets, but there weren't enough of the monster engines to go around and a number of 351 Clevelands were slipped in instead.

title from Ford that year and held it in 1969. With its racing effort back in control, Ford reclaimed the championship in 1970 with matching yellow fastbacks driven by Californians Parnelli Jones and George Follmer.

With many GT40 engine parts installed in the 302 racing blocks, Ford developed 500 reliable horsepower at an astonishing 9,000 rpm for Jones's and Follmer's cars. For production versions they reduced the engine speed and power output to 290 horsepower at 5,800 rpm, but even then a production engine could be tuned for an additional 20 horsepower at 7,000 rpm. The street 302 engine also adopted many of the technologies Ford engineering had invented and proven in the first 289 hi-po-based engines for the GT40s as well.

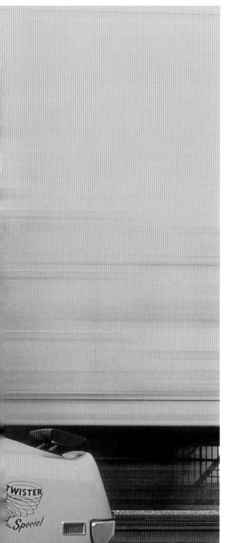

The engines played a roll in the success of the car, but its handling also won it rave reviews from journalists and owners. In *Mustang Boss 302: Ford's Trans-Am Pony Car*, author Donald Farr quotes a philosophy Bunkie Knudsen had brought with him from General Motors.

"If a car looks like it's going fast and it doesn't go fast, people get turned off," Knudsen said. "I think if you have a performance car and it looks like a pretty sleek automobile, then you should give the sports-minded fellow—the car buff—the opportunity to buy a high performance automobile." To help Ford division's cars look pretty and sleek, he imported his favorite GM designer Larry Shinoda. Knudsen's philosophy extended beyond just looks and engines, though. When the idea to market a street version of the Trans-Am 302 race car arose, Knudsen set his goal unmistakably. Farr reported that Knudsen dictated, "Make it absolutely the best-handling street car available on the American market!"

The promotion for these 96 Mach 1s was in Kansas City, famous for extreme weather. Half of the 428 SCJ equipped Twister Specials used C-6 Cruise-O-Matics, while the other half came with 4-speed manuals. This one rides on Magnum 500 wheels.

Cubic-inch call-outs that flank the Shaker Hood scoop left little doubt that the engine compartment was stuffed with good parts. The Shaker Hood scoop assembly was bolted to the engine, and when the powerplant would buck and quiver, so would the scoop.

(opposite) The interior of the 1969 Boss 429 was as low-key as the exterior. While the cabin was loaded with most of the available options, air conditioning was not allowed. High-back front bucket seats with Comfortweave fabric were standard.

The assignment descended from Knudsen to chief of light car engineering Howard Freers and then to Matt Donner, principal ride and handling engineer. Donner had worked on the Mustang chassis since the first production cars, and this project gave him the opportunity to take it further than any production-based Ford had ever gone.

By the time he had finished, Donner had solved a collection of unanticipated problems that had arisen during the process of making Knudsen's performance Mustang into a Camaro-killer. In some instances, it was shades of the 1964½ Mustang all over again. The biggest challenges involved trying to adapt fat tires to the package. The new F60 Polyglas tires were so stiff that when Donner put the car through its durability tests, it literally broke the front shock absorber towers. This had required him to significantly strengthen and modify the structure not only for Knudsen's hoped-for performance 302-equipped cars, but for all Mustangs. As Gary Witzenburg reported, engineer Howard Freers and his crew had to put substantial reinforcement into all Mustangs since it was not reasonable to structurally modify only some of the cars on the assembly line.

Former GM designer Larry Shinoda had an easier time. Shinoda had made several amazing GM show and development cars, including Chevrolet's 1960 CERV I single-seater. He also had completed all the production design work on Corvette's stunning 1963 Stingrays (derived from Peter Brock's originals), and designed the striking 1962 Corvair Monza GT fastback coupe, introduced at Watkins Glen the same weekend as Mustang I. His most recent achievement was his invention of the Camaro's rear spoiler and its reversed hood scoop.

His quick eye had caught the graphic treatment on the side of the Ford GT40 Mk IV, and he had adapted it to the race and street cars. However, one of his more visible accomplishments with the 302 was the car's name. Don Peterson's product planners had proposed calling the street cars "Trans-Am," but both Knudsen and Shinoda knew Pontiac division already had protected that name. However, the word "boss" had earned a connotation among young people. On the street, "boss" meant something undeniably good, something that was unquestionably at the top of everything else available. What's more, Shinoda always had referred to Knudsen as "Boss" and there was nothing wrong with honoring the boss.

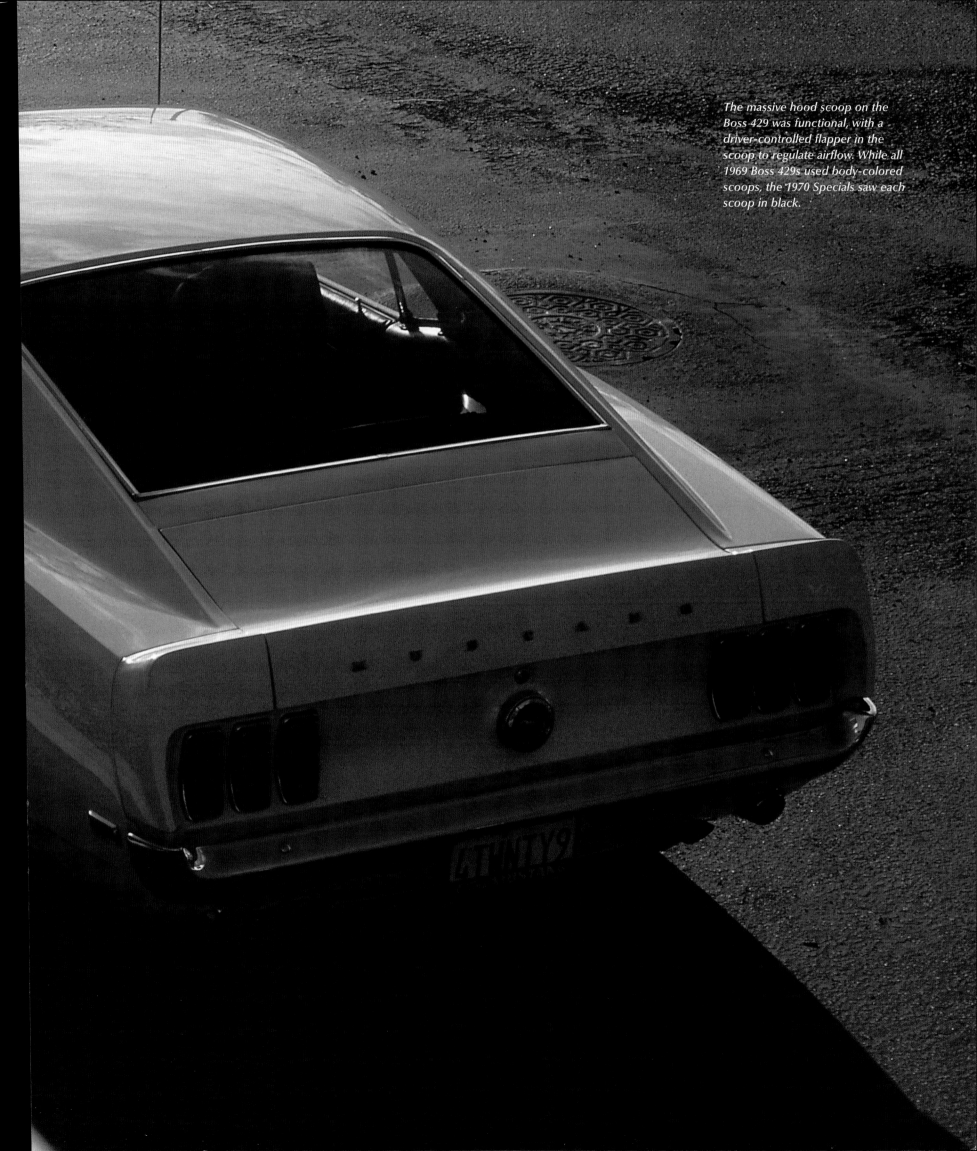

The massive hood scoop on the Boss 429 was functional, with a driver-controlled flapper in the scoop to regulate airflow. While all 1969 Boss 429s used body-colored scoops, the 1970 Specials saw each scoop in black.

Designer Larry Shinoda, fresh from the GM Styling Studios, created the tape graphics for the 1969 Boss 302. This was the closest the Mustang would come to a streetable race car. Rated at 290 horsepower, it would leap to 60 miles per hour in six seconds flat.

(opposite) The decals on the front fenders were the only external markings to identify the Boss 429. Magnum 500 steel wheels were standard rolling stock on the 1969 and 1970 Boss 429s.

Essentially a NASCAR racing engine squeezed into a street car, the Boss 429 suffered at the hands of most other muscle cars—until a bigger carburetor and headers were installed. Then all hell broke loose.

The Boss didn't stop at just 302. While Matt Donner was trying to tame the handling of the 302, the "boss-est" Boss was already in the works. If Ford meant for the Boss 302 to humble the Camaro Z/28 on the street and on the road circuit, Ford meant this one, the Boss 429, to humiliate Chrysler's 426-ci, 425-horsepower Hemis and GM's rare and exotic Central Office Purchase Order (COPO) cast-iron Mk IV 427-ci, 425 horsepower big-block V-8s.

As domination in SCCA's Trans-Am racing series had inspired the Boss 302, so did Ford's desire for superiority in NASCAR spark the idea for the Boss 429. While Ford's "tunnel port" 427-ci engines had been doing well enough on the Super Oval series, engineering had envisioned the 429 as the successor, due to its quasi-hemispherical cylinder heads. Chrysler had

Year two for the Boss 302 package was 1970, when a different tape and graphic package, as well as some engine and body tweaks, produced a stunning automobile.

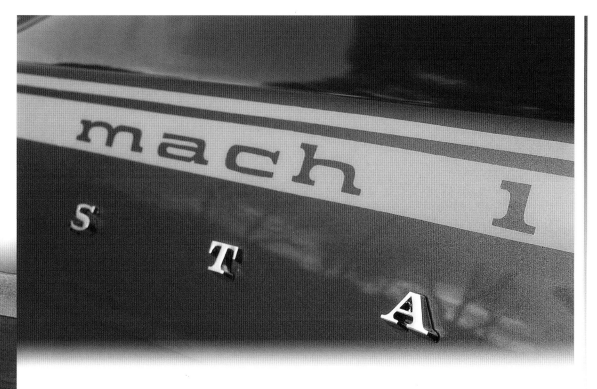

With a choice of three engine sizes, 351, 390, or 428 V-8, the 1969 Mach 1 could be tailored anywhere from mild to wild. The tape on the back of the rear spoiler and the side stripes were reflective.

introduced its hemi-head engines in the late 1950s for NASCAR and USAC events and they went into limited production for the street in order to legalize them for racing. Ford's engineers knew the domed head was the most efficient combustion chamber form because it left no hiding place for fuel to remain unburned.

Ford's 429 was a semi-hemi; the difference was that areas of the cylinder head where the valves were located were curved in the hemi, but were flat in a semi-hemi. Technical and philosophical arguments and benefits to each type still keep enthusiasts and engineers talking for hours. The semi-hemi is sometimes called a "crescent" head because the flat areas around the valve seats are crescent-shaped. NASCAR required minimum production numbers of any engine to qualify it for racing, so Ford offered the 429 in the Boss, beginning in 1969.

Ford assembled the first 279 of the Boss 429 street engines with hydraulic lifters and cams. Sometime in mid-1969, Ford had revised the engine to use a mechanical cam. Rated conservatively at 375 horsepower, these Boss engines were assembled in Ford's Lima, Ohio, engine facility. However, once engines were completed, car assembly became quite complex. Engines left Lima and went to Kar Kraft, a kind of official/unofficial Ford fabrication and racing shop that had first developed the Boss 302 and 429 engines for racing. Kar Kraft's pedigree came from its experience. Ford had transferred Roy Lunn, chief of the Mustang I project, to Slough Estates in England in order to take his race car enthusiasm and mid-engine expertise and apply it to Henry Ford's GT40 project. When Lunn had returned to suburban Detroit, he and a few other Ford performance engineers had recognized the need for a special, rapid-response facility outside Ford. An enthusiast magazine called *Car Craft* already existed (as did several other shops around the country), so co-founder Lunn and the rest of the group had chosen Ks for their spelling.

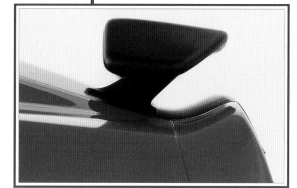

Everything was sent to the new, enlarged Kar Kraft facility, a space leased specifically for assembly of the Boss 429s, located in Brighton, Michigan. The engines came from Ohio and completed car bodies arrived from the Rouge plant. Complications arose because Rouge refused to build cars without engines, even though Kar Kraft didn't want the 428s the Rouge plant assembled. To keep peace, Kar Kraft accepted the Boss 429s off the assembly line with 428CJ engines installed, along with all the modifications necessary for the CJ package to become the big bosses. Lunn's people drove the cars onto transporters, trucked them to Brighton, and removed their engines, which were placed in storage. The Kar Kraft crews did some suspension modifications, installed the 429 engines and oil coolers, relocated the batteries to the trunk, and fitted the huge, black front hood scoops, racing mirrors, and decals. Then Kar Kraft returned the complete Boss 429s to the Rouge plant for distribution.

Ford and Kar Kraft produced 859 of the Boss 429s in 1969, but they only reached 499 in 1970. By comparison, the Boss 302 sold 1,934 in 1969. Magazine reviewers loved the performance, handling, and balance of the 302 version, and young buyers began wanting to identify with the Parnelli Jones–George Follmer racing successes. Production jumped to 6,318 in 1970. The Boss 302 was a $676 engine option in 1969, while the 429-ci engine added $1,208 to the sticker. In 1970, Ford product planners made the Boss 302 a separate package, pricing it at $3,720 (compared to the $2,771 base price for a "SportsRoof," Ford's 1969 and 1970 designation for its 2+2 Fastback body style). The 429 remained an option and its price went unchanged.

The 1970 Boss 302 that Parnelli Jones, racing for Bud Moore, drove to claim the SCCA Trans-Am title that year. The competition Boss 302s have campaigned in vintage races (shown here at Sears Point).

(opposite) In 1970, the Boss 302 could be ordered with the smooth hood seen here or with a Shaker Hood.

In order to meet the SCCA requirement for racing a production car, at least 6,500 Boss 302s had to be built. When the dust settled, Ford had cranked out 7,013.

In its debut year, the Mach 1 could be ordered tame as a grocery getter or brutal, especially when equipped with the 428 Cobra Jet. Shaker Hood, front and rear spoilers, and rear window slats all combined to project a tough street persona. Quad headlights were a 1969-only design element.

(opposite) *One of the joys of Mustang ownership is personalization of the pony. This very-Boss-like Mach 1 exemplifies that hobby, wearing Magnum 500 wheels, a rear wing, and rear louvers available on the 1969 Boss but not offered on the Mach until 1970 and 1971.*

The stockpile of unused, unwanted 428CJ engines continued to grow at Kar Kraft until, according to Anthony Young in his *Ford Hi-Po V-8 Muscle Cars*, the Rouge plant nearly ran out of Cobra Jet engines. Kar Kraft saved the day by selling them back truckloads. A stealth version of the CJ arrived in 1969, and Ford offered it only through 1970. Known as the Super Cobra Jet, buyers had to understand the dealer order forms to find it hidden among option codes. While it was never specifically labeled the SCJ, buyers received it when they ordered the Drag Pack Axle option. The base hardtop or SportsRoof retailed for $2,618 in 1969, and adding the normal Ram Air 428 Cobra Jet was a $421 option. After selecting the transmission and whatever other items the buyer desired, spending that last $155 replaced the CJ with the SCJ and added a 3.91:1 Traction-Lok rear end. If absolute performance with no road comfort compromise was the goal, Ford's knowledgeable dealers suggested spending yet another $52 for a 4.30:1 Detroit "Locker" differential and rear axle.

At the other end of the performance spectrum, Ford had quietly announced a Mustang Model E for model year 1969. This was a 250-ci in-line six-cylinder with a special automatic transmission, 2.33:1 rear axle, SportsRoof body, and a suggested retail of $2,905. Actually, only one was assembled, Ford's entry into the April 1968 Mobil Gas Economy Run. Its high-compression engine ran on premium, and Ford did a number of tricks for maximum economy.

Boss 429s, such as this 1970 example, were street cars packing a racing engine. The 15x7 Magnum 500 wheels were part of the Boss 429 package, as was a sizable front spoiler. Rear window slats and a rear spoiler were optional.

Bob Negstad obtained from Goodyear a set of 7.35x14 tires made of natural rubber with nylon cords. He took these to the engineering shop and inflated them to 110 psi. Then he took them to the paint shop where they baked in the paint drying oven at 180 degrees for the entire weekend. This stretched them round so that the tire patch was barely 2x3 inches per tire. With Ford leading on points, the Mobil Run got canceled at Indianapolis. Riots in protest of the death of Rev. Martin Luther King, Jr. on April 4, 1968, made Mobil conclude that it was too dangerous to continue across the United States.

Product planners provided performance options in abundance throughout the last years of the 1960s. If Mustang GT notchbacks with Cobra Jets or SportsRoofs with Drag Packs didn't satisfy buyers, if Boss 302s didn't provide enough motivation, and insurance costs for the Boss 429 were too much, Ford also offered still another jet-flight inspired option, the Mach I package.

The Mustang Mach I, introduced in 1969, came standard with a 250-horsepower 351W engine with a two-barrel carburetor. Buyers could choose optional engines all the way up to the 428CJ with its functional ram air hood scoop, a combination known as the 428CJ-R. For the Mach I, the GT390 was just a $100 option, but that was the farewell appearance for the

390; it disappeared from Mustang catalogs after 1969. The Mach I came with its own package of appearance cues, including hood pin latches, side body stripes, chromed wheels, and even a chromed racer-type quick-open, spring-loaded gas filler cap. The Mach I with 428CJ-R set its young enthusiast back $3,122 for the car and another $224 for the engine. Prices rose by $149 for the car and $152 for the engine in 1970.

Chassis engineer Bob Negstad had been part of the crew transferred from Dearborn with Roy Lunn to work on the GT40 project. Now back in Dearborn, his engineering bosses brought him in to replace Matt Donner, who by the time the 1970 Boss 302 development was nearly complete, had become quite ill. Negstad had lamented what happened to the Mustang in the years he, Lunn, and others were off fulfilling Henry Ford II's prime objective. As he had left for England, Negstad had heard the clamoring at the doors.

Parnelli Jones leads a Penske Javelin through a turn in the hotly contested 1970 Trans-Am season. Jones and teammate George Follmer won the Trans-Am title that year.
Dale von Trebra

Hurried pit stops were the norm for George Follmer. Here the Bud Moore crew tops up the fuel as a fire extinguisher is aim at the engine compartment. Dale von Trebra

Repairs are made underneath Parnelli Jones' 1970 Boss 302 race car during a practice session. Like the street Boss 302's, the rear wing was functional and adjustable. Note the dapper gentleman to the right; today's racing crowd is a bit more casual. Dale von Trebra

Parnelli Jones leads Mark Donohue through Road America's Moraine Sweep towards Turn 5. Bare knuckles racing was the rule in the 1970 Trans-Am season. Dale von Trebra

George Follmer talks with teammate Parnelli Jones during the 1970 Trans-Am series. Dale von Trebra

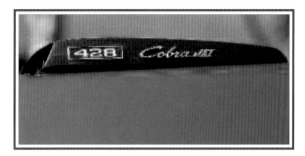

"Everybody in the company said, 'My God! Look at these guys. Look what they've done,' and they came in a rush to take over to show the troops how it really ought to be done. Everyone who was jealous of the success of the people that made the Mustang, they jumped in and said, 'Wait till we show you how to do this thing!'

"We just barely held on to the '69 and '70 Mustangs. The '69 Boss 302 was one of the finer ones. And the '70 Boss, they were outstanding cars. People that were into cars did those." Then Negstad frowned.

"But the baton was passed clearly to a bunch of guys who had discovered bigger and larger and heavier and flashier and gaudier. They said, 'Well, if they can do good, wait till they see what we can do.'"

The 1969 Trans-Am season saw considerable close racing. Here Parnelli Jones in a Bud Moore team car leads a Shelby team car driven by Horst Kwech. Dale von Trebra

chapter nine

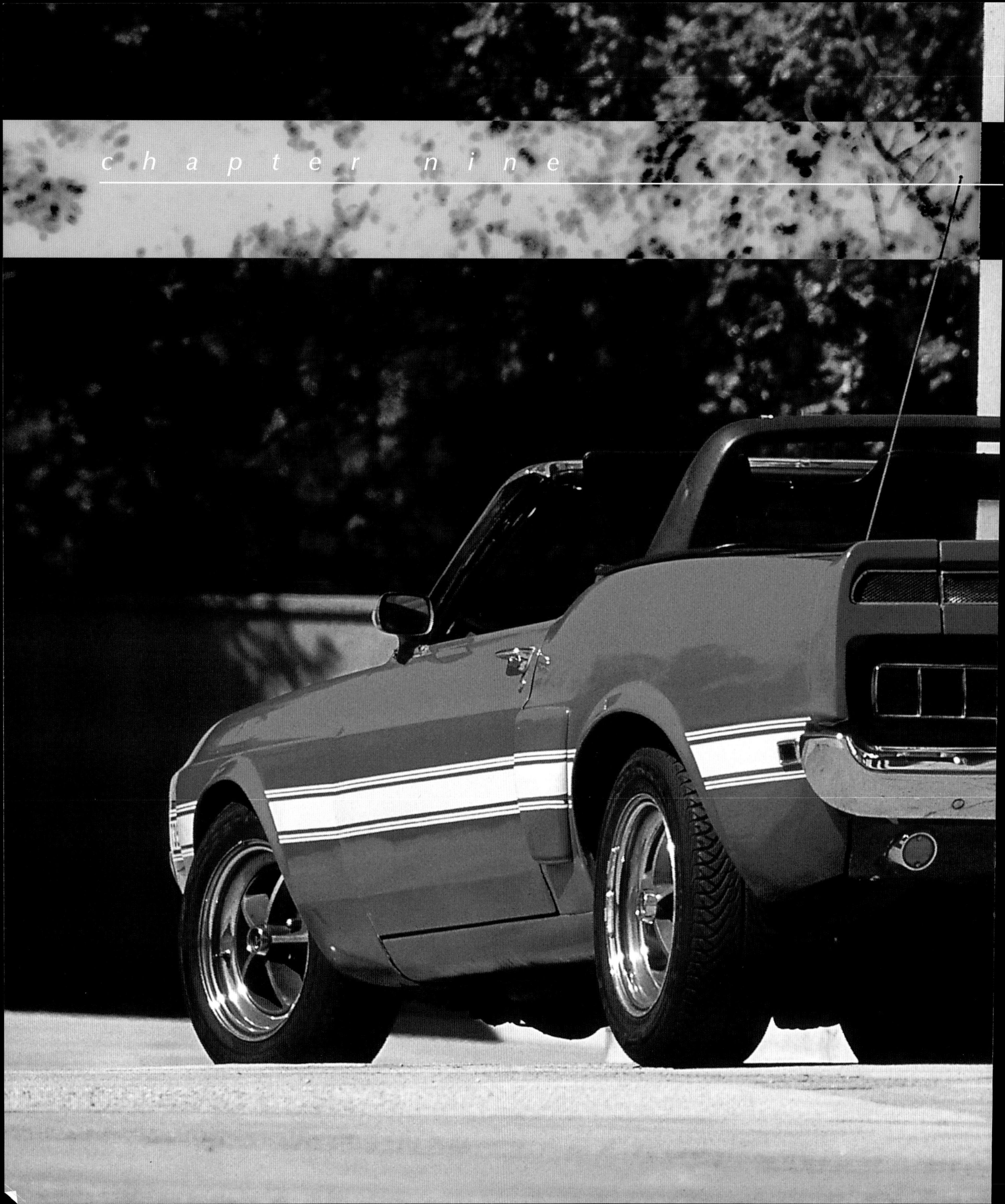

(previous) The 1969 Shelby convertibles were rare and used a bolt-in roll bar, unlike the welded units of years before. Cast-aluminum wheels were standard on the GT350 and 500. No optional wheel was offered.

Ford's bin of 1965 Thunderbird taillights was thinned considerably with Shelby's use of the parts on his GTs. In 1969, 306 Shelby de Mexicos were built by Mexican businessman Eduardo Velasquez at a factory in Nuevo Leon, Mexico.

(S h e l b y   M u s t a n g s   1 9 6 9 – 1 9 7 0)

REACHING MATURITY IN POWER, STYLE, AND AUDIENCE

It took 21 separate pieces of plastic and fiberglass to remodel and reshape the body of the GT350 and GT500 for 1969. One look at the cars made it clear that Ford division's emphasis now was on appearance. What had been subtle became outrageous. Designers sliced five NACA (National Advisory Committee on Aeronautics) ducts, adopted from jet aircraft, into the hood to maneuver air into the air cleaner and evacuate heat from the engine compartment. Ford designers had used some of their first ones on the GT40 FIA Appendix J prototype. Staff designers tested other Shelby appearance cues through the response of auto-show crowds toward Ford's "dream" cars. The 1970 Mustang Milano bore several elements adopted from Shelby's cars. These cues would strongly influence the final look of the 1971 production Mustang. This included not only the ducts, but also the wide, flat, rectangular grille opening. Bordinat and his staff sensed, from Knudsen's style and Shinoda's work, that the GT350/GT500 design would influence the next generation of Mustangs.

Engineering fitted the 290-horsepower 351W as the standard engine for the 1969 GT350. This replaced the no longer adequate hydraulic-lifter 302-ci V-8 used only in 1968. The GT500 continued with the 428 Cobra Jet, still rated at 335 horsepower with Holley four-barrels on its medium rise intake manifolds. Suspension for the cars, which featured Gabriel Adjust-O-Matic shock absorbers and Goodyear F60-15 Polyglas bias-belted tires, carried over the

In the February 1969 issue of Sports Car Graphic, *the staff ran a 1969 GT500 through the quarter-mile in 14 seconds at 102 miles per hour. The 428-ci V-8 made; 335 horsepower and 440 foot-pounds of torque.*

Mustang Mach I configuration. But prices had to come up, adjusted by marketing's decisions to make more options mandatory in order to sell the car as a Shelby. The GT350 SportsRoof started at $4,434, with a similarly unadorned GT500 going for $4,700. Of course, dealers, who would receive only a single model of each Shelby per year, loaded up their versions with options. They found buyers willing to pay for every creature comfort available. Fully equipped GT500 convertibles wore a sticker price in excess of $6,300. Few of these customers were baby-boomers, but many were their parents. With children finishing college, they were able, for the first time, to enjoy the rewards of their hard work and the abundance of a healthy economy.

Convertibles and SportsRoof models retained their integral padded roll bars, and the enclosed cars kept the two-piece shoulder harnesses introduced with the 1967 and 1968 models. By 1969, the nature of the Shelby Mustang had changed drastically. It had been Shelby's 1965 and 1966 racing homologation specials that *Car & Driver* writer Steve Smith had characterized

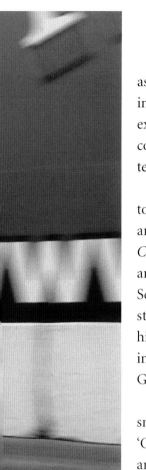

as "a brand new, clapped out racing car." By 1967 and 1968, Shelby and Ford offered the cars in a broad range of exterior colors, and for 1969 and 1970, product planners and marketing experts made sure there were abundant choices for interior options as well. The cars came completely carpeted and trimmed with chrome. Ford's interior designers applied imitation teakwood to the center console, door panels, and the dash.

The more the car evolved, the less charitably enthusiast magazines treated Shelby, failing to recognize or accept that nearly every detested decision was made by nameless committees and department managers miles from California and light-years from Shelby's philosophy. *Car & Driver* magazine's eloquent writer, Brock Yates, was a man with vast racing experience and originator of the legendary cross-country race, the Cannonball Baker Sea-to-Shining-Sea Memorial Trophy Dash. Though he had access to enough insider information to understand Ford Motor Company's intentions with its Shelby-badged cars, his strong love of high-performance automobiles led him to sadness and cynicism. He exorcised his frustration in print, his text published in tidy contrast to dramatic and eye-catching photos of a new GT350 convertible.

"And so we come to the 1969 edition of the Shelby GT 350," Yates wrote, "a garter snake in Cobra skin, affixed with dozens of name plates reading 'Shelby,' 'Shelby-American,' 'Cobra' and 'GT350' as if to constantly re-assure the owner that he is driving the real thing and not a neatly decorated Mustang (which he is)."

Ford designers penned the 1969 Shelby lines, including the lengthened nose. Shelby-specific fenders were stamped, and the grille was a Shelby exclusive. The scoops ahead of the rear tires fed cool air to the aft drum brakes.

The 1970 Shelbys were basically carryover 1969 models with black stripes on the hood and new VINs from the Department of Motor Vehicles. They were Ford designed, built, and serviced. The GT350 and 500 went out on a high note.

The huge fiberglass hood utilized five scoops. The front pair fed air to cool the engine compartment, while the back two vented warm air to the atmosphere. The center NACA scoop fed air into the air cleaner plenum.

Alongside a dramatic photo looking across the vast field of a hood interrupted by gentle rises, NACA slots, and NASCAR-style rotating hood lock pins, the caption skewered the car: "The original Shelby GT350 was a fire-breather; it would accelerate, brake, and corner with a nimbleness only a Corvette could match. The GT350, 1969-style, is little more than a tough-looking Mustang Grande, a Thunderbird for Hell's Angels. Certainly not the car of Carroll Shelby's dreams."

In truth, the car had gone beyond Shelby's wildest dreams. He really had invented a brand-new clapped-out sports car. It had been a homologation trick in order to go racing and bring glory to Henry Ford II, Lee Iacocca, the Mustang, and the Blue Oval. The legacy that had led to the 1969 and 1970 Shelby appearance was huge, but had also drawn in people of significance and influence, with style and taste of their own.

Ford President Bunkie Knudsen had been so taken with the 1969 car's appearance that he had gone to Gene Bordinat and ordered him to integrate "the Shelby look" into the styling for the 1971 Mustang. Even as magazine writers were lambasting the look, Bordinat's advanced designers stretched out new vellum sheets and went back to work.

On Wednesday, September 3, 1969, Ford introduced its 1970 models, including the carry-over Shelby GT350s and GT500s. For some time now, Bordinat's designers had been frantically adapting working drawings from fronts of 1969 Shelby-based prototypes to mold onto the 1971 Knudsen Mustang. Then eight days later, Thursday, September 11, Henry Ford II fired Knudsen. It had been a whirlwind 583 days. Unfortunately, the chairman was too deeply occupied with

209

other things to think about coming to Bordinat and dismissing Knudsen's legacy of design as well. Knudsen's forceful personality and his strong ideas had collided with Bordinat, and this, regrettably, had resulted in the next series of Mustangs that resembled Shelbys, and Thunderbirds whose noses resembled Pontiac Trans-Ams.

Some people closer to Henry Ford II claimed it had been a maelstrom. As Knudsen had roared down hallways always in a hurry to get things done, he had stepped on too many toes and collided with too many egos, shoving doors open too hard and moving on too fast. Others closer to the maelstrom said he simply pushed open Henry Ford II's door without knocking, signifying an assumption of equality that never had been nor could be.

Putting a 1969 GT350 in the driveway required $4,434 for the SportsRoof version. The fiberglass hood tended to warp from the tension of the hood springs.

One of those individuals who Knudsen had rolled over and who had threatened to leave was a man of equally strong personality and ideas. Lee Iacocca had grown more mature, though, after learning from McNamara and working for the Deuce. He had badly wanted the job that went to the GM executive. Fiercely loyal to Henry Ford II, Iacocca had rode out the 583 days of Knudsen while he had remained executive vice-president of North American Automobile Operations (NAAO). After Knudsen's dust had settled, Lee Iacocca was still there.

It was Iacocca who Carroll Shelby had turned to in the middle of 1969. Shelby, another man of strong personality and ideas, had seen battles closing in all around him. The cars that bore his name had sold more copies as convertibles with air conditioning and automatic transmissions than as unadorned performance coupes. Even the competitors—Camaro, Trans-Am, Barracuda, Challenger—now sold less muscle and more luxury across the line. Perceptively, Shelby had known cars bearing his name would also be competing against Ford division's Mach I and Boss 302 and 429. People within the corporation had resented that fact and some had tried to undermine his influence and his success.

Outside the car enthusiast world, voices of public welfare and strident safety activists, such as Ralph Nader, began questioning the need for 300- and 400-horsepower cars. Insurance companies simply punished the owners with premiums that sometimes equaled their car payments. Even the critical comments of friends such as Brock Yates had begun to sting. Despite all this, Ford division still sold 194 of the GT350 convertibles, and another 335 of the GT500 convertibles. Sales of SportsRoof model GT350 and GT500s brought the 1969 total to 2,364 cars.

Shelby de Mexico cars used a different hood than their American counterparts, as well as a changed C-pillar. Mexican regulations required that at least 45 percent of the parts be manufactured in Mexico. Rear axles, seat upholstery, and tires were some of the components made south of the border.

211

The long, aggressive nose of the 1969–1970 GT350 and 500 required the driver to have good depth perception. The vents behind the numerals were designed to feed cool air to the front brakes, but their effectiveness was questionable.

Unlike American Shelbys, the Shelby de Mexicos did not utilize functional rear brake-cooling scoops. The vinyl-covered rear roof silhouette makes the vehicle stand out from both Mustangs and Shelbys.

Twist-lock hood latches lent a competition touch to the 1969 GT350. Mesh screens kept large objects from slipping into the engine compartment, but the scoop that fed the engine air was wide open.

(opposite) Never one to shirk self-promotion, Carroll Shelby mounted his recognizable Cobra emblem wherever he could, including the C-pillar on the 1969 GT350. Rear quarter windows popped open about 1 inch, which was identical to the SportsRoof model Mustang that was the starting point for the GT350 and 500.

In the late summer of 1969, knowing the car and its sales would be nothing like the old days, and knowing that a major new body was due for 1971, Shelby went to Iacocca and Ford Division Vice President and General Manager John Naughton. He asked them to end the Shelby Mustang program at the closing of the 1970 model year. They agreed.

Throughout 1970, "production" reached a total of only 789 GT350s and GT500s. As Rick Kopec and his thorough researchers reported in the *Shelby American World Registry*, these cars really were leftover, unsold 1969 cars. Ford division gave them new number plates and fit the front spoiler and hood stripes their designers had developed for the car. This 789 figure was not even a measurable fraction of the record sales numbers the Mustang achieved in its first year. Then again, that accomplishment was never a goal for Shelby cars.

The Shelby Mustangs were intended for a limited audience with clear and particular taste. Up through their final evolution in 1970, these "personal" cars still fit precisely into the Iacocca "Fairlane Committee" concept of the Mustang as "Total Performance—Powered by Ford." In recognition of that achievement, Ford Motor Company named Iacocca its corporation president on December 10, 1970.

(previous) Although the fog lamps in the grille were faux, the shovel-like front spoiler was needed because the 351 Cleveland engine could get the 3,860-pound 1971 Boss 351 up to 60 miles per hour in under six seconds. Despite its bulk, the suspension had been refined to generate identical cornering forces as the Boss 302.

The 1971 Boss 351 was built after the wave had passed and was the last of the race-inspired Mustangs. Functional Ram Air scoops on the enormous hood fed ambient air to the potent 351 Cleveland V-8, delivering 370 horsepower at 5,400 rpm.

RAM AIR

(1971–1973)

KNUDSEN'S LEGACY: THE WRONG CAR FOR CHANGING TIMES

As late as the spring of 1967, when Gene Bordinat's designers began daydreaming about 1971 Mustangs, barely anyone in America could forecast what would become two major concerns of the early 1970s. The issues, one of political correctness and the other of environmental consciousness, did not exist in the public eye yet, but the slow-building storm was about to break over the auto industry. As time passed, both of these factors would play a role in the development and character of the 1971, 1972, and 1973 Mustangs, redefining it for the next decade of its life.

The Mustang introduced to the public for 1967 had grown slightly larger and heavier than its first-generation predecessor. Soon after, with short- and long-term engine plans already detailed in countless memos, Bordinat's designers knew only that they had to enlarge the car further. The horsepower war against GM and Chrysler was already causing engineers to cram 427-, 428-, and 429-ci engines into the Mustang and the Fairlane. What's more, product planners and market researchers were swamping design and engineering with studies and reports. These suggested perhaps as many as one-third of buyers wanted not only staggering acceleration, but they now wanted that acceleration with an automatic transmission. They also desired other creature comforts such as air conditioning and stereo radios capable of playing their favorite 8-track cassette tapes. A practical back seat would be nice.... Was real leather possible?

When the 1971 Mustang debuted, it looked bigger because it was. It measured 2.1 inches longer than the 1970 model and could comfortably carry any size engine in the Ford garage. While it was being developed in 1968, a performance war was underway, but by the time the fourth-generation Mustang hit the street, insurance costs and emission regulations doomed powerful engines.

Ford engineering and production could stuff the 428s and 429s into the current cars because no one believed the performance pursuit could possibly require anything larger. But following corporate acceptance of the big engines, there was not enough time or money left for Ford designers to reshape the cars to provide enough room for service personnel to work on them for 1967 or even 1970. Now that they could start over, the engineers and designers had to provide working room for the poor mechanics.

They stretched the wheelbase an inch to 109 inches, the first growth in the length of the platform even as the front and rear track spread for a second time, another 2.0 inches up front and 1.5 inches at the rear, to 61.5 inches and 60 inches. The body went through more than a dozen full-size clay prototypes until then-Ford president Bunkie Knudsen saw one he liked on January 18, 1968, and approved it on the spot. Nine months later, production engineering was too far along to change anything by September 11, when Henry Ford II fired Knudsen. By the time that 1971 model car rolled off the assembly line in time for the August 20, 1970, introduction, the Knudsen body measured 2.0 inches longer and wider than the 1970 model and had gained 600 pounds as well. Much of this came from the weight of optional engines and the required extra suspension and chassis pieces to support that performance potential.

The appearance was bold and evolutionary. J. Walter Thompson agency had teased the buying public with features of the new Mustang for months. A new Ford show vehicle, the Mustang Milano, had circulated North American auto shows beginning in early 1970. This wild purple sparkler had adopted the Shelby GT350-GT500 grille treatment that Knudsen had fallen in love with and carried over the Shelby's NACA ducts. It also had pre-saged the almost horizontal fastback SportsRoof line.

Engines continued to dictate the design decisions. The 290-horsepower 302-ci engine used in the Boss through 1970 was a costly engine to produce; Ford replaced it 351HO (high output), a Cleveland engine that was a little less complicated, a little less expensive, a little less noisy, and a lot more powerful. It developed 330 horsepower at 5,400 rpm. But for those demanding

The huge rear window was only 14 degrees from horizontal, but it directed the airflow well, which was ideal in a race car. Ford's withdrawal from competition at the end of the 1970 season meant the 1971 Boss 351 was a race car locked out of the race.

pure bravado, Ford replaced the 428 Cobra Jet with a new series of 429s, still called Cobra Jet, (CJ), Cobra Jet-Ram Air (CJ-R), and Super Cobra Jet (SCJ). The new CJ produced 370 horsepower with or without the Ram Air induction system, while the SCJ was a substantially different engine. Rated at 375 horsepower at 5,600 rpm, it used four-bolt main bearing caps instead of two-bolt caps as was common in all the other Ford engines except the Cleveland-built 351HO, and it relied on mechanical valve lifters instead of hydraulics used in the other two 429CJs.

The body style formerly known as the notchback now was called the hardtop. Design had taken the formerly more vertical lines at the back of the roof and faired them out into the deck lid, creating a kind of tunnel behind the rear window. This was another Knudsen-Shinoda adaptation from the Pontiac division half a decade earlier. The Mustang SportsRoof soon became known as the "flat back" because its line deviated barely 14 degrees off the horizontal. Ford carried over the convertible, and thus the Mustang began its eighth season. Marketing kept the Mach I in the Mustang lineup as it did with the luxury model Grandé, both introduced in 1969.

The new Boss 351 had evolved from the same legitimate racing heritage that had given birth to the 302 and 429 models. It had taken until opening day of the Detroit auto show, November 21, 1970, to ready this model for introduction. NASCAR had proposed a new displacement limitation of 366-ci, and Ford engineering had agreed to stretch and develop the Cleveland-built 351 to meet NASCAR's specification. NASCAR had later elected to apply intake and exhaust restrictors that would limit the power in larger displacement engines rather than force manufacturers to come up with completely new blocks. To keep costs under control for the

Boss 351 street version, engineering had adapted and modified its Boss 302 heads. The Cleveland engine used a cast-iron crankshaft but forged steel connecting rods and forged aluminum pistons. They had replaced the Holley 780 cfm carburetor they had used on the 1970 Boss 302 with an AutoLite 750 cfm model. They had coupled a Hurst shifter with a four-speed manual transmission and ensured power got to the streets by adding a locking rear axle.

Prophetically, the day before the show opened, the *Detroit News* published a story reporting that Ford Motor Company was withdrawing from all auto racing. Anthony Young quoted the story in *Ford Hi-Po V-8 Muscle Cars*. On Wednesday, November 19, Matt McLaughlin, Ford vice-president of sales, delivered a formal statement saying, in part, "We believe racing activities have served their purpose and [we] propose now to concentrate our promotional efforts on direct merchandising and sale of our products through franchised dealers." All competition plans and projects that divisions or dealers had in motion slammed to a tire-skidding halt, pulled off to the side of the track, and parked as a result of the Thursday, November 20, news story. In a country still reckoning with the horrors of Vietnam and still reeling from high

Even though the 1971 Mustang had been enlarged, the rear seats were still a painful place on a long journey. Only 6,121 convertibles were built in 1971, a far cry from the 72,119 ragtops sold in 1966. This would be the last year for a Mustang convertible for quite some time.

By 1973, performance in the Mach 1 consisted of tape graphics. Increasingly stringent emission regulations and escalating insurance costs brought the muscle Mustang down to earth. Some just say down because it was the sunset of performance for quite some time.

While it's now hard to believe, in 1973 the 14-inch Wide Oval was state-of-the-tire-art. Brushed aluminum hubcaps with trim rings were standard for 1973. Power front disc brakes were standard on 1973 Mustang convertibles and 351 V-8 cars.

(opposite) Weight was bumped up in 1973 with the addition of the federally mandated 5 miles per hour front bumper. The design increased the length of the Mustang by four inches. Vertical turn signals and a body color front bumper cover were the only exterior changes from the preceding year.

insurance costs for high-performance cars, McLaughlin's move reminded some of Harlow Curtice and the AMA ban in 1957; it betrayed racers and disappointed fans. McLaughlin and Henry Ford II understood, though. If an industry acts quickly enough, it might be able to claim credit for its own politically correct responses to public concerns while also heading off government scrutiny before they could possibly force those same actions anyway. Unlike the 1957 ruling that left open back-door loopholes, Ford shut all its doors tightly this time. This was part of an auto industry-impacting storm front that would hit Detroit like a one-two punch.

The second punch came on December 18, a month after McLaughlin's announcement and a week after Ford Motor Company named Lee Iacocca its new corporate president. That day, the federal Clean Air Bill passed both houses of Congress on a voice vote. The bill, first proposed during the summer as part of President Richard Nixon's National Environmental Policy Act, required automakers to develop, within six years, an engine that would eliminate 90 percent of exhaust emissions. As early as July 1954, a six-year study in California, Nixon's home state, had defined smog—auto exhaust and industrial emissions—as a major health hazard. On April 6, 1960, California's state legislature approved the nation's first smog control legislation. By late 1970, environmental consciousness had now become federal law.

Prior to the increasingly strict safety regulations and tough emissions standards outlined in the National Environmental Policy Act, Congress had tossed the carmakers and the buying public a bone six weeks earlier. Wanting to slightly soften the huge costs of implementing the new regulations, it had passed the Job Development Act of 1971 on November 8, 1970, which

Using an evolutionary design of the 1969 Mustang instrument panel, the 1973 Mustang was long on front-seat comfort. The Rim-Blow steering wheel was a $35 option, while an AM radio went for $59.

The Mustang lived up to its performance roots in 1973 with tape graphics from the 1971 Mach 1. Hardtop design was the most popular Mustang model in 1973.

had repealed the seven-percent Federal excise tax imposed on passenger cars and made it retroactive to August 15. Congress had suggested to Henry Ford II and his fellow industry executives that this $200-per-car tax reduction would surely spur auto sales. The other incentive of passing this act had been the hope that voters and car buyers might forget Nixon's Economic Stabilization Act of 1970, which had frozen wage and price increases effective August 15.

Unfortunately, Nixon's first policy didn't work and rapid fiscal expansion and high growth continued through 1971 and 1972. When this Act rolled into Phase II, it held maximum wage and price increases to 5.5 percent until April 30, 1974. The leading edge of the storm was holding tight over Detroit.

The storm hit again on February 3, 1971, when the members of the 11-year-old Organization of Petroleum Exporting Countries (OPEC) had reached a deadlock in negotiations with 17 western oil companies over OPEC's proposed price increases. Together, the 11 member nations decided to set oil prices themselves, no longer consulting with their customers in advance. Through 1971, the price of a barrel of crude oil increased almost 100 percent. OPEC cut production and export volume by nearly 75 percent by the end of 1973. Negotiations continued, but it would not be until mid-March 1974 when relations between the then 13-member OPEC nations and its Western customers would calm a little. By then, oil that had sold for $2.11 a barrel was going for $14.08. While gas prices held remarkably steady from 1971 to 1973, rising from $0.36 to $0.39 a gallon, gas jumped to $0.55 shortly after the beginning of the Arab oil embargo on October 21, 1974, and by year's end, lines were forming around gas stations.

Ford Motor Company money and personnel who had been used on racing now were needed for more socially, environmentally, and politically acceptable assignments, such as vehicle safety and exhaust emissions. Racing had attracted and occupied the minds of Ford division's best and brightest engineers and outside talents, beginning with the Fairlane Inn dinners, and flowing through to Jacque Passino, Roy Lunn, Carroll Shelby, and countless others. Those who remained at Ford would be equally challenged by the responsibilities ahead, but less excited by their achievements.

In the calm eye of this brewing storm, the Boss 351, producing 330 horsepower in 1971, accomplished in part through the use of an 11.0:1 compression ratio, had to be modified to run on unleaded gasoline for its 1972 production year. Engineering decreased compression to 8.8:1, which reduced power output to 266 horsepower at 5,400 rpm. They accomplished crucial, significant changes within the engines so they could run on the lower octane rating, thus improving their fuel economy and their ability to meet the emission standards already in place. Washington's highest and most influential policymakers selected Henry Ford II from the big three automakers, asking for his help and warning him of what they saw on the horizon. Ford Motor Company accepted and complied, and its designers and engineers looked ahead to a very different future.

Production of Mustangs had steadily declined from its peak of 607,568 in 1966. The numbers slipped to 317,404 in l968, and to 190,727 for 1970. The 1971 figures slipped further to 149,678, despite some renewed interest because of the car's fresh looks. Even with the excise tax repeal, this upward trend reversed only briefly. Ford produced just 125,093 cars in 1972. Dearborn was well inside the eye of the storm.

Ford tried to certify the 351-ci, 4-barrel engine in the the 1973 Mach 1 by using data from the 2-barrel Mustang engine. The government caught Ford in this subterfuge and left the Mach 1 with only a 2-barrel carburetor. The 248–horsepower, 4-barrel 351 engine, code Q, was available in any model except the Mach 1. A four-speed manual transmission was only offered with this engine.

Design work for the 1971 Boss 351 started in early 1967, with Semon E. "Bunkie" Knudsen giving the design his approval in February 1968. The 351 engine replaced the Boss 302 powerplant in 1971 because the larger engine was much cheaper to build.

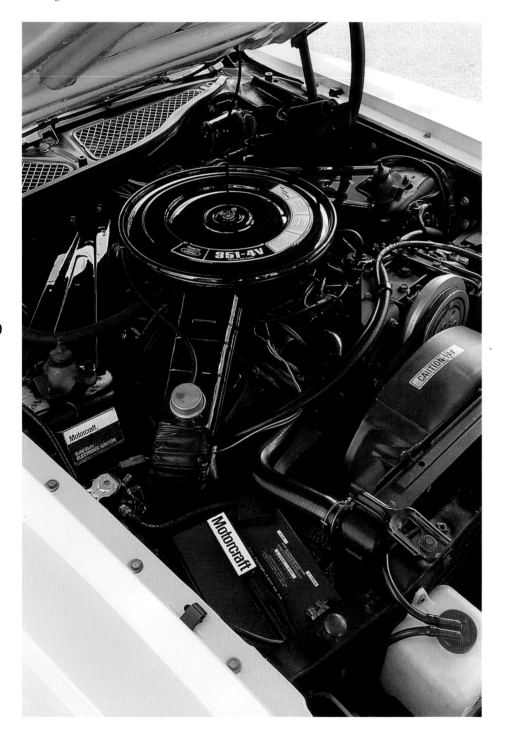

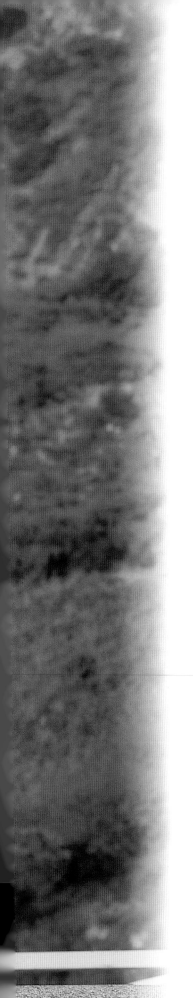

Throughout 1972, Ford's public relations releases and advertisements no longer announced horsepower figures or boasted performance statistics. Instead, they stated that Ford's engine exhaust emissions equipment cut unburned hydrocarbons by 85 percent and diminished carbon monoxide output by 60 percent.

For 1973, emissions certifications challenges eliminated nearly all the low sales-volume engine options, taking with it the high output 351. All three 429s had disappeared at the closing of 1971, and, by 1973, the hottest engine Ford offered was the 351C with a four-barrel carburetor and 7.9:1 compression that produced 259 horsepower at 5,600 rpm. Engineers fit emission control equipment—better known as pollution control devices—to all the engines and included exhaust gas recirculation (EGR) pumps in 1973, which returned some of the burned exhaust back to the cylinder. This combined with fresh, unburned fuel to reduce combustion chamber temperatures and decrease nitrogen oxides emissions, one of the key elements of smog.

Ford had produced 134,867 Mustangs throughout 1973, a nearly 6 percent increase from 1972. The pendulum that had gradually reached its limit with the 429 Super Cobra Jet in 1971 now had violently whipped back as the tail-end of the storm hit with full force. At the end of 1973, not only had Ford deleted the 351 from Mustang catalogs, but it had also cut the 302. The company had listened carefully to Washington's warnings and thus prepared wisely. Engineers and product planners also had paid attention, studying intently what information they could to determine which way the wind would blow, and in what direction they must head. The aftermath of the dark brooding skies would reveal drastic change.

When the sun finally shone down, the 1974 Mustang's largest optional powerplant would be a V-6 engine that displaced barely two-thirds of the littlest engine offered during 1973. It would appear in a car of equally reduced proportions.

An elongated honeycomb grille and 5 mile per hour front bumper was fitted to the 1973 Mustang, making it the largest Mustang ever built. The highest performing engine, the Q-code, was a $194 option fitted with four-bolt main bearing caps, a special intake manifold, and required a power front disc brake and competition suspension.

As vibrant as a bordello, the 1978 Mustang II King Cobra interior was a comfortable place to control the 134 horsepower generated by the 302-ci V-8. Genuine aluminum trim was used across the dashboard.

(1974–1978)

FOUR CYLINDERS AND 55 MILES PER HOUR

Mustang II's birth could be dated back to May 23, 1968, the day of the Ford Motor Company annual shareholders meeting. Board members flanked chairman Henry Ford II, then-president Bunkie Knudsen, and Lee Iacocca, executive vice-president of North American Operations. They presented their financial statements and answered questions from shareholders. In the audience, Anna Muccioli, an artist married to a Ford employee with 600-some shares of Ford Motor Company stock between them, raised her hand and addressed Henry Ford II.

"I have just one complaint," she began. "Thunderbird came out years ago. It was a beautiful sports car. And then you blew it up to a point where it lost its identity. Now the same thing is happening to the Mustang. I have a '65 Mustang and I don't like what's happening. Why can't you just leave a sports car small? You can't see the difference anymore. You don't know Ford from Chevy. In a few more years, I want a new one. I don't want a Chevy look." She sat down. Henry Ford II, seated at a table with a microphone, responded quickly and warmly.

He told her he agreed, that cars could get too big, but that they try to build cars to sell to most of the general public. Since not everyone likes the same thing, models proliferate. He told her they'd keep in mind what she had said so they would have a product to satisfy her. She rose again. "Just leave the Mustang small," she said. "Let's not blow that one up."

The Cobra II was available with any engine in the Mustang II lineup, from the 92-horsepower, 140-ci inline four to the 139-horsepower, 302-ci V-8. In 1977, the Cobra II option was $689, a $361 increase from 1976.

Observers remembered that applause had rolled through the auditorium, evidence of support from the other shareholders. Ford had whispered to one of his aides. Muccioli's name and address were in the records. In order to speak, she had to register. Anna's husband, Joseph, worked for Ford, hired in 1951. By 1968, he was in charge of electrical and climate control in the truck assembly division. His father had worked for Ford, and Anna and Joseph's son Ronald was a fairly recent hire as an engineer.

Anna Muccioli's sentiments reverberated through World Headquarters for the next 12 months and didn't die until Henry Ford II invited her back in August 1973 to personally see what her comments had created. Not until Bunkie Knudsen left Ford in September 1969 could the division address Anna's concern and completely remove the risk of a Chevy-look-alike. Two months later, at a retreat in West Virginia, Lee Iacocca, not yet Ford's president but now its highest officer, expressed his desire that the Mustang change as well. For 1974, he suggested something sporty, luxurious, and small.

Almost immediately, he launched two separate plans under a broader, long-term program known as Project 80. One created a small, sporty car code-named the Ohio and built off a shortened 1970 Maverick platform to be introduced for 1974. The second would slightly lengthen the 1971 Pinto platform and move it upscale. Called the Arizona, Iacocca wanted it ready for 1975.

Following the startling success of the Ford of Europe's Capri as a Lincoln-Mercury Division import, and influenced by the quick sales and public excitement of Japan's Datsun 240Z, Ford division began to measure the pulse of small car buyers. Nat Adamson, the advanced product planning manager, organized a show that displayed a 240Z, Toyota Corona, Chevy Camaro and Vega, Porsche 914, Opel GT, Triumph Spitfire GT6, MGB-GT, Ford Pinto, and three full-size fiberglass-and-metal push-around Ford Arizona concept cars. Thousands of market research phone calls brought 200 handpicked potential customers to the Long Beach, California, convention center. They concluded that if Ford built an Arizona, they would be interested. Adamson sent his designers and engineers home to begin fitting interiors and engines into an Arizona.

In San Diego, another 700 people provided similar reactions and results. Unfortunately, through the spring and summer of 1970, Bordinat's staff designers still were sketching Knudsen-inspired cars that were growing. Then in November 1970, Ford Motor Company bought 84 percent of Carrozzeria Ghia, the automotive design firm in Turin, Italy, from Argentine art-and-antique broker and carmaker Alejandro DeTomaso, who had acquired it in 1966. Ghia, DeTomaso, and Henry Ford II already had collaborated on the Pantera as Ford's pulse-pounding Ferrari-killer.

The Mustang II Cobra II's wheelbase was only 96.2 inches, a full foot shorter than the original 1965 Mustang. Quarter-mile numbers were a far cry from a decade earlier; 17.7-seconds at 77.6 miles per hour.

Each Mustang II Cobra II rolling out of the San Jose, California, assembly plant wore a decal boasting the fact that it was made in America. Imports were starting to make serious inroads into the U.S. auto market by 1977.

As if to say, "I'm not a real muscle car, but I play one on the street," the 1977 Mustang II Cobra II used vast amounts of graphics to whisper performance. Side sculpting hinted at the lineage between the 1965 Mustang and its diminutive successor.

Maintaining the Mustang tradition of a three-element taillight lens, the 1977 Mustang II Cobra II used a broad setup that somewhat resembled the taillights on the Shelby GT500.

A first for the Mustang line was the hatchback design that debuted in 1974. The rear seat back could flip forward to convert the rear seating area into a generously sized cargo area.

Far more luxurious than an original Shelby Mustang, the Cobra II interior was meant for day-to-day use, not occasional forays to a racetrack.

Soon after acquiring Ghia, Ford division commissioned the firm to develop a replacement for the German Capri. Ghia produced a full-size clay model of a glassy, classy fastback hatchback the designers had named the Diana after a secretary there who inspired them. In November 1970, when he saw it, Henry Ford II thought Diana went too far. He scratched into the clay some new lines that he felt better defined the Capri and he left. Iacocca liked the Diana, and after Ford left the studio, he suggested they develop something more acceptable to Ford and to Americans. In David Burgess-Wise's 1985 history, *Ghia: Ford's Carrozzeria*, he quotes what Iacocca said to them: "I'd like to see what you can come up with in the way of a nice little hatchback car in the best European tradition."

A month later, Ford's directors elected Iacocca president of Ford Motor Company. Less than a month afterward, only 53 days after Henry Ford II saw and rejected the Diana, Ghia delivered the Ancona, a drivable prototype, to him in Dearborn. Iacocca was stunned by its looks and by the speed in which the craftsmen had produced something "complete."

One question that Iacocca had answered soon after the November 1969 retreat was engine sizes for new cars. They would have no V-8s; because this new car would be smaller and lighter, a six-cylinder powerplant would be ideal. But should it be an in-line or Vee configuration? Don DeLaRossa, director of advanced design for Bordinat, disliked the straight engine, arguing that it would destroy the compact shape by making the car too long. He had an in-line six installed in a modified Pinto frame and then completed a drivable, mocked-up Arizona they could paint. It looked like a car. Unfortunately and unexpectedly, Bill Innes, who was promoted to

One steel-bodied and seven fiberglass "production" Monroe Handlers were built. Regular production 1977 Cobra IIs were used as a starting point. Dave Kent designed the swoopy bodywork, crafted the first one in steel, and made molds for the remaining seven cars.

replace Iacocca as North American Operations executive vice president, loved it. He recommended that the Ohio project, proceeding parallel to this Arizona car, be ended. In July 1971, Arizona would become the 1974 Mustang. Not exactly, though, for there still were thousands of details to resolve. In this case the details were major: DeLaRossa hadn't finished fighting the engine battle. That meant shape and design of the car still were undecided.

DeLaRossa created another full-size clay model representing how the car would look with an in-line six under its hood. Immediately after Iacocca had commented internally how important it was to make the next generation Mustang small, DeLaRossa invited him over for a look.

The strategy worked. Iacocca overruled Innes and killed the straight six. From this came an all-new 2.3-liter four-cylinder engine and a slightly enlarged version of the Capri's optional V-6. The little in-line four, to be assembled in the Lima, Ohio, plant that had produced 429 Bosses, would be Ford's first four-cylinder engine since Henry Ford II's grandfather authorized the last Model C in 1934. As a metric engine, it also would be the first one built in the United States.

While engineering based it on Ford of Europe's 2.0-liter Cortina engine, they did so many revisions that the two would share only nuts and bolts. Dearborn engineers fitted an overhead camshaft into its cast-iron head. They used a two-barrel Weber-Holley carburetor to feed fuel through its aluminum intake manifold. The engine developed 102 horsepower at 5,200 rpm with compression of 8.4:1 and weighed 319 pounds. The V-6 was a bored-and-stroked version of the 2.5-liter Capri engine enlarged to 2.8 liters that developed 119 horsepower.

Once DeLaRossa cleared the engine configuration hurdle, the focus switched to the car's appearance, which still nagged at decision makers. With unsatisfactory responses coming from design, Iacocca proposed another contest, this time inviting Ghia studios to participate as well. Between Italy and Dearborn, designers carved and shaped 50 clay models developed out of 150 drawings proposed before the three-month deadline ended. In December 1971, the final candidate from the Lincoln-Mercury design studio was a fastback with a tapered waistline below the door windows. Design chief Al Mueller's staff had done a car that bore

many Mustang cues, including a front-end treatment and side scoops strongly reminiscent of the 1964½ model. Iacocca loved it, finally choosing it over his own favorite, a notchback coupe of Don DeLaRossa's based on Ghia's Ancona.

With this decision made, the question of body styles emerged next. Ghia had provided both a fastback and a notchback coupe. Should Ford continue a convertible version? Should they offer only one coupe style so as not to confuse buyers with too many choices nor distract them from the message that this was a different car? Customer sampling was inconclusive. Surveys in Anaheim, California, virtually killed the notchback. Southern California, with its love for sportiness, strongly favored a fastback Arizona. At the last minute, product planner Nat Adamson included the Ancona notchback anyway, bestowing the nickname Anaheim in honor of its failure there. In a San Francisco survey, the tables were turned completely, dramatically demonstrating the difference between audiences. The Anaheim-reject scored best of show up north. Plenty of work would be required to redesign the notchback and make big expensive sheet metal items, such as its hood and doors, common to both cars. It was now only 16 months before Job One.

Another obstacle arose: what to name this all-new car? Arizona was its code. But it was important that car buyers understood what this car meant and recognized that Ford Motor Company was alert and responsive to trends and to their desires. Thus no one ever seriously considered any other names besides Mustang. Lee Iacocca once told *Motor Trend* writer and automotive historian Karl Ludvigsen that his most important "personal" contribution to the Mustang II was, "the name—not changing it."

Iacocca husbanded this new car as patiently and attentively as he had done a decade before. He understood "perceived value" and he wanted this car recognized as "a little jewel." Some four-cylinder cars from other makers delivered buzzing engines with harsh, uncomfortable rides.

Semi-black paint was baked onto the trim for durability. Jack Roush built the engines, enlarged from 302 cubic inches to 363. The result was 400 horsepower at 6,500 rpm and 400 foot-pounds of torque at 4,800 rpm.

Rolling stock on the 1978 Mustang II Monroe Handler was B.F. Goodrich GR50-14 T/A radials on Centerline 8-inch front and 9-inch rear wheels.

Iacocca wanted customers to value his little jewel as a diamond, not pressed glass. Glass rode like small cheap cars; diamonds rode like Mercedes-Benz.

Four-cylinder engine vibration would be unacceptable. At certain engine speeds, engineers perceived a moan that ran through the car, caused by harmonic vibration. Enlarging the diameter of the bolt circle to mount the engine to the transmission changed the harmonics and reduced the noise and vibration. Engineering made this change late in the development; it was a modification that cost millions. Using a stronger, 3.5-inch diameter drive shaft rather than the Pinto's 2.75-inch diameter shaft was the final polish to the gem. The additional mass of the shaft further dampened vibration.

To come up with the primary specifications for the Arizona, engineers had to cut a 94.2-inch wheelbase Pinto in two pieces right behind the windshield and, there, lengthen it 2.0 inches. Real luxury car-ride and handling would have required starting from scratch, something for which there was neither time nor budget. Making the Pinto ride, handle, and drive as an Arizona jewel fell to program engineers Bob Negstad and Jim Kennedy.

"We were not getting anywhere," Negstad recalled. "I was working for Charlie Veranian, an old-time Ford engineer. We were trying double-isolated tension struts, double-isolated number-two cross members, changing geometry. We got to trial number fifteen or so, building cars, riding them, and they were terrible.

"Charlie came down one day and said, 'I'm gonna throw in the towel. We don't have a viable solution to doing the Pinto. We'll vote to make the Mustang carry over.'" This meant someone would have to go before Iacocca and recommend to him that Ford Motor Company should NOT introduce a new little jewel for 1974 because it still rode like a Pinto.

Negstad had one more idea, and Veranian, recognizing that both their engineering futures were at stake, let him try. This was on a Friday. Veranian authorized Negstad to bring in a crew on Saturday and Sunday for overtime work and have the same engineers in on Monday. After that it would be too late. Over the weekend, Negstad and the others created a device from scrap steel that suspended the front-end suspension and engine on compression biscuits, resembling hard rubber hockey pucks, back to where the frame rails rose to meet the firewall.

"When the wheels reacted, it let this whole thing move around and average all the loads before it came into the body. It looked like hell. We got it together, put the car down. It was Sunday, late. I went for a ride, and it didn't feel like a Pinto. The guys couldn't believe this piece of scrap junk." He called Veranian at home late that night. The senior engineer came in and they drove it, and on Monday morning, others came in to ride it. At noon, it went across the street for a management review.

"'It's a good idea, affordable,' the company said. 'We still gotta crash it.' And then we had a design review. There were no drawings. We took this thing off the car. It was all dirty. There was a can of spray paint, and I sprayed it yellow lacquer. Chassis engineering said, 'This is the piece that's gonna save the Mustang?'

"And it got the nickname, because of its shape, the 'toilet seat.' That lasted a long time, it looked just awful and it went into production."

By the time Negstad, Veranian, Kennedy, and the rest of the engineers had finished, all that remained of the Pinto was its rear-wheel houses, the trunk floor, front-suspension arms, and the rear axle. It was less of a Pinto than their 1964½ had been a Falcon.

For Lee Iacocca, this was the re-invention of his dream. Ford staff designer Charles Keresztes created new Mustang logo sculptures of somewhat smaller horses running in the same direction as before. Viewer samples and marketing surveys once again pointed toward this being the right car in the right time.

As it had done a decade earlier, Ford began leaking information and pictures of the new car. A public relations staff memo in August 1972 officially named it the Mustang II. Iacocca publicly hinted that this car was so exciting and of such high quality that it might exceed the phenomenal first-year sales record of the 1964½ Mustang. Henry Ford II invited Anna Muccioli and the local press for her own preview of the car. She saw a white notchback, a model called the Ghia that replaced the luxury Grandé, with a white vinyl roof. A foot shorter than Muccioli's 1965 Mustang and not even 300-pounds heavier with its luxury equipment and new pollution and safety features, the new car impressed her. "Now that's more like it," she beamed. "That's the kind of car it started out to be." She posed for pictures and told Henry Ford II she would sell her 1965 and replace it with a Mustang II.

The King Cobra option in 1978 cost a hefty $1,277, $69 more than the Boss 429 package. The T-top convertible option cost $647 when fitted to the King Cobra, but $689 on all other Mustang IIs.

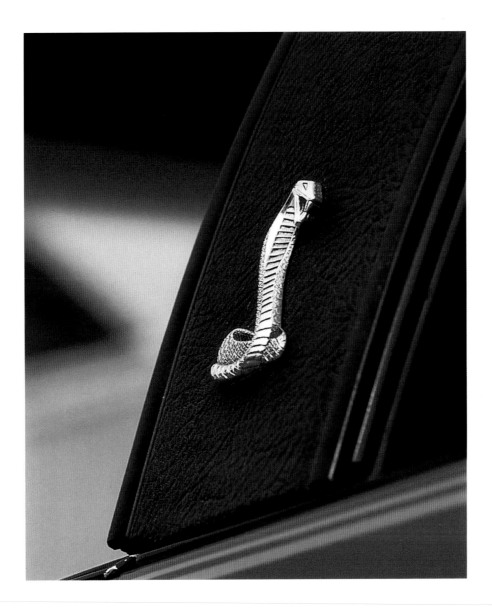

The 1978 King Cobra package included plenty of visual cues of past Cobras. This piece of trim, mounted on the B-pillar, was part of a high-visibility graphics package that set the King Cobra apart from its regular Mustang II brethren.

Before it hit show rooms in September 1973, the public had once again been let in on the secret. This time around though, they were underwhelmed and some felt betrayed. Buyers, anxious to see Iacocca's little jewel, found dealerships showing models of the $2,895 notchback with full options and price stickers reaching higher than $4,500. A base car at anything less than $3,000 was nowhere to be found. Buyers muttered and shrugged. Some settled for the hatchback Pintos or two-door Mavericks. Others left.

Barely 18,000 cars sold in the first month, very disappointing compared to 22,000 on the first day in April 1964. Enthusiast magazines were none too enthusiastic about the mini-limousine Ghia or the four-cylinder Mach I. Engineering had kept weight distribution equal to the 1973s—58 percent front/42 percent rear—and 2.8-liter track tests yielded 0–60 times of 13.8 seconds and quarter-miles of 19.4 seconds at 70.5 miles per hour. However, even the optional engine just didn't get the car moving out of showrooms. Through until mid-October, slightly more than 17,000 additional cars had been ordered.

Three days after the mid-October reports however, the Mustang II suddenly started to look very appealing all across the United States. Morning newspapers on the 17th reported that OPEC had decided to shut off oil delivery to nations that had aided Israel in the three-week Yom Kippur war. Lines at gas stations that briefly appeared in 1971 came back in frightening proportions when gasoline and heating oil producers predicted gloom and doom. The White

Tape stripes and rear window louvers were part of the $1,277 King Cobra option. A huge rear spoiler came in handy, as the top speed of the vehicle was near 120 miles per hour. Fuel economy was horrid and averaged 13 miles per gallon.

House responded with talk of gas-less weekends and no driving on Sundays (something Germany put into effect for a short while). A national "energy saving" speed limit slowed traffic down to 55 miles per hour for years to come. Gas prices that had averaged $0.386 per gallon, jumped to $0.527 nationwide within weeks.

Five months later, on March 18, the Organization of Arab Petroleum Exporting Countries (OAPEC) ended the embargo. Gasoline had risen another $0.06 to $0.58.7 per gallon. Inflation, already at a painful 6.2 percent through 1973, rocketed up to a record 11.1 percent in 1974. President Nixon's price controls had allowed two small increases that still fit within the 5.5 percent cap each year. By year's end, Ford had raised the price of the notchback Mustang from $2,895 to $3,134, and listed the Mach I fastback with optional V-6 at an additional $540. Despite the slow start, the year's sales total was not bad, aided immensely by the increasing cost of gasoline. By September 1974, with gasoline inching toward $0.60 and inflation slightly receding to 8.98 percent, 1974 Mustang II production totaled 385,993, nearly three times the 1973 big-car level.

The most exciting improvement for the Mustang II image was the 302-ci V-8 engine squeezed between its fenders for the 1975 model year. Ford offered it with the automatic transmission only, for there had been insufficient time and interest to certify a manual transmission version that met emissions. The new Mach I, ordered with the Rally suspension package, offered adjustable Gabriel shock absorbers and included larger diameter anti-sway bars and stiffer springs. This greatly improved the handling and the extra power cut 0–60 times to 10.5 seconds and got the car through the quarter mile in 17.9 seconds at 77 miles per hour. While this performance barely strained neck muscles, Washington had begun to look at fuel economy. Congress ordered the Department of Transportation (DOT) to establish Corporate Average

Fuel Economy (CAFE) standards for new cars starting in model year 1978 and light trucks the year after. Each carmaker would be required to meet fuel economy quotas across their entire fleet, a number which would increase each year.

Reminiscent of Ford's one-off 1969 Model E Mustang for the 1968 Mobil Gas Economy Run, Ford offered a 1975 Mustang II MPG model with a 3.18:1 rear axle ratio (compared to the standard 3.40:1), and fitted with a catalytic converter that was now required on all cars destined for California delivery. Ford literature quoted highway economy at 34 miles per gallon and city performance at 23 miles per gallon, following the EPA standards for testing. This kind of fuel efficiency counter-balanced the more profligate consumption of the optional 302.

Weighing 3,300 lbs, the 1978 King Cobra might not have snapped one's head back under acceleration, but the drag strip numbers of 16.59 seconds at 82.41 miles per hour were better than in earlier years, despite a 2-barrel carburetor. Pricey options tacked onto the King Cobra options could raise the price of the vehicle to a lofty $6,890.

For 1976, the catalytic converters mandated in California went nationwide. Engineering continued to improve fuel economy for all Mustangs. Ford made the 302 available with a four-speed manual shift after completing the mandatory 50,000- and 100,000-mile runs the EPA required of the engine-transmission combination. In addition, Ford offered a Cobra II appearance option, but this was savagely attacked in the magazines; in a product planning miscue, Ford regrettably provided the package with the four-cylinder engine as standard equipment. However, careful reading of the options list, just as in the late 1960s, could turn the little Cobra into a reasonably potent mini-muscle car.

Beginning in 1976, the public began to see gasoline prices occasionally spike to around $0.70 to $0.75 per gallon, especially during summer vacation driving season. Few people complained now that the lines had disappeared. It wasn't because salaries had doubled as gas prices had; it was simply because the United States is a nation of drivers. In America, more than anywhere else, driving was recreation, due largely to the affordability of gasoline. Going for a drive was a pastime. Americans began relationships, proposed marriages, started families, and ended their marriages inside their automobiles. With $0.75 for gas deemed as acceptable, the drama of interpersonal relationships inside the rolling "neutral territory" of cars resumed. The desire for larger, roomier cars resurfaced, so Mustang II production slipped to 187,567.

Befitting the "little limousine" that Iacocca dreamed of, the Ghia model used plush carpeting, rich-feeling fabrics, and genuine simulated woodgrain trim to evoke a luxury air.

Starting in 1977, performance made tentative returns. Monroe Auto Equipment Company reintroduced the concept of automotive flamboyance with seven identical promotional Mustang IIs, created mainly to promote their new Handler shock absorber. The cars eventually became showcases for the works of fabricators, painters, suspension designers, and chassis tuners with ample help from Monroe and a 400-horsepower 351W engine from Jack Roush Industries. *Hot Rod* magazine's Gray Baskerville expressed his desire for the car through his step-by-step production stories leading up to its debut as a 1978 show car. "Ahh," he cooed, "it's like shades of yesteryear." Yesteryear was coming back; Ford division knew it and prepared for it, even as 1977 ended with still smaller production numbers. Only 153,173 of the 1977 Mustang IIs moved off of Ford assembly lines before September, when the 1978 models appeared.

During the previous years, the Cobra II had turned into a respectable small performer. Ford division had rewarded enthusiast interest in the Monroe Handler by unveiling the King Cobra. It had been a $1,277 option that would, among other side effects, spark instant recognition of the owners from local police. It looked outrageous and performed nearly outrageously with its 302-ci V-8 and Variable Venturi Carburetor, an effective combination for fuel-economy consciousness and performance potential. The purchase price included a huge Pontiac Trans-Am decal laid out across the hood, removable-panel SportsRoof, rear anti-sway bar, stiffer springs, and adjustable shock absorbers. Ford cautiously rated its horsepower at only 139, but this figure was pessimistic even when using the new "net" SAE standards that measured power transmitted through all the running gear to reach the ground. It was a much more accurate measure of engine output, but it drastically deflated egos when King Cobra owners had to answer the question they dreaded most: How many horses you got under the hood?"

Aimed at the active lifestyle, the 1978 Mustang II Ghia hardtop looked snappy with its color-coordinated interior and tasteful exterior touches, such as wire-laced wheels, whitewall tires, and blacked-out grille.

The CAFE (corporate average fuel economy) specifications went into effect for 1978, enforced by the new Environmental Protection Agency (EPA). This began at 18 miles per gallon and would rise a mile per gallon per year. By 1985, the federal government wanted the average of all cars to be 27.5 miles per gallon. Total 1978 Mustang production jumped again, reaching 192,410. A very high proportion of fuel-efficient 2.3-liter four-cylinder and 2.8-liter V-6 cars weighed in against the lower mileage numbers developed by the roughly 5,000 King Cobras.

The buying public knew that a new Mustang was coming for 1979. The country had endured a dark-age of performance during the mid-1970s, suffering through product planning, design, and engineering missteps as American carmakers attempted to deliver what buyers thought they wanted or liked in Japanese and European imports. Detroit automakers tried hard, but suffered badly with hurriedly engineered products, such as the Chevette and Vega, the Pinto, the Gremlin, and the Omni and Horizon.

In the period between September 1969 and September 1979, everything in America reversed. Gasoline prices reached a full dollar per gallon, tripling within a decade. Engines got huge, and then cars got small. Engines got small, and then cars began to grow. Skirts rose and fell, a president who was re-elected later resigned, and his successor would then be voted out of office as the country tried to change course. In early 1974, Congress adopted Daylight Savings Time year-round in an attempt to conserve heating fuel and gasoline, but soon it repealed it. In an era of growing fossil-fuel consciousness, clothing and textile manufacturers promoted a new fabric that was highly wrinkle resistant and somewhat stretchy. It was called polyester; in perverse irony, it came from petroleum. The energy shortage took on a new meaning when New York City blacked out in late summer 1977. Some parts remained without electricity for as long as 25 hours. In the late spring of 1978, a new baby boom erupted in New York City, probably a result of excess energy of another kind that came with the heat and the dark during the city's electric failure.

It was through these times that Ford engineers and designers, product planners and marketing surveyors, Lee Iacocca, and Henry Ford II had gazed once again into a crystal ball. They had started looking for a new direction as early as 1972, just as Volkswagen replaced its long-lived Beetle with its Golf, known in America as the Rabbit. What could they use to chase a rabbit, they wondered? Throughout Dearborn, what Ford people had heard howling in their imagination was the Fox.

Lee Iacocca wanted the Mustang II to step away from the performance bent it had developed. With the 1978 Mustang II Ghia edition, Ford came closest to realizing Iacocca's dream to transform the Mustang into a "little limousine."

1979–1984½

(previous) Only 104 Turbo GT350 Anniversary Edition Mustang convertibles were built in 1984 with the 2.3-liter turbocharged inline four. This was the last Mustang to bear the GT350 name. Shelby had sold Ford use of the Cobra name, not GT350 or GT500, so Shelby sued Ford.

Standard tires on the 1984 GT350 Mustang were P220/55R390 Michelin TRXs that surrounded three-spoke, metric-sized aluminum wheels.

(1979–1984½)

A GLOBAL APPROACH REGIONALIZED

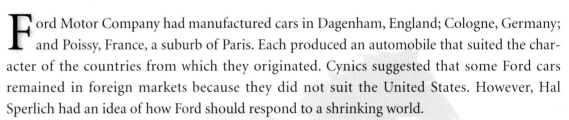

Ford Motor Company had manufactured cars in Dagenham, England; Cologne, Germany; and Poissy, France, a suburb of Paris. Each produced an automobile that suited the character of the countries from which they originated. Cynics suggested that some Ford cars remained in foreign markets because they did not suit the United States. However, Hal Sperlich had an idea of how Ford should respond to a shrinking world.

Marketing had made an analysis years before. Ernest R. Breech, the man who for years was Henry Ford II's mentor and his company's president, had initiated it. He was among the first to understand the accounting principles of cost analysis, and ultimately had become General Motor's problem solver. GM supplier Bendix Corporation had lost $3 million a year before Breech arrived in 1937. Within two years, Bendix earned $5 million in profit. The Deuce, as insiders have referred to Henry Ford II, knew that his grandfather's company was in financial trouble; insiders acknowledged losses approaching $50 million. Ford had coaxed Breech into joining him as company executive vice president in July 1946, several months after he had hired Robert McNamara and his fellow inquisitors. Breech, 48 by then, had possessed the skills required to save Ford's company, and the Deuce, at 28, had learned much from his new teacher.

Marchal fog lamps were housed in the front air dam that was part of the GT350 package in 1984. The GT350 received numerous suspension upgrades, including a four-link rear axle with special coil springs and gas-filled shock absorbers.

Eleven years later, Ford Motor Company had attempted to take on General Motors, "To be first in America," as Breech once explained, by adding the 1957 Edsel to its structure as a complete, separate division. The car's failure set the relative market share between Ford, General Motors, and Chrysler: All of Ford Motor Company would sell about as many cars as Chevrolet Motor Division of GM would sell; all of Chrysler Corporation would sell about as many cars as Ford Division sells. Lesser carmakers Nash-Hudson and Packard-Studebaker would sell as many cars as Plymouth Division.

For Ford to sell more cars, it needed a new marketplace. Easier than fighting with General Motors and fighting off Chrysler, Henry Ford II could expand into Europe. McNamara's Cardinal had been Ford's first attempt to make a World car. Lee Iacocca had maintained that the looks of the Cardinal killed its chances for U.S. sales. He figured the Mustang's success had distracted Henry Ford II from world market expansion for a short while, returning focus to the pursuit of Chevrolet. Even the Mustang's phenomenal sales had not been enough to overtake Chevy.

Then the Deuce had concluded that he could beat General Motors if he hired General Motors, represented in the person of Bunkie Knudsen. When that had failed, the chairman had known his next attempt would have to be plain, old hard work.

Near the end of 1972, as OPEC began taking on international prominence, Hal Sperlich became involved in a Product Planning and Research committee that peered into the future of a world economy that soon would be driven by petroleum. They understood the availability of petroleum would now be subjected to the political whimsy of a group of exporting countries that could be offended easily. The group analyzed what would happen if it grew worse.

Sperlich saw in his mind a car for both Europe and the Americas. With identical engines, suspensions and bodies, the car would sell on both continents. Casting molds and stamping dies would be the same. Ford engineering would make it fuel-efficient as well as manufacturing- and cost-effective because parts would be interchangeable worldwide. The group launched this project to develop a common platform that would support both a sporty car and a four- or five-passenger sedan early in 1973. They code-named it the Fox.

Ford's timing with the introduction of its gas-conscious Mustang II had proven to be perfect. But that car would take Ford only so far, through 1977 perhaps, or 1978 at most. Ford of England planned to replace its Cortina, and Ford of Germany was looking for its next Taunus. Dearborn was conceiving new cars to replace the Pinto and Mustang II. The Fox was the platform of choice. Engineering and design began concepts and development on a shorter,

The hood scoop was fitted to clear the top of the engine with the bottom of the hood. It did not act as a functional air inlet.

(continued on page 269)

263

A machined look was the style in Detroit in the mid-1980s. The federally mandated 85 miles per hour speedometer could be buried at will with the 145-horsepower engine in the 1984 Mustang Turbo GT.

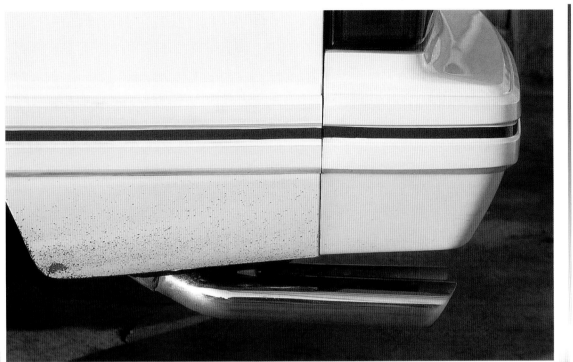

Once the boost came on under the hood, the turbocharged 2.3-liter, four-cylinder engine made 145 horsepower at 4,600 rpm. It was enough to coat the bottom the rear quarter with expensive rubber. All of the 20th Anniversary Edition GT350 Mustangs were built in 35 days, and each one was painted in Oxford White with red trim and a red interior.

While the folded convertible stack did not slip completely from view, it did let the occupants hear the whine of the non-intercooled turbocharger in the Turbo GT350's 2.3-liter, inline-four engine.

While structural rigidity took a back seat to alfresco fun, the 1984 GT Turbo Convertible was a lifestyle automobile that could find its way around a corner. Drivers wanting a serious canyon-carver tended to pony up for the hardtop. American Sunroof Corporation (ASC) did the initial hardtop conversion into a convertible, but Ford eventually brought the process in-house.

266

The GT Turbo Convertible sold for a staggering $13,441. It was not as strong a seller as Ford wanted. Only 3,000 Turbo GT hatchbacks and 600 convertibles were sold in 1984, so FoMoCo pulled the plug after two years.

(continued from page 263)

100-inch wheelbase upon which to base the Pinto/Cortina/Taunus replacement during the summer of 1973. Through the next year, work advanced on the Fox Pinto and commenced on a Fox Mustang. But in 1974, the problems of achieving Sperlich's theoretical world car proved overwhelming. Safety standards differed from country to country, and no nation was willing to yield its regulations to another's. The hugely different production techniques between European and U.S. factories were an insurmountable hurdle to the same-car-everywhere project. Still, the platform on which to base a Pinto/Mustang/small sedan began to look more viable in the United States. Early in spring 1975, North American Automobile Operations (NAAO) took over the Fox program from Sperlich's group. As an authorized, approved, and funded program, NAAO set Fox introduction dates: a new sedan called the Fairmont for 1977, and a new Mustang for 1979. (It deleted the Pinto from the program altogether.)

As NAAO set the specifications for the new Mustang, designers began to work. While the Fox might be a U.S.-only Mustang, NAAO wanted European influences to contribute to the car's appearance and handling, fuel economy, and overall size and weight.

The electronically fuel-injected Turbo GT had a compression ratio of 8.0:1 and a bore and stroke of 3.781x3.126 inches. With the 2.3-liter engine came 3.45:1 gears in the differential.

The hood scoop on the 1984 GT Turbo was for engine clearance and not for ingesting cool ambient air. The return of the 5.0-liter V-8 over-shadowed the turbocharged engine, as the larger mill developed 30 more horsepower yet cost $200 less.

Ford, Lincoln-Mercury, Advanced Vehicle Development, and Ghia design studios all went to work on the appearance of the new sedan and the Mustang. Fritz Mayhew, Light Car Design Manager, produced some striking early proposals. These wedge-shaped sports cars with large glass areas derived more of their lines and shapes from DeTomaso's Pantera than from any existing Ford product. Then NAAO specification writers established "hard points," the basic measurements that could not be altered, for wheelbase, tread width, overall length, height, width, cowl and radiator heights, and other dimensions that virtually defined the shape of the car without actually drawing lines. Thereafter, the appearance grew less daring. Each proposal bore some resemblance to the next, with hard, tall, flat sides and deck surfaces that took too much from the 1971–1973 Mustang designs and the coming Fairmont sedan.

Designer Jack Telnack had returned to Dearborn in April 1976, following several years in Germany as design vice president for Ford of Europe. Now as executive director of North American Light Car and Truck Design, his ideas were a breath of irreverent fresh air. He simply cheated.

For Telnack and his counterpart in engineering, Bob Alexander (promoted to product development vice president), the only "real" hard point of the new car's front-end dimensions was the height above the ground of the engine's air cleaner. Anything else might not be so hard.

Telnack wanted to decrease the car's frontal area, which would improve its aerodynamics and increase its fuel economy. He could lower the nose by pivoting the hood line over the air cleaner, but that meant elevating the hood at the windshield, or cowl line. It startled management because, as Telnack said to Gary Witzenburg, "No Detroit designer ever asks to make anything higher." But Gene Bordinat agreed to try it, knowing it would require a different support to lower the radiator (and understanding that this change might eventually cost more than $1 million to develop).

Once Telnack did that, he slightly narrowed the nose as well. He swelled the fender wells gently at the axles in the interest of aerodynamics; this gave the car a very slight coke-bottle effect. He favored a louvered grille treatment that induced better airflow through the radiator, though customer clinics disliked its appearance.

The sleeker lines of the mid-1980s Mustangs was evident by the taillight design that spanned most of the width of the car, yet kept a clean, crisper look.

Design again relied on clinics to sample potential customers' reactions. Consistent with a dozen years of Mustang, the audience divided nearly equally on their preference for coupes or fastbacks. Following these late winter and spring sessions, Telnack's crew created the "semi-fastback", a design recalling the 1965 and 1966 2+2 cars more than the 1967-and-later SportsRoof full fastback designs. Then, in a repetition of history, just as Gale Halderman's designs for the 1964½ cars had gone virtually unchanged from drawing board to sales floor, so the Telnack team proposal for the 1979 model moved nearly unscathed through all the processes.

The design demonstrated its merit once it went into the wind tunnel. They had configured the fastback deck to wrap over the edge of the body, similar to contemporary

The cast-aluminum pieces found on the 1984 GT Turbo were essentially the same wheel that had been available since 1978. They were designed to use only metric-sized tires.

The woefully inadequate speedometer in the 1984 Mustang GT Turbo could be put past the 85 miles per hour mark with relative ease. Crisp white-on-black instrumentation allowed for rapid reading of the dials at speed.

Honda Accords and VW Sciroccos. Manufacturing balked; they had never done a car that way before, but Bob Alexander insisted on it. Hitting the University of Maryland wind tunnel, which Ford used for testing its cars, resulted in a 6 percent reduction in drag.

By September 1976, engineering had its first three prototypes running. Besides ride and handling characteristics, engineers worked on noise, vibration, and harshness (NVH). Bob Alexander's staff ran the Fox prototypes through the same durability tests that had broken the 1964½ cars and necessitated the "toilet seat" on the Mustang II.

Ford Mustangs had been shod exclusively on U.S.-made tires in the past. Telnack's and Alexander's European experiences suggested to chassis engineers that other tire options bore consideration. Engineers within Ford had tested Michelin's high-performance TRX and a metric-dimension wheel for some time.

The third generation of Mustang was built on the Fox unit-body platform, shared with the Ford Fairmont and Mercury Zephyr, in an attempt to amortize costs. The wheelbase grew 4.2 inches to 100.4, which enabled the interior to be enlarged and smoothed the ride.

Now they developed three separate chassis options: a handling package that introduced the TRX tires, an intermediate version using a variety of domestic and imported mid-level radials, and the baseline car running on economical bias-ply tires. Alexander wanted the suspension to adopt some European hardware, thus Bob Negstad and Jim Burns developed a hybrid MacPherson strut to fit within the lowered hood line. Engineering had tolerated the sedate performance of Iacocca's mini-limousine-vinyl-roofed Mustang II Ghia, introduced in 1974. However, by late 1976, the pursuit of performance had once again become an admirable goal. Ford now offered six engines, starting with the baseline 2.3-liter overhead cam, in-line four-cylinder from the Mustang II, and ranging up to the now-10-year-old 302-ci 5.0-liter V-8. European high technology had brought a turbocharger to the 2.3-liter four, creating a light-weight engine with 132 horsepower that would provide much better weight balance than the more-powerful 302.

The turbo was a mixed blessing, however, delivering the high-end horsepower that a V-8 might make without the heavy fuel consumption. At lower engine speeds, such as getting off the start line, the turbos turned too slowly to be effective, and the engine simply moved on its own barely adequate four-cylinder torque. In Europe, where the stoplight "grand prix," the impromptu drag races that arose on Saturday nights among performance car owners, didn't exist, high-end horsepower made for fast cruising speeds on autoroutes and autobahns. In the United States, still stuck with the national speed limit of 55 miles per hour, Ford division had to offer the 302. At the time, just a few makers, such as Porsche, Saab, and Buick, offered turbochargers. Their engineers were only beginning to recognize that the distance needed for the exhaust to travel from engine block to the turbo affected the condition known as turbo

The trim 1980 Mustang sedan was basically a carryover from 1979. The 302-ci engine was downsized to 255-ci, as its power output fell to 119 horsepower. This car, the last vehicle owned by actress Bette Davis, was purchased to allow her to travel unrecognized.

lag: the longer the pipe, the greater the lag. However, magazine tests of the turbocharged Mustang-engine car recorded 9.1 seconds for 0–60 miles per hour and quarter miles of 17.4 seconds at 82 miles per hour. In comparison, the 302's best performance was 8.3 seconds to 60 miles per hour and quarter-mile times of 17.0 seconds at 84.8 miles per hour.

Worse, owners of all makes experienced oil lubrication problems that caused some turbos to fail and others to ignite. For the 2.3-liter turbo to become a performance package to reckon with took several years. Even then, it would never match the V-8's gross torque, and its appeal would remain among drivers who favored high speed runs through twisty roads, where the turbo's lighter front-end weight improved handling.

Ford public relations invited the enthusiast magazines to Dearborn for their annual ride-and-drive introductions in mid-June 1978. Writers liked the new styling and the car's size (overall, it was 4.1 inches longer, with a 4.2-inch longer wheelbase, yet it weighed nearly 200 pounds less than the comparable 1978 Mustang II model). Magazines interested in handling and road holding praised the Michelin TRX package, but criticized the 60 percent front/40 percent rear weight-bias of cars equipped with the 302-ci V-8 engine. Those publications that only promoted short distance, straight-line travel loved the 302 but they complained that the Michelins were not up for the torque that the engine produced. The rear tires broke loose and hopped awkwardly until the car caught up.

Vertical taillights were incorporated in the 1979 Mustang design to continue the visual heritage of the original Mustang. The taillights now wrapped around the rear corner of the vehicle and acted as a rear side-marker light.

A plastic grille with rectangular holes was a Ford styling cue used across virtually the entire Ford line. The entry-level sedan was bereft of excess graphics and trim in an effort to hold the retail price at $4,494.

A month later, as the journalists toiled with their stories and editors tried to match product release dates with printing schedules, all of them—daily newspapers, television news, and magazine editors and writers—went back to their typewriters. On July 13, 1978, Henry Ford II fired Lee Iacocca from Ford Motor Company. The Deuce did allow Iacocca to stay three months until his 54th birthday, enabling him to qualify for full pension benefits. Even though Iacocca had remained deeply loyal to his boss, his charismatic personality had led journalists and the public to identify Ford Motor Company more with him than with the aristocratic chairman, Henry Ford II.

The l979 Mustang reached Ford dealers one month before Lee Iacocca's grace period expired. The car now was in its mid-teens, reaching a kind of youthful maturity. Ford offered the third-generation car as a two-door or three-door fastback/hatchback coupe. Ford's "flip up, open-air roof," was a hinged sunroof, and it was as close as 1979 buyers could get to a full convertible. Marketing staff still applied the Ghia name to its upgraded trim and appearance option.

Indy 500 race promoters selected the new Fox to pace the race on Memorial Day 1979. Goodyear Tire & Rubber Company's alliance with the Speedway forced Ford to run Goodyear Wingfoot tires instead of the usual Michelin TRXs. Engineering performed a slight chassis modification to accommodate the change. In order for the pace car driver and assistant to be visible to the racers, spectators, and television audiences, the car and its identical backup received prototype T-roofs. Fully adjustable Recaro seats made the ride more secure and a number of spoilers, wings, and graphic treatments rendered the car more visible to everyone. Ford hired racer/engine magician Jack Roush to enhance the pace car 302s, enabling them to run much longer than a full 500 miles at 125 miles per hour in the worst-case scenario. Various internal modifications brought the pace car engines to more than 260 horsepower,

The Fox-bodied Mustangs that debuted in 1979 were noted for their clean interior, with spare lines and easy-to-read instruments. While base Mustangs came with a carpeted transmission tunnel, a console was available for $140.

compared to the street version's 140. Roush revised the transmission to handle the speed and power, and fit larger front disc rotors and station wagon oversize rear drums instead of the stock brakes.

To commemorate the occasion, Ford division produced another 11,000 Indy Pace Car replicas without Roush's modifications. Buyers did get the form-fitting Recaro seats, which introduced reclining buckets to the Mustang. In all its versions, pace car and otherwise, Ford produced 369,936 Mustangs through the 1979 model year, nearly doubling the 1978 total of 192,410.

For 1980, the Cobra option included the Recaro seats as well. This barely compensated for the bad news under the hood. In efforts to close in on Ford's corporate average fuel economy (CAFE) figures, engineering reduced the 302's 5.0-liter displacement to 255 cubic inches, 4.2 liters, by decreasing bore from 4.00 to 3.68 inches. This decreased horsepower from 140 to only 119 SAE net. Ford continued through 1981 with the 2.3-liter turbo, which, ironically, was now Mustang's most powerful option at 132 horsepower, but reliability problems led Ford to withdraw it at the end of the model year. Mid-year, Ford introduced a much-welcomed four-speed-plus overdrive (effectively a five-speed) manual shift transmission. On the auto show tour, Ford showed its 2.3-liter turbo-powered Mustang IMSA, named in honor of the International Motor Sports Association, the sanctioning body in which Ford was qualifying Mustangs for competition. The car looked very stock except for widely flared wheelwells that barely contained enormous Pirelli tires. It served as an announcement: While advertising for 1979 had promoted the new cars as "The Next Generation," many racers and enthusiasts saw hints of "Total Performance" returning again. Through 1980, Ford produced 271,322 Mustangs.

The SelectShift automatic transmission was a $307 option. Cigarette burns on the carpet are reputed to have been caused by actress Bette Davis.

Ford offered the official Indy pace car T-roof as an option for 1981. While early brochures listed the 2.3-liter turbo among engine choices, the division withdrew it just before the 1981 introduction. This left them with only three engines: the base 2.3-liter four cylinder with normal carburetion, the 3.3-liter 94-horsepower six, and the 4.2-liter V-8 which, with its two-barrel carburetor, rated an anemic 120 horsepower. Engineering now offered a Traction-Lok rear axle, a limited-slip differential without the noise or aggression of the late 1960s versions, and buyers could add this to the five-speed transmission introduced in the previous spring. The Traction-Lok finally addressed the rear-wheel spin and axle hop of hard-acceleration standing starts, even though engines now produced barely enough power to need it. With only the 4.2-liter V-8 for power, Ford discontinued the Cobra package at the end of 1981. Altogether, the division produced 182,552 Mustangs for 1981.

The Indianapolis 500 Pace Car replicas were offered only as three-door hatchback models. However, they could be purchased with the lift-up sunroof or the removable-panel T-top.

The front suspension used a modified MacPherson strut system that relocated the coil spring off the strut and a front anti-sway bar. The Indy Pace Car replicas and the Cobras were equipped with the top-of-the-line Special Suspension that incorporated Michelin's TRX low-profile tires and metric cast-aluminum wheels.

Sometime in 1981, aftermarket car stylists and body shops began cutting the tops off T-roof coupes and cobbling together not-always sturdy nor good-looking convertibles. Individual operators and even small corporations that lacked the budget to prepare full-size clay models produced cars with awkward and incorrect proportions. Only the best of the shops understood the chassis-stiffening requirements of an open car. Modifications cost as little as $1,000 and as much as $5,000. Ford division noticed this trend but did not respond publicly to these privateers.

The success Mustang, Camaro, and Firebird had achieved in returning performance to the streets led law enforcement to take an interest in the cars in the early 1980s. Their attention went beyond making the cars radar targets. Michigan's state police did an annual evaluation of pursuit vehicles available from the manufacturers. Their findings influenced dozens of state and local police agencies in their purchases. The California Highway Patrol (CHP) especially was interested in finding a "pursuit" car that could keep up, and they asked their Michigan colleagues to add a Camaro and a Firebird to their test. Ford learned of the request and asked to be included. On the day of the scheduled evaluation, neither Chevrolet nor Pontiac showed up. The Mustang performed very well, and the CHP quickly added them to their fleets, especially along the well-traveled and tedious Interstate 5 run from Los Angeles to San Francisco and Sacramento, and along I-15 from Los Angeles to Las Vegas. With their top speed of 137 miles per hour, the Mustangs developed a reputation as "Porsche catchers."

For civilian use, test drivers and engineers stayed busy completing 50,000- and 100,000-mile engine emission certification runs. Ford completed EPA certification on several engine, transmission, and rear-end combinations. This paid big dividends to enthusiasts when Ford published its catalogs for the 1982 model year. The division reintroduced the 302, now called the 5.0-liter HO (high output), which it rated at 157 horsepower. In addition, it brought back the GT package with a choice of red, black, or metallic-silver body paint, complete with spoilers and a large nonfunctional hood scoop. Body designations changed as two-door coupes got more substantial B-pillars and became two-door "sedans." Ghia's named disappeared, but, in addition to the GT, there now were L, GL, and GLX packages. It was the first year that a fully optioned Mustang cracked the $12,000 barrier.

If 1982 had been good for power and performance, 1983 was good for the spirit. Ford division reintroduced the convertible after a ten-year hiatus. Engineering got the all-glass rear window to fold itself. Overnight, dozens of variously skilled body-shop men with cutting torches went out of the convertible conversion business.

Ford also broadened its Mustang engine lineup, dropping the 3.3-liter in-line six but replacing it with a new 112-horsepower 3.8-liter V-6. Performance engines grew more plentiful. The turbo returned, now as part of the three-door Turbo GT package, after engineering had thoroughly reworked it, adopting Ford's new electronic fuel injection (EFI) to yield 145 horsepower. Engineering replaced the insufficient two-barrel carburetor on top of the 5.0-liter HO engine with an updated 1980s version of the 1960s Holley 600-cfm four-barrel. This combination raised output to 175 horsepower.

Mustang's second pace-car appearance at Indianapolis came for the 63rd running in 1979. The car was as different from the previous Mustang II as the first production Mustang was from Ford's other products in 1964. Something like 11,000 replicas were manufactured.

To keep this power on the ground, GT-package tires ballooned from the 185/75R14 radials to 205/70 high-speed-rated radials. Design slightly changed the appearances of all the cars with redone grilles and taillights. Total production amounted to 120,873 cars.

For 1984, Ford introduced its Twentieth Anniversary GT wearing a GT350 logo where it had been 19 years earlier. The division offered this commemorative edition with either the turbocharged in-line four, still developing 145 horsepower, or the 5.0-liter HO. Available as a three-door sedan or a convertible, the cars were strictly Oxford White with Canyon Red stripes and interior. Ford built a total of 5,260 in open and closed configurations.

The steering wheel wore the early Ford Motor Company logo while the instrument maple resurrected the machine-tuned appearance of racing cars from the 1930s through the 1950s. The full instrumentation was part of the GT package. The Recaro seats were completely adjustable.

For noncommemorative cars, engineering had at last rid both the 3.8-liter V-6 engine and the 5.0-liter HO of their temperamental and environmentally questionable carburetors, fitting them with a new throttle-body electronic fuel injection. While it decreased the horsepower rating of the 5.0-liter from 175 to 165, it improved everything from cold starting to throttle response to fuel economy. In addition, engineering introduced a sophisticated on-board engine management system on all 1984 Fords. This fourth-version electronic engine control (EEC-IV) furthered Ford's pursuit of ecologically conscientious performance.

On April 17, 1984, nearly 500 Ford Mustangs congregated for an enormous show and new product introduction near Burbank, California. In the center of the Griffith Park Equestrian Center polo grounds, Ford Public Affairs staff carefully directed owners and collectors to their parking spaces, forming a design they could only see later that night on local and national television news—a giant 20 surrounded by a circle all made of Mustangs. News

The 140-horsepower, 5.0-liter V-8 first appeared in the 1975 Mustang II. Power remained unchanged, although numerous changes improved cold start, drivability, and fuel economy. The new four-speed-plus-overdrive manual transmission offered a 0.70:1 gear ratio in fifth. Carburetion was still only a two-barrel.

media helicopters buzzed overhead. Hollywood film and entertainment celebrities turned up and told stories of first dates, first kisses, and first loves in Ford Mustangs. This inaugurated a now-annual regional gathering called Fabulous Fords Forever that encompasses and invites examples from every Ford Motor Company automobile product line.

Commemorative GT350s with new electronics were not the only product revelation of mid-April 1984. A small group of dedicated people had worked at taking the familiar Mustang in a different direction since 1980, creating a car outside of the mainstream. This result struck some enthusiasts as another breath of fresh air. Others never understood the thing, nor did they want it.

chapter thirteen

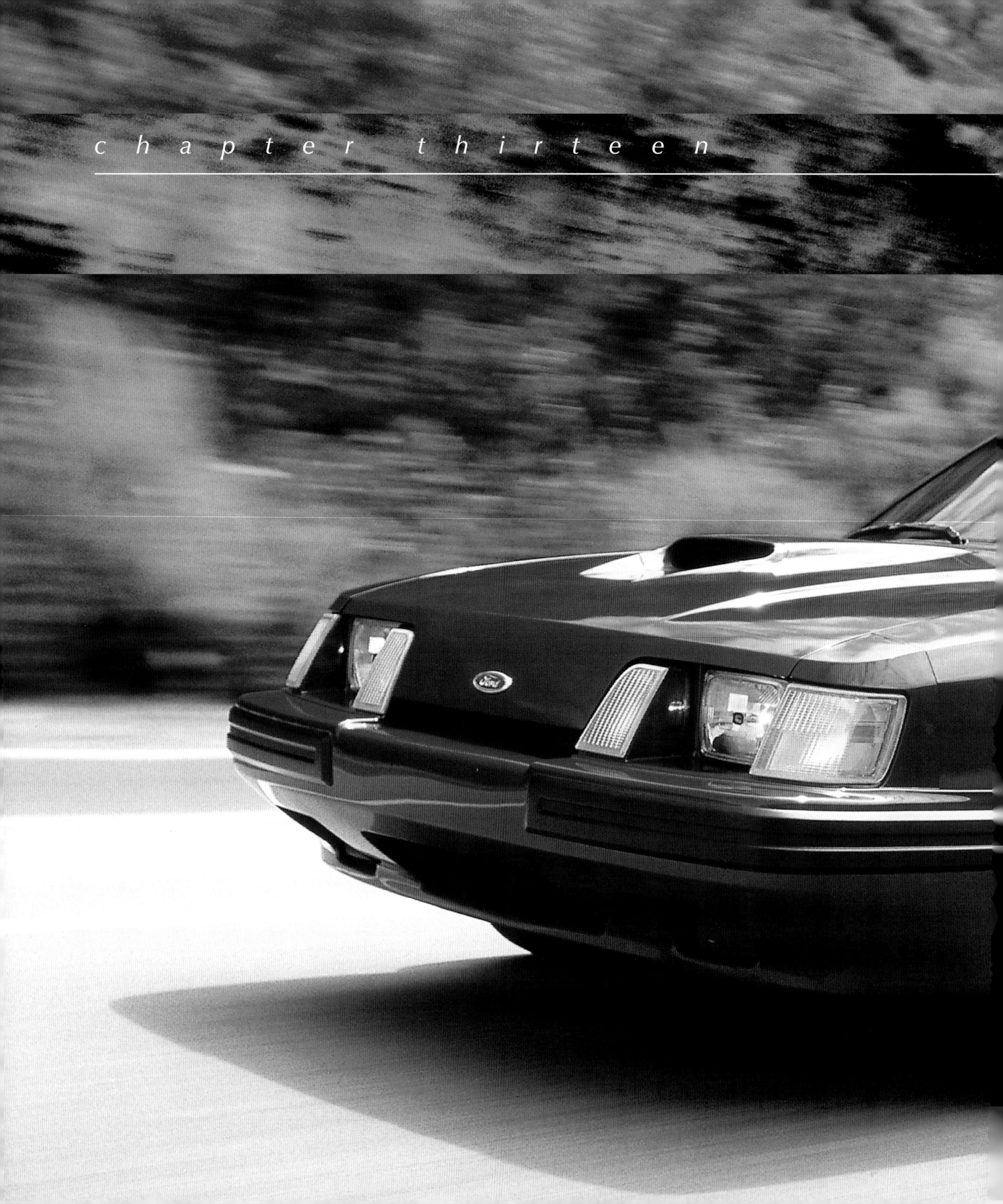

1984½–1986

The large NACA duct was fitted into the hood, slightly offset toward the passenger side. It led outside air through the air-to-air intercooler, boosted power, and kept the fuel economy of a regular four-cylinder.

(1984½–1986)

SVO: SOME VARIATION OBSERVED

Mustang's IMSA show car not only told race fans and competitors that Ford was back in racing, it also spoke to the United Auto Workers (UAW) and to Mazda Motor Company, Ford's Japanese partner. Some Ford product planners and corporate board members had proposed letting Ford division exhaust the Fox platform's usable life as a Mustang. Then Ford could import Mazda's front-wheel drive, four-cylinder MX6 and re-badge it as the 1983 or 1984 Mustang. It would save the corporation billions of dollars. Division planners moved the idea far enough along to reassign plants that had supplied Mustang parts to manufacture pieces for other vehicles. It made financial sense, yet it struck some people within Ford Motor Company as profoundly wrong.

Michael Kranefuss, a German who had run Ford of Europe's competition department as director of motorsports starting in 1972, had shown enthusiasts, journalists, and the corporation outstanding performances from small cars called Zakspeed Capris. When Ford division concluded that it was time to take Ford Mustangs racing again in the United States in 1980, it invited Kranefuss to Dearborn to command the effort.

The SVO was designed to accommodate flush "aero" headlamps. Following its introduction in mid-1984 with standard sealed-beam headlights such as these, it was not until late June 1985 that models were able to take advantage of a relaxation in federal standards that allowed aerodynamic "composite" headlights with a separate bulb and lens/reflector system.

Ford suffered severe damage to its credibility in the racing world after November 20, 1970, the day when Henry Ford II ordered Jacque Passino to scrap all the racing parts and discontinue all support, and abruptly withdrew the company from all motorsports. Kranefuss inherited the challenge of rebuilding Ford's reputation. The company named him director of Special Vehicle Operations, SVO. Ford division had paid attention to the ways and the speed with which outside "vendors," such as Shelby American, Ghia design studios, Jack Roush's organization, Kar Kraft, and Detroit Steel Tubing, accomplished their goals. Even though SVO was definitely part of Ford division, upper management thought that placing it outside the Dearborn "campus" might enable it to operate more efficiently.

Part of SVO's support came from Walter Hayes, former manager of public affairs for Ford of Europe. Hayes, a distinguished Englishman, had controlled the purse strings for the GT40 program under the umbrella of public affairs. The racing in Europe had benefited engineering developments for their road products as well as furthered Ford's image. Following the successful attacks on Le Mans and victories over Ferrari, Henry Ford II brought the dour, ambassadorial Hayes to the United States and named him vice president of Public Affairs.

SVO was no secret, but Ford did not widely publicize the fact that Walter Hayes' public affairs budgets supported it; there were those in management and on the board who had been embarrassed by their Pinto and the tragic propensity for its gas tank to ignite in certain types of rear-end accidents. They hoped that a successful racing program at home might distract public attention.

Hayes endowed Kranefuss with three methods of accomplishing his task. First, SVO would encourage Ford involvement in motorsports and supervise its activities, as Kranefuss had done in Germany. This would be done through a small factory effort involving Mustangs, wherein Kranefuss would select promising private teams and provide them with a great deal of assistance in engines and parts, technical back-up, and even financial support. Second, just as in the mid-1960s, SVO would expand the racing- and high-performance street parts program for Ford to market under the banner of Ford Motor Sports.

The third part of SVO's "mission" was perhaps the most complex, paralleling operations such as Enzo Ferrari's in Italy and Porsche's in Germany. In order to support its own racing

Its most controversial feature was its twin-deck—or bi-plane—spoiler. Some within Special Vehicle Operations felt it was too distinctive and ran the risk of being the single feature people would remember best if the car failed, like the exotic grille of the Edsel more than 25 years earlier. In the end, the idea prevailed.

Special Vehicle Operations (SVO) burst upon the scene in 1984 with the debut of the Mustang SVO. Patterned off the increasingly popular European sport sedans, this Mustang gave notice that Ford was going to be a presence in motorsports again.

operation, Hayes expected Kranefuss and SVO to develop and manufacture a limited-production, high-performance passenger car. The public purpose simply would be to transfer SVO's racing successes to the streets of America. Ford's larger and ulterior motive, good publicity, rendered the toughest challenge to Kranefuss: the division expected SVO's street car sales to generate the profit necessary to fund its racing programs without calling on Ford Motor Company or approaching outside sponsors for financial assistance. This meant that racer Kranefuss could not merely plan from race to race. Businessman Kranefuss had to plan and project two, three, and even five years into the future, shrewdly postponing or delaying one thing to accomplish something more important sometime later.

By mid-1982, SVO and Ford Motor Sports had ventured into every form of racing in the United States, from NASCAR to showroom stock, from Indianapolis to the prototype category of IMSA. SVO also had decided what its "production" car should be. Kranefuss and Hayes had brought in Glen Lyall as SVO engineering manager, and imported Bob Negstad as their chassis engineer because he had, by that time, 20 years of experience making Mustangs handle, the prime objective for this group.

SVO carried out some of its racing efforts using Ford's 2.3-liter four that it turbocharged and intercooled. Lyall, Kranefuss, and the growing SVO team decided to develop a detuned version of the racing engine for the street car. This version would introduce multi-port fuel injection to Ford engines and intercooling to American production cars. The intercooler decreased the fuel-air mixture temperature from the turbo compressed-and-heated 300-degrees Fahrenheit down to a more effective and denser blend at 175 degrees. Even with the extra plumbing, the entire engine assembly weighed 150 pounds less than the 5.0-liter V-8 that produced the same power. The weight difference would clearly benefit handling.

Ford used discreet badging on the SVO. With the huge polycarbonate twin-deck spoiler and smooth front end, the vehicle didn't need splashy graphics.

Cast-aluminum 16x7-inch wheels were wrapped in Goodyear 225/50VR16 BSW NCT tires. This metric tire was used because the 1984 Corvette utilized the Goodyear Gatorback tire that Ford wanted to use. Chevrolet and Goodyear signed an agreement that prevented the Gatorback to be used on anything but the 'Vette. Goodyear told Ford they had this tire from Germany that Porsche was using on the 928.

The 1984 Mustang SVO was the first 'Stang that didn't have a "proper" grille. It was one of the first American cars that pulled the majority of its cooling air from under the front bumper.

292

The SVO group was headed by Michael Kranefuss. The fascinating styling features included a smooth front end with improved aerodynamics, which is important in any vehicle capable of running 140 miles per hour.

"People who are into GT cars just love the SVO," Negstad said. "Its directional stability is outstanding. But for people who measure whether a car is good or bad with a stopwatch...the first half-a-car length, a V-8 will beat it. We studied why this happened. The V-8 has a heavier flywheel. So we took an SVO and put a heavy flywheel on it. It would come out of the hole just like a V-8. However, it wouldn't pick up speed as well in mid-range because it had to turn the bigger flywheel. It came down to another decision: Do you want a car to burn rubber, or do you want to have a car that feels good at the top end? Ford already had a car to burn rubber. It was already called a Mustang, a 5.0-liter HO. We saw no need to build another."

As early as January 1981, SVO vehicle planning manager John Plant had set out targets and objectives on paper to define terms to engineers. Two months later, Lyall and Negstad had worked out program assumptions. These were the catalog of parts that they would carry over from production Mustangs or other Ford products, and those that would be new for a car called the 1982½ SVO Special Mustang. Then Ford division temporarily killed the Mustang because it planned to replace it with a car based on the Mazda MX6. In the several months before the division brought it back, SVO had shredded its papers for its 1982½ programs. Now its Special Mustang would be a fall 1983 introduction for the 1984 model year.

A feature exclusive to the Mustang SVO was the bi-level rear wing assembly, which was effective in generating −0.011 lift versus +0.085 for a base Mustang. The top wing was designed to spill the airflow rearward, so that the air would tumble onto the rear lip of the lower wing and push the vehicle down, improve gas mileage.

SVO set production at a maximum of 10,000 cars for its first year. Being produced in relatively small volume created problems for SVO. Ford's shock absorber plant turned out more shocks in a week than the SVOs would need for a year's production. Fortunately Koni, the Dutch company that had been Ford parts suppliers in the early days of Shelby Mustangs, was glad to provide such small quantities.

At the same time, Chevrolet was working on its fourth-generation Corvette, and Goodyear was developing 16-inch Gatorbacks using GM's proprietary tread design. Negstad wanted something similar, and SVO found Goodyear's NCT European tire that was available. NCTs got the SVO tooled and running with a 16-inch wheel. Later, Goodyear developed a separate Gatorback for the SVO. Lyall and Negstad even looked at 17-inch wheels and tires, but the technology wasn't ready yet.

SVO was small, 30 people by this time, and final decisions stemmed from barely a dozen of them. This allowed them to react quickly, to seize opportunities. Sometimes it left them with little clout or strength, but when they were fortunate, they found chances to prove themselves. One huge challenge was brakes. Plant, Lyall, and Kranefuss all agreed the SVO Mustang had to have four-wheel disc brakes. Bob Negstad adapted rear discs from the Lincoln Versailles, the high-end Fox chassis sedan. It required special modifications, including fitting a slightly larger rotor at the rear rather than the front to accommodate an emergency brake system that would pass federal tests.

Glenn Lyall's engine development team faced similar challenges with their computer program for engine calibration. They developed a two-stage spark advance so someone could take the car into Mexico and not burn up the engine while using lower octane gasoline. Another part of the program controlled turbo boost for the same reason. The computer would hold boost to 10 psi, 0.7 atmospheres below 2,500 rpm. Above that speed, boost would increase to 14 psi, one atmosphere. SVO placed a switch on the dashboard to manually limit boost that would accommodate poorer gasoline.

The intercooled and turbocharged SOHC 2.3-liter four produced 175 horsepower at 4,500 rpms and 210 foot-pounds of torque at 3,000 rpms. The seal around the top of the intercooler fit flush with the bottom of the hood, where a scoop directed cool air across the heat exchanger to cool the air up to 125 degrees.

In the midst of SVO's development, another significant battle went on within Ford Motor Company. While former product planner Donald E. Petersen, whom the board had named corporate president, was a car enthusiast, his boss, chairman Philip Caldwell, was cost-conscious in the mold of Ernie Breech and Robert McNamara. Ford's middle management was populated with decision makers who tended to work harder at keeping their jobs than producing fine cars. The board authorized the creation of a "blue-ribbon" panel to determine, among other things, how far down the corporate hierarchy major decisions could be made. Buried in the project was the unuttered question: Just how few people would it take to produce a car? Each battle that SVO's small group won reinforced the philosophy of the blue-ribbon committee. Most of SVO's 12 decision makers all worked in the same low-walled room; designers and engineers could shout a question over a divider, get an answer, make a commitment, check something off a list, and move on.

From the mouse-hair dash panel to the short-throw shifter, the Mustang SVO's interior was designed for sport driving. Recaro-style seats and ample legroom meant that a comfortable position could be achieved easily.

296

The Ford ad boasted "Never have so few done so much for the enthusiast." A relatively small outfit, Special Vehicle Operations blended racing know-how with production line procedures to build a car many Ford employees felt would never happen.

Chassis engineer Bob Negstad recalled, "People who are into GT cars just love the SVO. It's directional stability is outstanding. But for people who measure whether a car is good or bad with a stopwatch . . . the first half-a-car length, a V-8 will beat it."

The Dearborn Assembly Plant had no facility to mount and balance SVO's new 16-inch tires. Micropoise Company developed an automatic machine to do the entire task.

Introduced with 175 horsepower, the 1984-1/2 SVO sold for $15,585. With Ford's Traction-Lok differential and final drive of 3.45:1, magazine testers accomplished 0 to 60 times of 7.5 seconds and standing start quarter-miles in 15.5 seconds at 90 miles per hour.

"In 'Mainstream,'" Negstad explained, "those decisions could literally take months. We talked to each other, were friends with each other. We had our staff meetings and discussed where we needed help or where we could give ground and where we couldn't and why not...."

SVO's Mustang, like any other, was made up of millions of decisions that Kranefuss, Lyall, engine-wizard Dave Domine, marketing manager John Clinard, electronics-genius Bob Stelmaszczak, and body engineer John Rundels made on a daily, sometimes even minute-to-minute basis. This group chose solutions based not on what the car should cost, but on what it should be.

They could get a gearshift knob through "Mainstream" for 39 cents. Kranefuss, Lyall, and Plant found a shift knob of hypercord hydron rubber formed inside a leather knob that was baseball stitched and embossed with the shift pattern on the top. It felt great and looked the way they wanted the entire car to appear. Each one cost SVO nearly $6.

Borg-Warner worked and reworked its T-5 transmission, finally achieving the feel that Lyall and Kranefuss knew was necessary for a car to go head-to-head against BMW's 3-series coupes. Hurst massaged and finessed its T-5 shift linkage with the same goal. SVO made Borg-Warner and Hurst understand that if they couldn't achieve the proper feel, Michael Kranefuss knew a company in Germany, Getrag, that could do what he wanted. This heavy-handed approach was necessary. While it not only resonated through the blue-ribbon committee, these little differences were things the buyers would feel every time they took the car for a drive.

SVO engineers aligned gas, brake, and clutch placement for heel-and-toe pedaling during gear changes and placed a "dead pedal" where the clutch foot rested naturally. After looking at and pricing Recaro seats, Lear-Sigler's articulated, reclining versions were chosen because they comforted and supported the driver and passenger equally well while providing better value for SVO's investment dollars.

Body engineer John Rundels wanted the fascia, the front piece of bodywork, to accept aerodynamic, faired-in headlamps. Ford knew these were less than a year away from governmental legalization, but, until they were, SVO would have to make do with standard flat-glass sealed

The Mustang SVO perfected the four-bar link rear suspension system, the first arrangement to effectively tame wheel hop in acceleration as well as greatly improve cornering and road-holding.

beams. SVO's decision makers wanted the aero look, but they could not afford retooling a big complex piece after the first few thousand cars. They faced a huge chore to fabricate a fascia that would accept both styles of lamps, along with the car's innovative below-the-bumper air intakes and fog lamp mounts that had to incorporate federally mandated safety bumpers. Rundels had to call his old friend, Bob Stone, out of retirement. Stone had done chassis work on the 1964½ Mustang and, before that, had worked on the vast sheet-metal surfaces of the big cars of the 1950s. Stone had friends far and wide within Automobile Assembly Division. He came in, looked at what SVO had done so far, and threw it away. Then he visited his friends, they pulled in outside vendors, and SVO had a "grille-less" front fascia that would accept both types of headlights, bounce off barriers at 5 miles per hour, and allow the engine to cool.

In its two-and-a-half model years, only 9,842 Mustangs SVO were sold, which was less than the first-year target of 10,000 copies. It was conceived as a low-volume image builder, and it exceeded its break-even point of 8,500 cars in total.

Then there was the controversial bi-plane rear wing. A drag racer from the 1960s named Al Turner was involved in the grass-roots racing promotions that SVO was doing as part of Ford Motor Sports efforts. Turner had spent time in Europe and Australia for Ford, and he was familiar with Ford of Europe's Sierra XR-4i sports coupe series that wore a distinctive two-level rear spoiler. He recommended it and pushed hard for its adoption to the Mustang. Older staffers within SVO who had witnessed the distinctive grille of the Edsel warned Turner that high-visibility features could hurt a car as much as help. After toning down the spoiler design from the Sierra (on which the top wing was aligned level with the roof line), everyone finally agreed that it probably did fit the GT image, even though it never would be appropriate for the tire-squealers.

Ford division's late decision to carry over the Mustang delayed SVO in getting started. Then Kranefuss and the others decided to postpone it intentionally so that it would not arrive with other 1984 models and get lost in the flurry. The SVO Mustang became a 1984½ introduction, reaching dealerships in mid-April.

Through the next two years, the reputation of the SVO Mustang for quality had become solid, and they had managed to maintain it. SVO's managers working out of the Whitaker Building, located on Southfield Road in Allen Park, had put their effort and their limited budget into obvious performance and subtle appearance. Ironically, while reviewers noted the performance features that SVO had spent money on, they criticized the car for its tame styling, just as others before them had wanted flamboyance on Shelby's Mustangs. Still others thought its handling was too tame.

Negstad created a car with good road manners. He had developed an innovative rear suspension system that utilized two of the low-pressure gas Koni adjustable shock absorbers in normal vertical position, plus two other shocks mounted nearly horizontally off the top of the rear of the solid axle. These led back to the SVO subframe. This quad-shock system, plus a 0.67-inch diameter rear anti-sway bar, helped cornering immensely and almost completely tamed rear axle hop during hard acceleration.

"So for '85," Negstad recalled, "I tightened the valving so it felt like it was hard. And in '86 I hardened it again because people assumed you were supposed to pay a little punishment for this love affair of driving this car. It can't be that comfortable!"

The 175-horsepower 1984½ SVO sold for $15,585. With Ford's Traction-Lok differential and final drive of 3.45:1, magazine testers accomplished 0–60 times of 7.5 seconds and standing-start quarter-miles in 15.5 seconds at 90 miles per hour. While total Mustang production amounted to 141,480 cars, only 4,508 of them were the three-door, black-trimmed SVOs.

For 1985, SVO replaced the black body trim with charcoal grey. At mid-year, for the car's first anniversary, they introduced more significant changes. Electronics-master Bob Stelmaszczak and engine builder Dave Domine improved the engine's manners and power as well as its mileage, now up to 21 miles per gallon city and 32 miles per gallon highway. Output increased 30 horsepower to 205 horsepower. Rundels replaced the recessed sealed beam headlights with flush-mounted halogen lights, which made negligible difference in the car's 0.38 coefficient of drag (Cd), but great difference in visual appeal. Goodyear's P225/50VR16 Gatorbacks and a new 3.73:1 rear axle ratio introduced at the beginning of the model year shortened quarter-mile times by nearly half a second and raised trap speed by more than 4 miles per hour. Negstad quickened steering response by changing steering ratio from 20:1 to 15:1 for the 1985 cars. SVO also managed to reduce the price to $14,806. Sales still dropped precipitously to only 1,954 cars.

For 1986, there were no major changes to the car although the reality of lower-octane gasoline required Bob Stelmaszczak to reprogram the EEC-IV module; this slightly decreased the power rating to 200 horsepower. SVO moved the suggested list price back up to $15,272, but as word of mouth began to spread favorable comments, production nearly doubled to 3,382.

But 1986 was SVO's final year. The question of killing the Mustang altogether had been bouncing around once again inside the division in late 1983. Mazda's MX6 had better EPA numbers that made meeting Ford's CAFE requirements easier. Performance packages had also improved the MX6's sporting image, and it was selling well. Ford division informed Kranefuss and Lyall that the Mustang would be dropped at the end of 1986. So the SVO group had asked for a Thunderbird. They could be perfectly content, they had decided, tackling a new challenge. Ford's Design Center and "Mainstream" had responded: Well, how about a really dramatic-looking car with a much lower cowl. Maybe a rear engine two-seater, maybe a mid-engine? Perhaps all-wheel drive? Harold "Red" Poling, head of NAAO, would be funding it.

As SVO had started work on its aero-T-bird and the mid-engine sports car, the strength in the numbers of the UAW spoke to Ford. If the Mustang is replaced with a car built outside of the United States, they told Ford management, a great number of Dearborn workers may lose their jobs. Their union brothers and sisters who work at other Ford plants around the United States might not take kindly to this. There might be some rough times. Ford signed an agreement with the UAW to keep Mustang production in Dearborn at least through the 1993 model year.

A rare model of an already rare car: the code 41C, with the competition "delete radio" option. While this option deleted the radio, it also took off the power door locks, power windows, and the air conditioning with its heavy compressor and additional plumbing, which saved nearly 100 pounds (and credited the buyer with $1,253) over the standard SVO.

Swooping down Laguna Seca Raceway is the IMSA GTP Ford Mustang, belching fire from its exhaust as the throttle is momentarily shut during a down shift. Although the DOHC four-cylinder engine only displaced 1.745 liters (106.5-ci), it generated 600 horsepower at a lofty 9,000 rpm.

Leather was an additional option to upgrade the interior of the SVO. As intriguing as the few options available to add to the SVO was the option for deleted equipment. Called "comp prep," designation "race" use, it was not offered in 1984-1/2. Production was limited to 40 models for 1985, and in 1986 only 83 were built.

In its two-and-a-half model years, SVO had produced only 9,842 Mustangs, fewer than the first-year target of 10,000 copies. Ford division had conceived it as a low-volume image builder, though, and it had exceeded its break-even point of 8,500 cars in total. Ford had meant for the SVO Mustang to set a benchmark for what could be created using a small, fuel-efficient four-cylinder engine. The division had meant for the SVO to express its commitment to those engines for the future.

The SVO Mustang had established several other things. Magazines referred to it as the "best handling, most balanced Mustang ever sold." It never received such raves from European reviewers who came over to drive it. Even though it was so well equipped that it only offered six options—air conditioning, power windows, power door locks, leather seats, flip-up sun-roof, and AM/FM stereo/cassette radio—it never drew into the showrooms any of the 3-series

The addition of the air-to-air intercooler (in between the Garrett AiResearch turbocharger and the cylinder head) produced a 30 horsepower gain to 174 horsepower at 4,500 rpm, with 210 foot-pounds of torque at 3,000 rpm from the 2.3-liter electronic fuel-injected inline four-cylinder engine. Power remained the same for 1985, but in mid-1985, dual exhaust, a wilder camshaft, and increased turbo boost lifted the power to 205 horsepower at 5,000 rpm and 248 foot-pounds at 3,000 rpm.

BMW owners SVO had hoped would appear. Worse, the American car buyers who went in ready to buy an SVO found the dealership personnel didn't understand the car. Still, they could close a deal on the GT with its 5.0-liter HO that didn't need to wait for the turbos to wind up for its identical 200 horsepower to arrive. Even better, buyers didn't have to spend an extra $4,170 to get it. In the end, its stablemates defeated the SVO as much as any other car on the market.

On top of that, the Mustang GTP racer disappointed all who bet on it. The Ford Motor Sports high-performance street and racing parts supply and the racing operations remained under SVO control until 1988. Ford Division then took all Mustang manufacturing back in-house.

1985–1993½

(previous) *Only 160 Saleen SSCs were built in 1989, and were stuffed with the best performance equipment Steve Saleen could lay his hands on. The chassis was stiffened, 16-inch wheels were installed, Monroe adjustable shocks were fitted, and power was bumped up to 292 horsepower.*

While Mustang GTs finally dumped the 85 mile per hour speedometer in 1989 for a 140 mile per hour unit, the Saleen SSC of that year boasted a 200 miles per hour speedo. Top speed was only 156 miles per hour, but notice the cruise control buttons on the steering wheel.

(1 9 8 5 – 1 9 9 3 ½)

THE FOX, REVISITED

As SVO struggled to reinvent the wheel, as it tried to demonstrate to American car buyers what a performance car could be, most of those buyers looked at its price and its engine and said, "I'd rather have a V-8." The high price for high performance from a small engine never caught customer's imaginations.

Buyers not only preferred the V-8, they also opted for the 3.8-liter V-6 and even the normally aspirated 2.3-liter four much more often than the high-tech turbocharged-intercooled SVO. Ford division had dropped the Turbo GT in 1985. While the 2.3-liter one-barrel carbureted standard engine retained its 88 horsepower, the 3.8-liter held at 120 horsepower, and Ford made it the standard engine with the LX convertible package. It was an adequate mix for buyers needing the bare minimum of power required to enter the freeways, but who were not willing to accept higher insurance rates or fuel consumption of the 5.0-liter or the GT package.

SVO tricks bled through, though. In 1985, the 5.0 received real dual exhausts and, ahead of the catalytic converter, the big V-8 received real 1960's era stainless-steel-tube headers. With a longer duration cam and hydraulic valve lifters, power output increased to 210 horsepower. Magazine testers loved the 5.0-liter GT three-doors with its four-barrel carburetor. They made great photographs for the covers with their back ends enveloped in billowing white tire smoke. Reviewers obtained 0–60 times of 7.1 seconds and quarter-mile elapsed times of 15.5 seconds

Not what most drivers wished to glimpse in their mirrors, 5.0L Mustangs were used by law enforcement for many years. While Ford produced a Special Service Package, Steve Saleen provided the Seal Beach (California) Police Department with a 1990 5.0L LX hatchback model, which was ideal for collaring perps on Interstate 405. Robert Genat/Zone Five Photo

at 89.7 miles-per-hour. The 3,000-pound car would average 17 miles per gallon under their mixed (make that hard) use. Ford produced 156,514 Mustangs in 1985.

Road & Track magazine published a comparison of Ford's 1986 GT and Chevrolet's IROC-Z. The results must have helped the sales of Mustangs because, in each acceleration measure, 0–30, 0–60, 0–100 miles per hour, the Mustang arrived a full second ahead of the Camaro. While fuel economy figures were nearly identical, fully equipped costs were about $3,500 different with the advantage going to Ford's three-door. The only test where the Camaro out-performed the GT was on the skid pad. The Camaro cornered at 0.845 g and the GT made only 0.792, a fact that *Road & Track* attributed to wider, fatter Goodyear Eagle P245/50VR16s on

Getting ready to bring irresponsible behavior to a halt, a Seal Beach police officer finds the driver's seat a snug, but adequate, work space. The CHP purchased 400 5.0L V-8 notchback models equipped with oil and transmission coolers, heavy-duty battery, and a 140 mile per hour calibrated speedometer. Robert Genat/ Zone Five Photo

Steve Saleen tweaked his heavily tweaked Mustangs into a law-enforcement tool. Decals were affixed to the rear side quarter windows. Robert Genat/Zone Five Photo

MUSTANG SB/S
Law Enforcement Specialty Vehicle

314

The 1987 Mustang GT 5.0L used lower body cladding extensively, including faux front brake cooling scoops. There was no arguing with a quarter-mile time of 15.3 seconds at 93.0 miles per hour. The top speed was 148 miles per hour.

The hatchback design proved helpful to the Seal Beach Police Department for carrying the multitude of equipment needed for the job. Robert Genat/Zone Five Photo

The 90-degree, 5.0-liter high-output engine cranked out 225 horsepower and 300 foot-pounds of torque.

Louvered taillights were a stylistic touch that most people either loved or hated. Regardless of your leanings, there was no mistaking the Mustang at night for any other vehicle. The functional bumpers were nicely integrated into the overall design.

the Camaro, while the GT wore 60-section tires, Goodyear Eagle P225/60VR15s. Through the slalom, the Mustang ran 60.9 miles per hour while the Camaro made 59.7 miles per hour. The Mustang weighed 240 pounds less at 3,355 pounds and produced 20 horsepower more at 210.

Ford performed big changes for 1987; most noticeable was the tenth edition of the Fox platform's facelift. All Mustangs became "bottom breathers," moving their major radiator air intake below the front bumper. The GT adopted the drooped nose hood of the SVO with its aero-headlamps and halogen bulbs. It also inherited their major handling improvement, the quad-shock rear-axle suspension. Engineering had perfected the electronic fuel injection (EFI) introduced during the 1986 model run. The new injection helped pull 210 horsepower from the 5.0-liter engine, and 225 horsepower from the 5.0-liter High Output. Product planners dropped the 3.8-liter V-6 so only the base 2.3-liter single-barrel and the EFI-HO remained.

They made the five-speed manual transmission standard on all models, its low final overdrive gear benefiting mileage figures; in reality, only the LX convertible, which inherited the 2.3-liter as its standard engine, suffered from the loss of the 3.8-liter V-6.

Road & Track revisited its comparison of the Mustang GT and the Camaro IROC-Z, tackling both 1987 models in its October 1986 issue. The IROC-Z was up to 220 horsepower while the GT was rated at 225 horsepower. The weight spread was nearly the same as the year before, at 3,720 pounds for the Camaro, 3,500 for the GT. Final drive ratios—3.27 for the Chevy, 3.08:1 for the Ford— remained unchanged as did tire sizes. The Camaro had made good use of the extra 30 horses under its hood.

Acceleration times now were within tenths, the GT beating the Z to 60 miles per hour by one-tenth of a second—6.7 seconds versus 6.8. However, going on to 100 miles per hour, the Camaro's sleeker shape gave it a four-tenths advantage, getting there in 18.4 seconds compared to 18.8 for the GT. Fatter tires got the Camaro around the oval at a higher G-load, yet the GT got through the slalom at 63.6 miles per hour compared to 63.3 miles per hour for the Camaro. Both cars came within one mile per hour at top speeds: 149 for the Camaro, 148 for the Mustang. The only dramatic differential was in price where once again, the smart money decision put $1,350 back in Mustang GT buyers' pockets. Chevrolet priced the Camaro at $12,675 while the GT listed at $11,324.

The GT also contained several distinctive appearance features lacking from the LX, including multi-louvered taillights and front and rear air dams as well as a side-aerodynamic valance with scoops to front and rear brakes. Englishman Trevor Creed, who had designed the interior of Ford of Europe's Scorpio imported by Lincoln-Mercury as the Merkur, and then did interiors for the Taurus and Thunderbird, brought tasteful functionalism to the Mustang's interior.

Road & Track reviewers captured the essential differences between the Mustang and Camaro. In brief comments, they summed up Ford's approach: "Ford chose ride quality; Chevy chose handling ability." In 1987, Ford built 159,145 of the cars. Nomenclature changed with the body styles. Gone were the three-door sedans, replaced by two-door hatchbacks.

The Japanese-produced MX6-based Mustang concept reared its head once again in 1987. Again Ford division felt the UAW's impressive force and the MX6 moved off Mustang drawing boards and out to Flat Rock, Michigan, for production as the 1988 Ford Probe.

Mel Nichols, reporting in *Automobile*, likened the new 5.0-liter GT hatchback to the 302s of 17 and 18 years earlier. In 1970, 0–60 miles per hour came in 6.0 seconds; in 1987, it was 6.1 in his tests. In 1970, the top speed was 118. Nichols experienced 145 miles per hour in 1987. For 1988, everything was better yet. *Road & Track* headlined their profile of the GT in their 1988 Performance Cars Special, quoting a lyric from singer Carly Simon: "Stay right here, 'cause these are the good old days."

Remember back to the bad recent days, the dark ages induced by OPEC. In September 1974, Henry Ford II had shown Anna Muccioli a little jewel with a white vinyl roof with Ford's first new four-cylinder engine since the 1930s. Now, it could only seem as if this was a renaissance. The dark ages were over. The lights were back on in Dearborn and fire was in the eyes of

the buyers for the 211,225 Mustangs that Ford produced in 1988.

The next year, Ford chose to ignore the calendar. While it had proudly produced the Mustang II in the tenth anniversary year of the car's birth and while the 1984 GT350s were called Twentieth Anniversary Commemorative models, there was no 25th anniversary special edition in 1989. The official reason was that the company had begun to consider that the April introduction was really half-a-year early for the 1965 model. It began referring to "early and late" 1965s instead of 1964½ models. As had been the case between 1987 and 1988, there were virtually no significant changes between previous year and new model cars.

As the production engineers readied the 1988 Probe for Job One, concern in Dearborn turned ever more acutely to the future of the Mustang. Ford division planners had concluded that any Japanese-based Mustang without a V-8, even if assembled completely in Michigan, would hurt Mustang sales. In the latter days of supply-side Reaganomics, it was thought that a Japanese-based Mustang also might hurt Ford's sales of all its products.

The competition between Chevrolet's Camaro Z28 and the Mustang GT was inevitable. Taut styling and aggressive engineering combined to make the 1987 GT the top pony car of the day whether it was on stock wheels and tires or these aftermarket American Racing mag wheels.

Most of the changes in the 1990 Mustang were federally mandated, such as the driver-side airbag and rear seat shoulder harnesses. Ordering the 5.0L LX the buyer received the same suspension and tires as the GT model without the ticket-baiting spoilers and air dam.

The rear luggage rack on the 1990 Mustang LX was not really meant to carry luggage, but it did provide a mounting position for the center-mount brake light. Base price for a LX 5.0L convertible was $17,681.

A longer hood, flush rear quarter glass and headlights, and a new grille were some of the changes the Mustang incorporated in 1987. A Traction-Lok axle was now available on the GT model.

To commemorate the 25th anniversary of the Mustang, Ford fitted this special badge to the passenger side of the dashboard. Except for the lettering, it is the same badge the Mustang has worn since day one.

On September 29, 1987, Henry Ford II died of pneumonia. In the years preceding his death and the decade that lead to Ford's awareness of the threat from Japanese competition, the nation had grown more world-aware and had continued to evolve. Filmmaker George Lucas' young Luke Skywalker had taught us what it meant to use "the force." Big Blue, the computer giant known as International Business Machines, IBM, had appointed a small Washington state software company, Microsoft, to create its computer operation system. In Iran, in November 1979, the Ayatollah Ruhollah Khomeini had shown us and president-elect Reagan another way to measure force, holding 52 U.S. embassy employees hostage for 444 days. A new death-wielding plague had received a name, acquired immunodeficiency syndrome, AIDS. In March 1983, President Reagan had defined the Soviet Union as the "focus of evil in the modern world." In January 1984, the federal antitrust courts had shattered American Telephone & Telegraph, AT&T. In early 1985, the Communist Party had named Mikhail Gorbachev its General Secretary, priming the world for a realignment of force that had lifted hopes for world peace. Those who had not been elated enough by this political change had found that Prozac, approved by the Food and Drug Administration on December 29, 1987, lifted their hopes for a better day. Stories in the newspapers had begun to reveal the history of a small team of wildly creative Lockheed aircraft engineers. They had produced the remarkable U-2 and SR-71 surveillance aircraft and the nearly invisible Stealth bombers out of a clandestine group operating at Burbank airport in California. This was an idea and a concept that Ford's Mustang program manager Ken Dabrowski greatly admired.

Dabrowski resurrected the idea of a small, streamlined SVO-type organization to conceive of the car that would replace the Fox chassis. Federal safety standards required automakers to provide not only a driver's automatically inflatable passive supplemental restraint system, an airbag, but also one for the front-seat passenger. Ford engineers knew they could easily fit a driver's bag into the steering wheel; to make it work, Ford sacrificed the tilt-wheel option. The

325

(opposite) *Basking in the southern California sun, the Dearborn-built 1990 Mustang LX 5.0 retailed for $17,796. Total production that year was 128,189, and 26,958 were convertibles.*

The 1989 Saleen SSC was available only in white. All 160 units built enjoyed the yellow and gray accents.

passenger bag required more engineering, and as it learned that many other carmakers would have new cars surrounding this feature, Ford division set the same goal.

Ford's newest group would ultimately call itself Team Mustang, and the crew set out to conceive of its new car while the company continued with barely changed models through 1989 to 1990. It produced 210,769 Mustangs in 1989. After 15 years, Mustang speedometers finally could acknowledge the cars would exceed 85 miles per hour; GTs and the 5.0-liter LXs, now called LX 5.0L Sports (in sedan, hatchback, and convertible), got new speedometers marked to 140 miles per hour. Production of all Mustangs for 1990 slipped to just 128,189 cars. This included the 1990 Limited Edition Mustang 5.0L LX Convertible with white leather interior. Ford planned to limit production of these emerald-green models to 2,000 copies. Ford fitted all the 1990 Mustangs with a tri-bar logo on the dash saying "25 Years." While the convertible listed for $19,878, it was so appealing and so successful that the division ultimately produced 4,103 examples.

The U.S. economy had been doing its own version of a brake fade test, stopping and starting and stopping again. In 1986 gas prices had tumbled down to $0.90 and then held at $0.93 through 1987. When Reagan had proposed repealing the CAFE laws, calling them harmful to U.S jobs and competitiveness, the stock market revealed American industry had far more serious problems than CAFE laws. On October 20, 1987, the Dow Jones industrial average had dropped 508 points, 22.6 percent of its value. A year later, with gas still at $0.93, Congress had

passed new laws to encourage manufacture of alternate fuel and bi-fuel vehicles. The average hourly wage that had been $8.17 in 1979, actually had slipped to $7.40 by 1990, the same year in which the DOT learned that while one-third of all American households had one car, one-half the households had two or more. Inflation had subsided from a devastating 13.5 percent in 1980 to 5.4 percent in 1990. Many economic historians generally agree now that the market crash of 1987 had been a "readjustment" in a 25-year-long bull-market that had begun in August 1962, yet many Americans remember 1988 as the year that their savings and loan failed. A year later the Berlin Wall fell, which economic historians credit as a victory for market capitalism.

For 1991 Mustang production had fallen again, to 98,737 cars, while the prices had risen again slightly. Still, the division had managed to keep the base price of the 2.3-liter four-cylinder LX two-door sedan at $10,157, even though it had come equipped with five-speed manual transmission, power front disc and rear drum brakes, and P195/75R14 radial tires. The price of the GT convertible—$19,864—had been nearly double that of the base LX, but now it would run on 16-inch tires and wheels.

For many years, Ford had left technical and engineering features, and the appearance of Fox platform Mustangs, largely unchanged. For just as long a period, Mustang buyers and performance car enthusiasts had heard and read about the uncertain future of the car beyond 1993. Sales continued to slip. The success of the Limited Edition Emerald Green convertible sparked a new version for 1992, in Vibrant Red, while repeating the white convertible top and white leather seats of the 1990 car. It was an $850 option that 2,196 buyers selected. Production of all Mustang models in 1992 reached 79,280 cars.

For model year 1993, Ford introduced three more limited edition cars: a yellow LX 5.0-liter convertible with white interior (1,419 produced); a white-on-white-and-white convertible (1,460 produced), both available from the start of the year; and a new Cobra beginning in 1993½. The Cobra's tweaked 5.0-liter V-8 produced 235 horsepower at a time when new SAE standards reduced the horsepower rating of the standard by 5.0, to 205. As a premium-priced ($19,990) limited-edition car, it was produced by Ford's Special Vehicles Team (SVT) which had assumed the marketing, training, and customer relations operations that SVO previously had handled. A second group, Special Vehicles Engineering, SVE, under John Coletti's direction, did the hands-on development and manufacture of the Cobra. Ford division formed both groups in late 1991, and model year 1993 marked their first product release. The SVT Cobra bore Jack Roush's performance improvements. The Cobra sold 4,993 cars in half a

329

Discretion behind the wheel is suggested with the high-profile stance of the 1989 Saleen SSC. The base price was a whopping $36,500, and today they are collector items.

MUSTANG · FORTY YEARS

Saleen massaged the 1989 SSC engine with an enlarged throttle body, improved rocker arm ratios, ported and polished heads, an AirSensors TPO unit, and stainless steel headers. Walker Dynomax mufflers and special exhaust tips were at the far end.

model year, just seven cars shy of its projected total production run.

Road & Track recorded 0–60 times of 5.9 seconds and the quarter mile slipped past in 14.5 seconds at 98.0 miles per hour. With its extremely long overdrive fifth gear of 0.68:1, 2,000 rpm yielded 65 miles per hour and the division quoted highway mileage at 24, impressive for a car that could be driven somewhat less frugally to nearly 150 miles per hour. Despite huge 245/45ZR17 Goodyear Eagles, the ride comfort was actually higher than standard GTs, due to interesting blends of standard LX springs with stiffer-than-GT bushings.

For serious racers, SVT and SVE created the final variation of the Fox-4 chassis in its 1993 Cobra R Competition Package. SVT intended this car to be strictly for competitors racing in SCCA's World Challenge Series in class B, and in IMSA's Firestone Grand Sport series. Improvements made the car stronger, modifications to the 351-ci 5.8-liter engine made it faster, and deletions made it 150 pounds lighter than the SVT street Cobra. Ford completed

Dual exhaust was part of the 5.0L package, whether it was installed in an LX or a GT. Retail price on an LX 5.0 hatchback was $15,150, and provided a lot of grunt for the buck.

Ford changed the method of rating engine output in 1993, which resulted in the 5.0L V-8 coming in at 205 horsepower, down 20 from the year before. This was the final year of the venerable Fox platform.

A minimalist grille and aero headlights helped the 1993 Mustang LX reduce the drag coefficient to 0.39. For states that require a front license plate, the factory bracket was supplied at no charge.

Sales of the Mustang in the last year (1993) before a major restyle were excellent, and 114,228 rolled off the showroom. This was the first year that a CD player was on the option list ($629).

Ideal for highway pursuit, the CHP did not use its Mustangs for the graveyard shift, when two officers had to be in the vehicle. The pony car was just too small for a pair of officers and their gear. Robert Genat/Zone Five Photo

One of the criteria used by law enforcement was a vehicle's ability to accelerate briskly from 60 to 90 miles per hour. The SSP Mustang needed only 8.07 seconds to accomplish the feat. Top speed was 137 miles per hour. Robert Genat/Zone Five Photo

The U.S. Air Force used Mustangs to assist U-2 spy planes when landing. It was a critical evolution because the aircraft didn't want to land and the pilot had a difficult time judging distance to the runway. A U-2 pilot would drive down the runway in the 1988 5.0 Mustang and radio instructions to the U-2 regarding distance from the ground and if a wingtip was starting to dip. Robert Genat/Zone Five Photo

just 107 of the cars on a temporary production line. They sold for $25,692 and some ended up in collector's garages as well as racing pits.

While the 1993 Mustang Cobra carried its maturity well, clearly it was aging. Ford division had discontinued the Special Service Package police car modifications for the Mustang at the end of 1993 after a nearly 12-year run. The 1992 and 1993 models, with their "slick tops"—roofs devoid of flashing light bars—loaded with an officer and gear, were capable of speeds into the mid-140s. In civilian dress, the interior and the body, which now boasted a very noticeable rear spoiler, had been around for 14 years. The car accomplished two goals. First, it made a statement to the enthusiast world: Quality may be Job One, but Performance was clearly Priority One.

At the 1993½ Cobra introduction, Ford announced that there definitely would be a 1994 Mustang and that it would be a new car. So the second purpose that the limited-edition, high-performance Cobra hatchback served was to deliver the same kind of hint that Lee Iacocca had dropped 30 years earlier: the Cobra was something "to show the kids that they should wait for us because we had some good, hot stuff coming."

The stenciling on the underside of the U-2 chase Mustang translates thus: "88B 9971" is the U.S. Air Force license number, while "AFE RAF A" stands for United States Air Forces Europe, Royal Air Force, Alconbury. Fitted with essentially a police equipment package, this Mustang chased aircraft until 1999. Robert Genat/Zone Five Photo

(1994–2003)

RESTORATION
OF FAITH

uring World War II, when Lockheed Aviation had established a top-secret Advanced
Development Projects group, founder Kelly Johnson and his colleagues had called it the
Skunk Works. This name had first appeared on a cabin in syndicated cartoonist Al Kapp's "L'il
Abner." All manner of amusing, startling things would emerge from this shack, all meant to
"skunk" the outsiders. Johnson's group had intended to do just that with their aviation inno-
vations. In 1994, when author Ben Rich published *Skunk Works*, his history of Johnson's
group, he stated that it also had served as the model for what Ford's Ken Dabrowski would
establish with Team Mustang. For Johnson, Roy Lunn, Michael Kranefuss, and now
Dabrowski, this simply was the most efficient way to do their jobs.

Mustang program manager Dabrowski formed his own ad hoc Skunk Works in late 1988.
He knew he had about $1 billion to fund the new car from concept to dealer delivery. Mustang
engineering design manager John Coletti had suggested that, with a dedicated Skunk Works
team distant from "Mainstream," it might be possible to bring in a new car for just half that
price. Meanwhile, they had enough time to do a proper car, starting four-and-a-half years
before Job One.

It took another year, until early August 1989, however, just to get this Skunk Works group
approved. That happened just after Ford's board promoted Alex Trotman to executive vice

(previous) For a platform over 20 years old, the 2001 Mustang GT has enjoyed constant refinement. The large hood scoop was nonfunctional and the rear spoiler was primarily for show. Cruising down Pacific Coast Highway at sunset with the top down is reason enough to own a Mustang convertible.

A driver side air bag and steering wheel-mounted cruise control buttons are part and parcel of SN-95 Mustangs. A 4.6L V-8 Mustang GT could put the needle into the upper reaches of the speedometer.

president of NAAO. Trotman had been manager of Product Planning for Ford of Europe through the 1960s. His experience with the German Capris and American Mustangs had convinced him of the necessity of investing in the project. Dabrowski's Skunk Works team, many of whom already had begun laboring on the project on their own time after hours, now continued their labors on the payroll. In an engineers' version of Iacocca's Fairlane Committee dinners, they met at 4 P.M. on Thursdays in Coletti's office in Ford's engineering building No. 3, and, like Iacocca's group, there were eight members in all. Meetings regularly ran late, and they often ordered in dinners. Coletti and Dabrowski enlisted design manager John Aiken to immediately begin a full-size clay model, one they wanted to look more like a Taurus rather than a Fox-Mustang. SVO-alumnus Ron Muccioli represented product planning, Mike Ferrence joined them as sales and marketing manager, Bo Kovacinski was finance manager and Joe Corvaia moved in as purchasing manager. Dia Hothi handled body and assembly, Sid Wells covered body and chassis engineering, and another SVO graduate, Tom Logar, took care of powertrain engineering management. Together, they established their product's description and program objectives.

They knew from Ford's union obligations and from the loud reaction to the Mazda Mustang that their car must remain front-engine and rear-wheel driven. They would offer a V-8 engine no matter what

When Ford revised the Mustang for 1994, it used design cues that harkened-back to the original Mustang of 30 years earlier.

343

(opposite) The Roush Stage 3 Mustang is little removed from the racetrack. Inside the huge 18-inch aluminum wheels are 14-inch rotors and 4-piston Alcon calipers in the front, and 13-inch rotors and 2-piston PBR calipers in the rear. The base price for a Roush Stage 3 Mustang is $39,500.

With its 1994 redesign, Ford breathed new life into the still-capable Fox chassis.

baseline powerplant they selected. They understood it needed to look entirely different inside and out, that it must conform to all the expected governmental safety and environmental regulations, that its build quality must be much better than before, and that they had to offer coupe and convertible models.

Styling and design manager John Aiken worked with a hastily assembled team, including designers Dave Rees, John Doughty, and Mark Conforzi, to produce a full-size concept model of what the car could look like. Coletti sent Bo Kovacinski, Joe Corvaia, and their groups off to work with any outside vendors to obtain better products and still, somehow, cut costs by a substantial 25 percent.

By June 1990, design groups had completed two separate body-styles created around the same hard point specifications. One body

An air dam with integral fog lamps was part of the 2003 Mustang Cobra package. Also part of the package was a 0 to 60 time of only 4.86 seconds, and a quarter-mile performance of 13.12 seconds at 109.6 miles per hour. Base retail price was $38,460.

The Cobra name has been part of the Mustang brand for many years, and the 2003 model has a supercharged 4.6L DOHC V-8. Power is an impressive 390 horsepower at 6,000 rpm and 390 foot-pounds at 3,500 rpm. Standard transmission is a six-speed manual, while the rear-axle ratio was a 3.55:1 gear set.

proposal had come from Aiken and his colleagues, the other from Ford's West Coast design shop, the California Concept Center (CCC), in Valencia, California. In a design clinic in June 1990 held in Pomona, California, viewers concluded the CCC car was too mild visually and urged designers to make Aiken's Dearborn prototype more radical.

Aiken and his team labeled their silver car the "Bruce Jenner" for its lean, muscular, clean-cut body form that reminded them of Jenner, Olympic-decathlon winner and sometimes race car driver, when he was at his physical peak. Aiken and Mustang design manager Bud Magaldi encouraged Rees and Doughty to let their imaginations flow further out. They then created an evil, dark-hearted sibling, also in silver but with lines that dove down from the tail to the nose where Jenner's lines remained closer to horizontal. They dubbed it "Rambo," and it provoked immediate responses from people who thought it went too far. Blending Rambo and Jenner, the design team created the car christened "Arnold Schwarzenegger." This became the design, and Tom Logar and Sid Wells supervised quick assembly of two drivable prototypes.

The chassis would be a heavily modified Fox

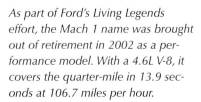

As part of Ford's Living Legends effort, the Mach 1 name was brought out of retirement in 2002 as a performance model. With a 4.6L V-8, it covers the quarter-mile in 13.9 seconds at 106.7 miles per hour.

monocoque unibody, different enough to be named Fox-4. Coletti and Dabrowski hired Bob Negstad, retired by this time, to consult, and he recommended some chassis changes, including his own 1986 proposal for a full independent rear suspension (IRS) version of the Fox chassis. Once again, management overruled the IRS as too costly, but Negstad's other suggestions improved steering and stability. The Skunk Works group produced one chassis prototype with Negstad's changes, and a second with slightly less modification. Following several evaluations, Ford Automotive Group President Allan Gilmour asked to see the car in May 1990. He ended up taking one of the prototypes for a vigorous drive around Dearborn's tight handling course and was impressed. He recommended showing the car to Harold "Red" Poling, Ford's chairman of the board, who, after seeing it, also expressed his satisfaction with the progress.

At that point, Coletti returned to Alex Trotman and suggested they continue on the same path with very little additional funding until their final design clinic in San Jose, California. There in October 1990, several groups would see Jenner, Rambo, and Schwarzenegger. As approval grew certain, the Mustang Skunk Works knew it would need a home to finish the car. Coletti's proposal of a staff free from other assignments, working under one roof together off campus, was sure to be accepted as well; his choice of personnel already had proven itself on this project. They estimated needing something in the neighborhood of 45,000 square feet to house the next phases of their operations. In late June 1990, they located a recently converted Montgomery Ward warehouse on Southfield Road in Allen Park, not far from SVO's home. Jack Roush had facilities in what had become a high-tech complex nearby, and the team selected Roush, a long-time friend of Bob Negstad's, to assist in the mechanical and engineering prototype creation. In August 1990, the design team moved into Suite 600 in the complex. By the time Trotman approved the car, Team Mustang already was at work on further development, and they had nearly completed renovation of the raw warehouse into offices, studios, and garages. Trotman gave them a $700 million budget and set Job One for December 1993.

Coletti's Skunk Works team officially disbanded, their job being done. Nearly all of them then joined "Team Mustang" to continue the project. Ford now internally coded it SN-95 to track prototype and pre-production status of the project. "S" designated "Specialty" vehicle, and "N" referred to North American Automotive Operations, which was responsible for the primary design of the new Mustang.

They lengthened the Fox wheelbase 0.8 inches to 101.3 inches to make Fox-4. They increased front and rear track 1.9 inches on the GTs, to 60.6 inches front and 59.1 inches rear. Fitting four wheel disc brakes, 10.8-inch front rotors and 10.5-inch rear rotors with Bosch's ABS2U anti-lock braking systems became options they would offer on both the GT and the base-model car, which would feature the Taurus- and Thunderbird-proven "Vulcan" 3.8-liter V-6. This engine used a great number of aluminum components. As a result, it was nearly as light as the 2.3-liter four it replaced while still producing 145 horsepower. Engineering again improved the 5.0-liter HO, modifying the intake system to fit a lower hood line, which also improved breathing and increased output to 215 horsepower. Both engines had operated with the EEC-IV electronic engine management system in place since 1987, but they received updated programs for emissions requirements. Ford offered its four-speed automatic-overdrive transmission for both engines while making the five-speed Borg-

The 1970 Mach 1 logo was resurrected for the 2002 Mach 1. The rear spoiler is an optional piece, styled to evoke the original from 1969. Dual exhaust and a modern version of the Magnum 500 wheel is a standard part of the package.

Base retail price on a 2003 Mach 1 was $29,330 and included rocker panel stripes, a styling cue picked up from the 1970 Mach 1. Like its earlier namesake, the Mach 1 has a diminutive rear seat.

An important part of the 2002 Mach 1 option is the functional Shaker Scoop. Like its 1969 counterpart, it is mounted directly on the engine, bucking and vibrating with every push of the accelerator.

The Shaker Scoop vibrating in the middle of the 2003 Mach 1's hood is more effective at evoking memories of Mustang's past than it is at increasing performance.

Warner T-5 standard and the Traction-Lok an available option.

During the early discussions of the car's appearance, chassis engineers observed that it always had been difficult to provide a rigid chassis in a three-door or hatchback body style. These observations convinced Coletti and his Skunk workers to produce only a coupe and convertible. Aiken's designers created the coupe's roof line based on another early product decision to make a detachable hardtop roof for the convertible; now it would be ideal if the finished design closely resembled the fixed roof line. The finished removable top weighed 84 pounds, and Ford eventually offered it as a $1,000 option, finished with interior head liner and dome light. From a distance, it was nearly impossible to differentiate this top from the coupe. Under the hood, they resurrected the mid-1960s Export Bar triangular brace that linked front strut towers to the firewall.

In May 1992, Coletti learned that Chevrolet and Pontiac Divisions would introduce their new Camaro and Firebird to the public during the January 1993 Detroit and Los Angeles auto shows. His SN-95 would not arrive till a year later. With his competitive juices flowing, he wondered how to "skunk" GM. He recalled what Mustang show cars had done in the early days to tantalize customers and frustrate competitors: Mustang I in 1962, Mach I in 1967, Mach II, the wild mid-engine concept car in 1969. He conceived a Mach III as an open car after the style of the two-seat Mustang I. To further skunk GM, which often had done simple push around show cars powered by GM personnel back and leg muscles, this new car also had to be drivable just like Mustang I.

Mach III project manager Joe Laura and John Coletti sketched ideas akin to Rambo, but some exaggerated even beyond that. They selected the 4.6-liter modular V-8 because, first, it was a V-8, and second, it was Ford's newest high-tech showpiece engine. Advance powertrain engineering assistant chief, Jim Gagliardi, supercharged the show car version and fit it with intake manifolds intercooled with ethylene glycol—essentially antifreeze—to reduce intake fuel-air mixture temperatures by about 75 degrees. When it was all done, Ford claimed 450 horsepower for the engine, which Gagliardi mated to a six-speed Borg-Warner T56 transmission. Masco-Tech, a concept- and show-car builder based in suburban Mt. Elliott, Michigan, completed the show car. Coletti's idea, Laura's shape, and Gagliardi's engine lured viewers away from GM. In the Los Angeles show, Ford and Pontiac shared the same hall, and the Mach III's vivid, red paint grabbed and held onto show attendees before they ever saw Pontiac's deep blue Trans Am.

Ford introduced its 1994 Mustang on December 9, 1993, but as early as the May 1993 issue of *Road & Track*, Detroit-based writer Ken Zino produced a seven-page comparison of the future Mustang and Camaro, featuring water-color illustrations of the two cars. Zino did not hazard a conclusion because there were still too many unknowns about Ford's new car. But in November, Zino drove the car and summed up his reactions:

"On first drive, there's no question that the 1994 Mustang is sufficiently improved to keep the Ford pony car tradition growing for a few more years. Sporty, not radical, styling, good power and a distinctively American rear-drive character are Mustang's attractions once again."

The 2000 Cobra R can use its 385 horsepower to propel itself to a top speed of 186 miles per hour. It has recorded a 0 to 60 time of 4.8 seconds, and a quarter-mile performance of 13.0 seconds at 108.5 miles per hour.

In *Road & Track's Sports & GT Cars* annual, author Tom Wilkinson compared the Mustang GT with the Camaro Z-28, both as convertibles. With its fully optioned test price at $27,225 compared to Camaro's $25,852, and with Mustang's 5.0-liter producing 215 horsepower compared to Chevrolet's new environmentally corrected LT-1 (the new 5.7-liter replacing an older, dirty engine) cranking out 275 horsepower, it was easy to understand how the Mustang came up way short. Ford knew the Camaro was coming, even knew its specifications, but division product planners and marketing staff decided to leave their car as configured. If they had substituted the planned 240-horsepower SVT Cobra engine, it would have left the company with nothing more powerful for its traditionally more powerful designation. When the Indianapolis Motor Speedway selected the 1994 Cobra as pace car for the 78th Indy 500 on May 29, Jack Roush prepared three official pace cars, and Ford created another 105 non-Roush-modified convertibles for use by officials and Indianapolis 500 race VIPs during the month. The division manufactured an additional 1,000 as replicas, which were sold for $24,010.

Then SVO's successor groups SVT and SVE produced a run of 250 cars named the Cobra R. These arrived at the dealer sans air conditioning, radio, and most of the insulation because Ford division built them for racing purposes. They became a second-year instant collector hit among well-heeled customers, and quite a few

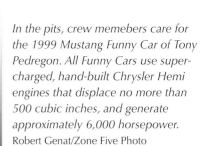

(opposite) *Tony Pedregon lights up the tires in the burn-out area to heat and clean them. A Funny Car burns about four gallons of nitromethane and alcohol fuel in the brief burnout.*
Robert Genat/Zone Five Photo

359

In the pits, crew memebers care for the 1999 Mustang Funny Car of Tony Pedregon. All Funny Cars use supercharged, hand-built Chrysler Hemi engines that displace no more than 500 cubic inches, and generate approximately 6,000 horsepower.
Robert Genat/Zone Five Photo

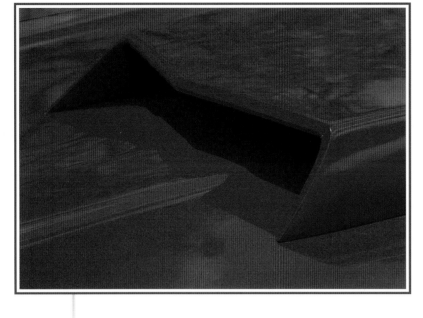

ended up racing from stoplight to stoplight. Ford had done it right for 1994. Despite the performance and price disadvantage of the GT versus the Camaro Z-28, Mustang's base models always outsold GTs and Cobras two-to-one, helping to maintain healthy production totals. In the 1994 model year, Ford produced 137,074 Mustangs, a 20 percent increase over 1993 production of 114,228. The 1994 figures were one-third greater than Chevrolet's Camaro and three times Pontiac's Firebird.

To rectify the "problem" of 1994 Cobra R models ending up on the streets and to remain in the good graces of governmental emission and safety compliance watchdogs, Ford required any potential 1995 R-customer to show a valid competition license and copies of their racing resume. Priced at $35,499, Ford manufactured the 250 R models almost entirely on the Dearborn assembly line, only adding the racing fuel cells and special engine cooling packages after initial assembly. It was a no-frills package with hand-cranked windows and no insulation, radio, or back seat. Ford provided minimum trim level seats so racers could install their own competition buckets inside their roll cages. Ford quoted delivery weight at 3,325 pounds and offered it only in Crystal White.

The most exciting news for the racers was that Jack Roush Technologies had developed the 351 Windsor 5.8-liter engine to produce 300 horsepower at 4,800 rpm. He replaced the Borg-Warner gearbox with a stronger Tremec five-speed and 3.27:1 final drive. Steve Anderson, Ford's Cobra R chief engineer also revised the suspension, putting Koni adjustable shocks on Mustangs once more and mounting special compound P255/45ZR17 B.F. Goodrich Comp T/A tires around 17x9.0-inch alloy wheels.

By year's end, Ford division was satisfied with its new Mustang. Throughout the model year, Ford's advertising emphasized the car's 30-year heritage, something even interior stylists, such as Emeline King, concentrated on, resurrecting the 1964½ car's dual-pod cockpit motif. Magaldi's designers had carved a c-shaped cove into the side panels to remind new buyers of the first two-seater and first four-seaters.

The next model year ended an era when Ford retired the aging, thoroughly developed 5.0-liter engine. It had enjoyed an interrupted 27-year run; it disappeared in 1974, 1980, and 1981

(opposite) The square outline on the hood in front of the scoop of John Force's Castrol Mustang Funny Car is the burst panel required by NHRA rules. In case of an engine explosion, it allows the pressure to be vented through the panel and prevent the body from blowing off. Robert Genat/ Zone Five Photo

when certification and CAFE requirements made it impractical. While Ford division had intended to offer its removable hardtop as an option for the convertibles beginning in 1994, early engineering problems and later supplier difficulties limited production and sales to just 499 examples. Ford only sold removable hardtops with SVT Cobra convertibles before it discretely withdrew the option. Production through 1995 soared 30 percent above 1994 levels, to a total of 180,356, including 4,255 Cobra coupes and 1,003 Cobra convertibles.

The most significant change for 1996 was Ford's regular production introduction of its 4.6-liter (281-ci) modular V-8 with a single overhead camshaft that permitted engine speeds of 6,000 rpm. The 4.6 engine was a proven product, powering Crown Victoria and Mercury Marquis sedans since 1992 and the Lincoln Town car since 1991. With horsepower and torque output identical to the 5.0, the smaller engine offered better fuel economy and cleaner emissions. Along with the "new" engine came new transmissions, a stronger Borg-Warner five-speed T-45 and the car's first performance automatic, the four-speed 43R70W. To keep this improved Mustang secure, Ford introduced a specially coded ignition key and steering column switch, part of its Passive Anti-Theft System, PATS. Using even a correctly duplicated, yet not encoded, fabricated key would send the new On Board Diagnostic II (OBDII) system an "error code" that indicated an attempted theft. The OBDII would cut off fuel feed and spark, allowing the starter to crank rapidly without ever starting the car. In all, Ford produced 135,980 of the 1996 models; owners, unsure of the coming 4.6-liter engine, had stocked up the year before. The winners were SVT Cobra buyers, all 10,006 coupe and convertible customers, who found 315 horsepower under their hoods, courtesy of the new "Romeo" dual overhead cam (DOHC) 4.6 liter engine.

Some observers claimed that while Cobra owners won with their engines, they lost with an $815 paint option introduced in 1996 for Cobra coupes alone. Called "Mystic," it was a "mystery" paint developed by GAF.

Lunging off the starting line, John Force aims his 1999 Mustang Funny Car down the track at the 1999 Nationals at Pomona, California. The huge rear Goodyear tires are 36 inches in diameter and have an operating pressure of 5 pounds. Robert Genat/Zone Five Photo

Light conditions and angle of view changed the color from blue to green, purple to black, or combinations of all those at once. It was eye-catching but did not appeal to everyone.

Overall production slipped further in 1997 to 108,344 coupes and convertibles. Ford introduced 17-inch wheels and tires as an option on the GT. These had been standard equipment on the SVT Cobras since 1994. For 1998, the division introduced a new GT sport group that included the 17-inch aluminum wheels and tires, and the division's engineers performed a slight modification that coaxed another 10 horsepower out of the engine. This bumped output up to 215 horsepower for the GT variations. Gasoline prices had been averaging about $1.15 per gallon for regular-grade from 1995 through 1998, yet four states—New York, Massachusetts, Connecticut, and California—had developed more severe emissions standards than the federal government EPA regulations. In recognition of those recent requirements, Ford qualified its base 3.8-liter V-6 and its four-speed automatic transmission as a Low Emission Vehicle (LEV) in each of those states. Production jumped up in 1998 to a total of 175,522 coupes and convertibles.

For 1999, Ford celebrated the Mustang's 35th anniversary with some new, more-aggressive sheet metal, enlarging the side scoop nearly to the dimensions of the 1962 mid-engine car. Clear lenses with simplified, highly polished reflectors and prominent-looking bulbs gave the headlights new power and a very novel look. Chassis engineers reinforced the convertible floor pan using subframe connectors, increased floor pan sealing, and packed the rocker panels with foam to reduce noise and vibrations. With a higher-lift camshaft, enlarged intake and exhaust valves, a better breathing intake manifold, and coil-on-spark plug ignition, Ford pulled another 35 horsepower out of the 4.6, bringing it to 260 at 5,250 rpm. Utilizing the same improvements on the V-6, engineers extracted 190 horsepower. For the SVT Cobra, output rose to 320 horsepower. The 35th anniversary generated a commemorative model option for GT coupes and convertibles only. Ford offered this model in black, silver, white, or red. The anniversary edition's body styling, with its large hood scoop and its more elevated rear wing, presaged the redesign that would appear in model year 2001. Ford limited the production of the commemorative editions to just 5,000, while overall factory output settled at 133,907. In 1999, the

Only 300 Cobra Rs were built in 2000, each one intended more for track duty than grocery runs. Massive Brembo brakes and B.F. Goodrich g-Force KD 265/40ZR-18 tires conspire to stop the Cobra R from 60 miles per hour in only 116 feet. Exhaust pipes exit in front of the rear tires, while a 7-inch-high rear spoiler is functional, especially at the triple-digit speeds this road rocket can generate.

A bulged hood was necessary for clearance for the 5.4: DOHC V-8. A massive plenum topped the engine, while an aluminum intake manifold used tuned equal-length runners to ensure good flow up to the 6,500 rpm redline. While needed for track work, the functional splitter could be removed by twisting the Dzus fasteners.

Fitting the Speedster top to the Saleen S281 eliminated back seat capacity. The fiberglass cover evoked the open air style of earlier days.

Cobra convertible cracked the $30,000 price barrier with a price of $31,470.

The last decade of the century had witnessed the creation of an international information system known as the World Wide Web, an information pipeline operating without borders or tariffs. In 1993 and again in 1995, terrorists both foreign-born and homegrown, had captured America's attention by bombing the World Trade towers in New York City and the Alfred Murrah Federal Building in Oklahoma City. March 1998 had seen the anti-impotence drug, Viagra , a medication originally patented to deal with angina, rising to meet the challenge of male discontent. At the end of the year, the end of the century, and the end of the millennium, it had taken all nine Supreme Court justices to elect a president who had failed to win the popular vote.

As 1999 drew to a close, Ford introduced the model year 2000 Mustang. While it differed little from the 1999 model, enthusiasts noticed that the race-pedigree buyers of a Cobra R now got a 330-ci, 5.4-liter Roush-built engine that developed 385 horsepower at 6,250 rpm. Ford fit the car with a

much higher rear wing, one clearly meant for racetrack benefits. Repeating a practice that Ford had experienced before, buyers flocked to the showrooms to view the redesigned model, and the division delivered an impressive total of 215,400 Mustangs, among them just 354 Cobra coupes and only 100 Cobra convertibles. It helped everyone's peace of mind (and didn't hurt Ford sales at all) when alarm clocks went off, computers started up, and airplanes landed safely on New Year's morning despite apocalyptic predictions that all computers would cease functioning when the clock struck 12:01 A.M. on January 1, 2000. All the Y2K worries had been unnecessary, it seemed.

For 2001, the entire Mustang line received styling updates, picking up cues introduced on the 35th anniversary models in 1999. Product planning had studied sales histories of special edition cars, from the 25th anniversary models through to its recent 35th celebratory Mustang, and concluded that this technique offered the corporation additional profit possibilities. For 2001, the latest of these limited-production runs celebrated the Mustang's role in a popular Steve McQueen 1969 film, *Bullitt*. Los Angeles racer/car builder Max Balchowski was a close

The 2001 Saleen S281 packed a 4.6L, two-valve per cylinder engine. However, Saleen worked his usual magic, installing a supercharger, 13-inch Brembo brakes, and 18-inch wheels shod with Pirelli P Zero tires.

friend of cinematographer Haskell Wexler. Wexler had led Balchowski to numerous jobs preparing and driving cars for film. Balchowski modified McQueen's two 1968 model 390-engined GT fastbacks and two other Dodge Chargers for the film, getting only vague indications that McQueen also needed these cars to fly. Balchowski heavily reinforced the suspension, chassis, and engine mounts; still the stunt drivers broke one of each car during hard landings from long jumps over San Francisco's hills. For the 2001 Bullitt, Ford lowered the standard GT suspension and selected 17-inch American Racing aluminum wheels that recalled the magnesium wheels McQueen and Balchowsky had fit to the movie cars. McQueen's car for the film was painted Highland Green; Ford reissued that color and also offered the car in blue and black. Using the 4.6 modular engine standard in the GT, Ford found an extra 10 horsepower

Under the Series II Saleen Supercharger is a 4.6L V-8 delivering 365-horsepower and a healthy 400 lb-ft of torque. The low-profile Rootes-style blower fit under the hood with minimal interference.

for the Bullitt replica, rating the engine at 270 horsepower. The various modifications, badges, special paint, and wheels added $3,695 to the cost of a base GT and Ford offered the Bullitt, all 5,582 copies, in coupe form only. Total production reached 163,818 cars.

In mid-2001, new vice president of design J. Mays assigned his design groups to consider the Next Mustang. As Greg Hutting, project manager at Ford's California Concept Center, CCC, explained, "Former vice president of design Jack Telnack liked a lot of derivatives to come in to him, one from us, one from Ghia, one from Dearborn. These were early directions into what would usually be a vaguely defined project, often with only the basic seating package and a wheelbase. It gave us a lot of freedom along with occasional missteps.

"With J. Mays now, he has a direction for each project in mind. Now we take one car, one concept, and invest an entire year in something. Then we get to see the public's reaction. The Dearborn studio now thinks of itself as Ford's Living Legend advance studio. Larry Erickson, the manager, and his staff, they did the new Mach I, the new Boss 302, the new GT40. And J. asked us to take on the concept for the 40th anniversary car. That was a cool day. Everybody here knew we were going to be part of Mustang history."

In Dearborn, Ford had real 2002 cars ready to be presented. The division made few changes. Most enthusiasts already knew the Mustang would be around for its 40th birthday, and the 38th year cars would be good. To rekindle that faith however, Ford introduced its model 2003 Cobra coupe on February 7, 2002. Ford supercharged the 4.6-liter dual overhead camshaft (DOHC) V-8, reaching horsepower output levels not seen since the 428 Super Cobra Jets. Ford rated this new version at 390 horsepower at 6,000 rpm and mated it to Ford's first six-speed transmission. This forced other changes, including revising the suspension and brakes to better contain the power, reconfiguring the hood with functional flow-through scoops to better withdraw engine heat, and switching from an aluminum to a cast-iron cylinder block to better handle the anticipated use.

Back in November 1994, *Automobile Magazine* had hinted that the Fox-4 would remain in production until perhaps 2004, a fact that customers and enthusiasts now know to be true. The magazine had also hinted there would be a replacement before or around then, in time for the 40th anniversary of the Mustang in April 2004. Rumors had emerged and submerged regarding the adaptability of the 4.6-liter V-8, and figures had simmered near the surface to hint that the 1995 Cobra R horsepower rating may be what buyers could expect even before the year 2000. This proved true as well. As the 2003 calendar year moved into fall, and the model year moved toward its end, sales of the more-than-20-year-old chassis held steady. In magazines throughout the world, enthusiasts saw the future. Not only would there be a Mustang, but also, if the concept cars were any indication, World Headquarters must once again be thinking, "Stick around, we've got some *more* good, hot stuff coming."

chapter sixteen

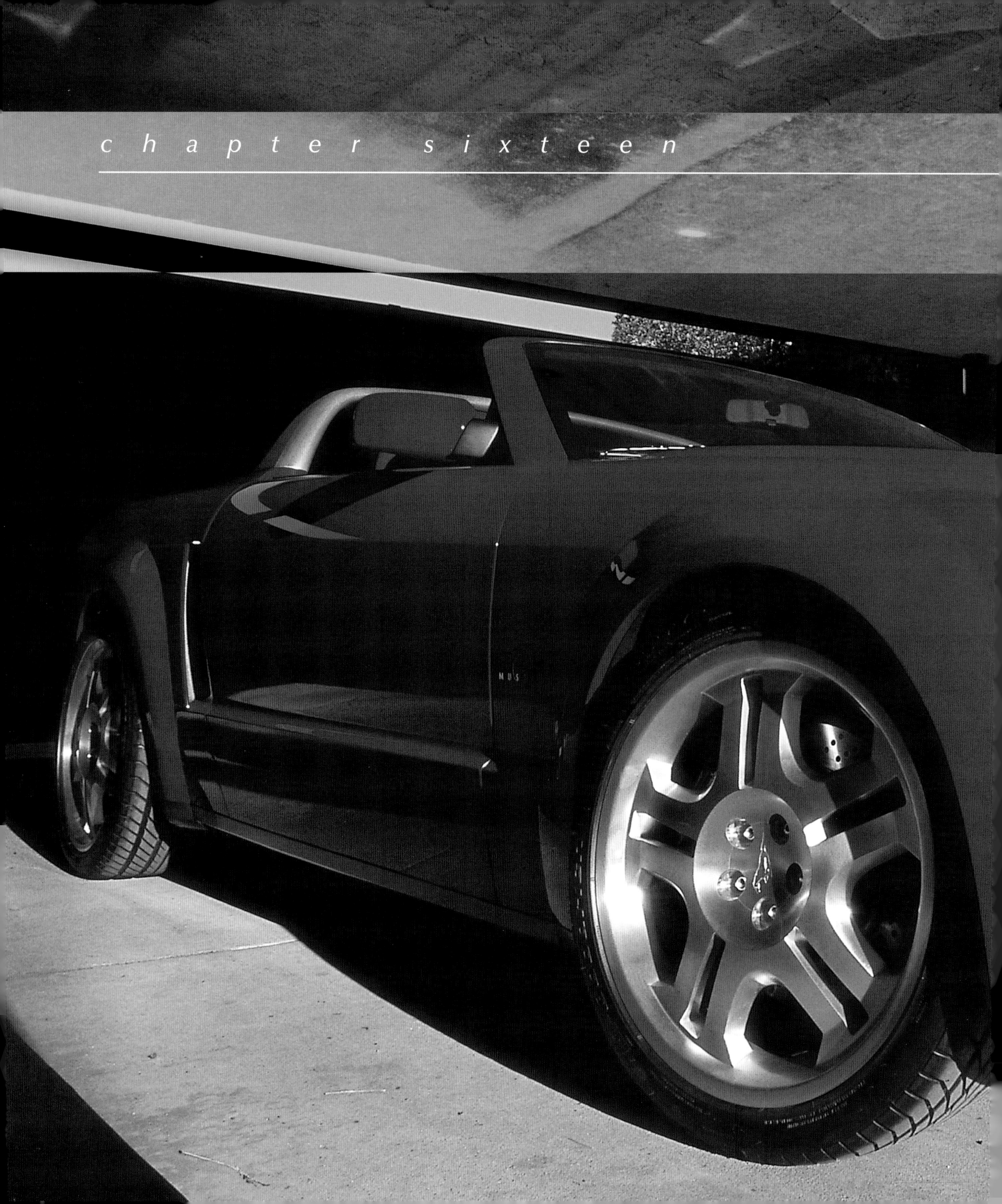

(*previous*) *Like Mustangs before, the 2005 Mustang concept vehicle features a honeycomb grille and a galloping pony. Leading-edge hood scoops are functional and feed air to the 90-degree modular 4.6L V-8. This engine uses a belt-driven supercharger in conjunction with a liquid-to-air intercooler to generate 400 horsepower and 390 foot-pounds of torque.*

The flashy interior of the 2005 Mustang concept vehicle uses billet-aluminum hardware and bright plastics and fabrics to create a visually exciting space. Cluster gauges feature round, optical-inspired faces to present information and impart a "heritage" feel.

(2003–present)

A GLANCE BACK, A LEAP FORWARD

"There are at least eight million Mustang enthusiasts who are going to hold us to a higher level of responsibility and accountability," Greg Hutting, project manager of Ford's California Concept Center (CCC) and author and design parent of Ford's new 2005 Mustang GT concept, said. Hutting had worked for more than a year under that scrutiny. "We got the assignment in early February 2002. We felt a lot of responsibility.

"When we started thinking about this, we tore up lots of books, magazines, catalogs. We threw everything up on a board, and we decided to pick out the best design features of all the Mustangs we loved. Any of us had veto power: my brother Dick (chief designer), Mark Gorman, Jon Trickey, Brian White, or me. Any feature any of us didn't like came down with just one vote.

"The 1967–68 regular production car front end with its sloped-back shark nose, that stayed. We loved the Shelby 1968 GT500 nose slits. We identified all the Mustang design cues through its history, but we executed them with modern surface language. The profile of the GT coupe is the 1965 fastback roof line; and our C-scoop and the roof scoop on the coupe match in style. If you meet someone on the street and ask them to draw a Mustang, they'll make a bad drawing, but they'll get the C-scoop on the car."

Greg and Dick Hutting co-founded the CCC in 1983 as an independent design shop. Since

1984, they have worked for Ford Motor Company exclusively. Ford acquired the facility in 1997. On this project, they worked hand in hand with Dearborn's Living Legends studio and chief designer Larry Erickson. The assignment to make the new Mustang came from vice president of design J. Mays, who spoke about the car with Matt DeLorenzo in *Road & Track* magazine.

"This is a muscle car," Mays said. "The original Mustang was a pony car, but, in 1967, it went to the next platform, or rather ladder frame, and became a true muscle car. That's when it started to get the big block 428s and 429s.

"If you dissect the cues that people associate with the Mustang, most of them gravitate to the 1964½, to the 1970 models. Those are the vehicles lodged in most people's minds as the iconic Mustangs. We wanted to take those cues, and what we filled in between them becomes the modern part."

Mays has been an open-minded student of everyone's design. He was not beyond studying a bit of outside influence for further cues on this new project. In January 2002, following the Los Angeles auto show, he had an opportunity to tour the Mattel Design Center. More than a

Styling cues from a number of past Mustangs, as well as fresh design work, are evident in the 2005 Mustang convertible concept vehicle that debuted at the 2003 North American International Auto Show in Detroit, Michigan. Painted Redline Red Metallic, it shared the spotlight with a Tungsten Silver coupe.

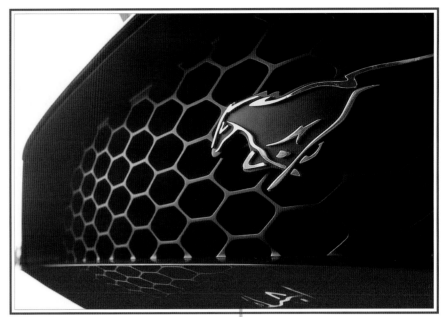

dozen automotive designers create between 800 and 900 different Hot Wheels cars each year, with production on the order of 3.5 million cars every week. After wandering the rows of CAD-CAM computer-aided design-equipped offices and work stations, and commenting that they used the same technology at Ford Design, he settled back in Hot Wheels' reconstructed 1950s gas station, a sort of conference room and visitor's lounge on the east wall of the large facility. Speaking with Mattel Vice President of Design John Handy, Chief Designer Larry Wood, and former Director of Design, now-New Products Licensing Vice President Carson Lev, Mays continually glanced around the walls while he unwound from the hectic week of press introductions and media interviews. Shelves on two walls displayed Hot Wheels cars in several scales, and one of the small cars caught his eye. He hopped up and reached past Carson Lev.

"What's this?" he asked.

Lev knew. It was the work of one of his designers in a new program called "Plausible Original Design." This concept gave Hot Wheels designers the freedom to "think about what Detroit would be doing if Hot Wheels designed the next generation" of any production car. Mark Jones had looked at the SN95 Mustangs and wondered where it might go from its current production. Others had done Camaros and Chevelles, even a GT40 that Mattel called "40 Something." Before Lev could answer, Mays asked another question.

"Are there more of these?"

Lev and Handy said it was a brand-new car, and there was a "master carton," one containing as many as 256 of the cars, in their store packages somewhere in the design center.

"Could I get a dozen of these? You know, we're redoing the Mustang for 2004. We're taking a look at every inspirational piece of the car's history. We're not sure at this point which Mustang we'll do as a retro-reinvented car, but I want this one. I want to take it back and show it to the guys." By the time Mays left, he had the cars in his bag. He didn't get to meet Mark Jones who had worked at Ford design years before Mays arrived, but Mays learned that Mattel called the car "Pony Up."

As Dick and Greg Hutting began whittling down design influences, they quickly moved into three dimensions, beginning their first clay model within a month of getting their assignment. Mays had given them a few "musts," including, for the convertible, the two-seat configuration and

Ford stylists have assured the public that the concept vehicles are 90 to 95 percent accurate at depicting what the production Mustang will look like. One change to be made is an additional six inches of length between the firewall and the front wheel centers to enlarge the engine compartment and give the car better proportions.

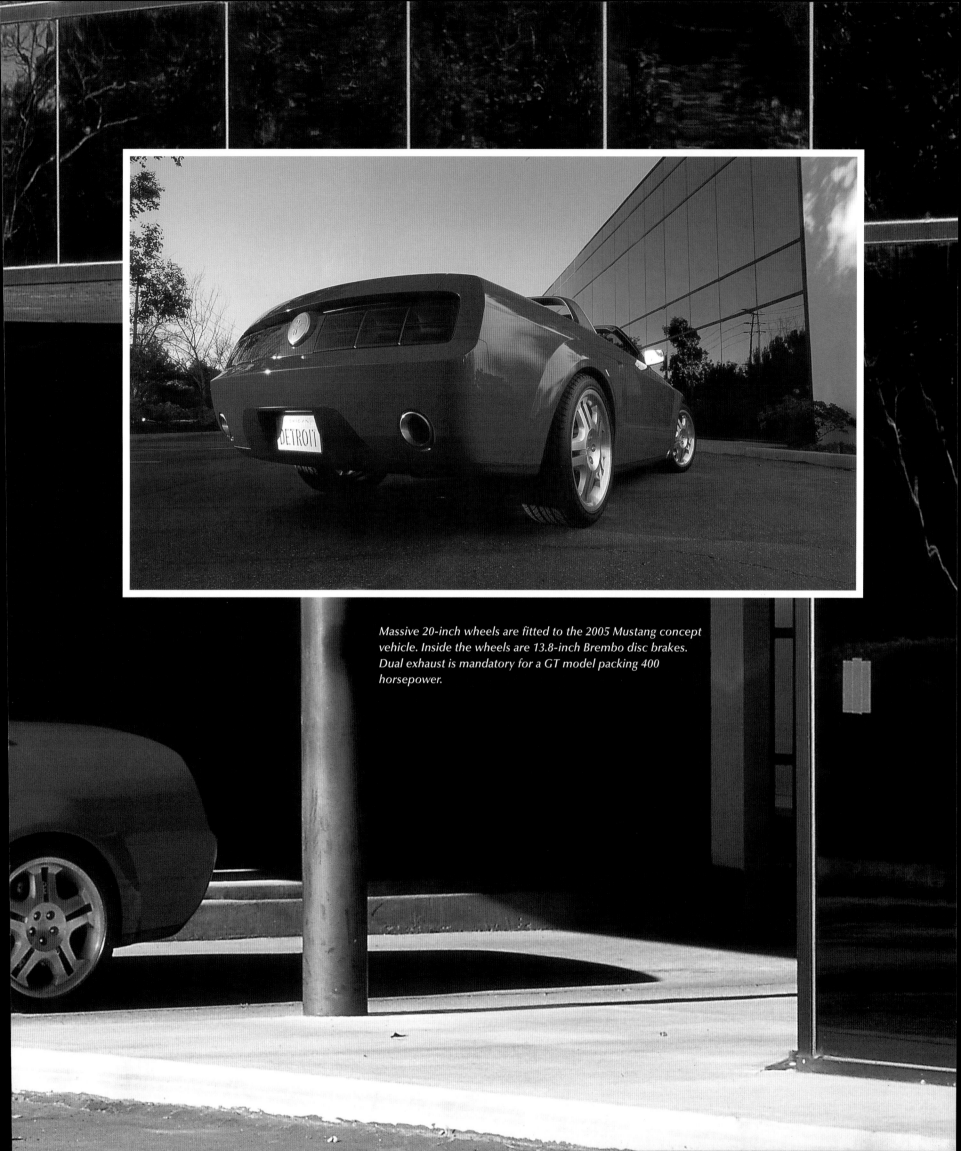

Massive 20-inch wheels are fitted to the 2005 Mustang concept vehicle. Inside the wheels are 13.8-inch Brembo disc brakes. Dual exhaust is mandatory for a GT model packing 400 horsepower.

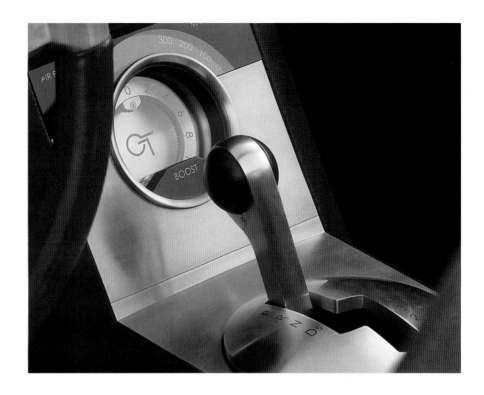

The 2005 Mustang convertible concept vehicle used a five-speed automatic transmission, and the coupe concept was equipped with a six-speed manual. The boost gauge located at the bottom of the center stack allows the driver to keep an eye on the supercharger output.

Similar to the 1965 Mustang, the 2005 Mustang concept displayed three-element taillights. Spanning almost the full width of the vehicle, only a center-mounted gas cap interrupts the flow of red plastic.

the overhead roll bar taken from the first 1962 Mustang I. Mays also wanted CCC to adopt the inside-mounted spare tire and wheel from Carroll Shelby's 1965 GT350s for their coupe, and the sequential rear turn signals from the 1969 and 1970 Shelbys to each body style. Mays gave them the basic seating package and told them to build their prototypes on a slightly modified Thunderbird DEW85 platform. Selecting this platform meant production base trim cars would retain their solid rear axle, although GTs and Cobras would get an IRS. While the concept show cars are both two-seaters, the production cars will grow on a six-inch longer wheelbase, adding body length at the cowl to accommodate rear seats and legroom. CCC received design approval in early July, just five months after their assignment began.

"It's retro," Greg Hutting concluded, watching the red convertible in golden light during yet another photo session, "but it's really new. It pays homage to all that heritage, but in the end, we have a very modern Mustang."

"No matter what kind of object you are looking at," Mays told Paul Lienert in *Automobile Magazine* back in 1998, "you break it down into shape, color, material, and texture. And when you reassemble it, whatever the hierarchy of those individual elements, it creates your final design. So, if you have a high contrast between those things, you end up with a bold or raw design. And if you have a sophisticated combination of those elements, it can go toward elegance."

"I think the surfacing on this car is significantly more geometrical," Mays summarized in *Road & Track*. "It is more technical. The overall feeling is more milled than the romantic, voluptuous Mustangs you remember. The overall tautness, rigidity of the bodywork, and construction techniques have brought it into the next century. This is a huge step forward for the Mustang."

Circular headlights returned on the 2005 Mustang concept vehicle. However, these adaptive headlights use a computer to rotate two concentric rings in a helix pattern to zoom in and out and change the light pattern to fit driving conditions.

INDEX